Klaus Hinrichsen

NCIS Season 1-12
NCIS TV Show Fan Book

* * *

May 2015

Klaus Hinrichsen

The book is based on articles from magazines, newspapers and other books as well as the Internet. Although the author never intended to use any lines from the various sources without stating so, it cannot be totally ruled out, that the one or other great line, read in the odd article, found its way into the book by pure chance. With this book the author only tried to give all the NCIS fans a complete book on the NCIS-TV-series seasons 1-12. The author holds no connection what so ever with Belisarius Productions, CBS Broadcasting or Paramount Pictures.

Hinrichsen, Klaus
NCIS Season 1-12
NCIS TV Show Fan Book

May 2015

Klaus Hinrichsen

***

Herstellung und Verlag: BoD - Books on Demand, Norderstedt
Produced and published by BoD - Books on Demand, Norderstedt, Germany
Printed in Germany

ISBN: 978-3-7347-9506-0

Content

Content

Content

Premise

NCIS (Naval Criminal Investigative Service) is a special unit to investigate any offenses that are finally brought to the Navy court concerning members of the Navy or Marine Corps at home and abroad, and it is unimportant whether the concerned are involved as perpetrators or victims. In everyday life in addition to the most absurd criminal cases the special agents are in particular involved in the fight against terrorism, and also tasks of protections against espionage are part of their daily business.

Previously, the NCIS investigation authority in contrast to FBI and CIA investigations were rather unknown, but this has changed due to the massive success of the TV series. The use of special advisers, especially of real NCIS agents during the filming convey to the viewer an intense authenticity and regularly provides exciting entertainment.

After a sluggish first series start NCIS is now the world's most successful television series ever and has now completed twelve seasons which each enjoyed huge viewership, the final of the 12th Season was aired in the U.S. on CBS in May 2015. In Germany, the current Season 12 runs since the beginning of January 2015 on SAT 1.

The concept of the television series is basically nothing new - previously there were already successful series like CSI, CSI: Miami and CSI: NY, all based on the exciting, audience captivating investigations in the crime lab with all its technical aspects. Excessive success of NCIS is not necessarily due to the cases which are certainly full of suspense, but it is probably owed to this incredibly well put together NCIS team, led by the rotten mouth, edgy, strict but also very fair special agent Leroy Jethro Gibbs. Each figure in the team has a unique character, with all the associated strengths and weaknesses, who the audience feels quickly attracted to and perhaps secretly dreams to be able to belong to such a dream team in real life. So one can easily ignore a perhaps less exciting case and enjoy the always funny dialogues of the team members, i.e. the viewer can almost always be fascinated in a humorous way. Another important point of difference to the CSI franchise is that NCIS is not confined almost to one specific place, but in particular the investigations outside the lab play an important role.

The previously aired 282 episodes in 12 seasons offered compelling, exciting entertainment. Besides tragic, sometimes even sad moments, the series offered a dash of dry humor that made the audience, whatever the generation they belong to start to love each member because of his/her personal charm.

Based on this success, a branch of NCIS was created in 2009. NCIS: Los Angeles is set in Los Angeles and the 7th season is coming up in 2015. In season eleven, NCIS led to second spin-off series, NCIS: New Orleans.

The Book

The always thrilling and entertaining cases of Leroy Jethro Gibbs (cover shot), played by Mark Harmon, and his NCIS-crew have been keeping a vast amount of followers all around the world glued to their seats and have made this series to one of the most successful in our times. Most likely being the absolute number one series on TV in the USA and in many other countries.

This fan book, covering season 1-12, includes all the vital and necessary information on the series, short summaries of all episodes, coverage of the role vitas and the famous actors and - it goes without saying - Gibbs, Tony, Kate, Ziva, McGee, Abby, Bishop, Palmer, Ducky's best lines.

TV Broadcast USA

Seasonal rankings (based on average total viewers per episode) of NCIS.

Note: Each U.S. network television season starts in late September and ends in late May, which coincides with the completion of May sweeps.

NCIS is the most watched TV series that airs during both halves of the television season in the United States, followed by CSI: Crime Scene Investigation. Both shows are from CBS. In 2011, NCIS was voted America's favorite television show. The series finished its tenth season as the most-watched television series in the U.S. during the 2012–13 TV season

On January 15, 2013, NCIS surpassed its previous series high in viewers from Season 8 episode "Freedom". The Season 10 episode "Shiva" attracted 22.86 million viewers, making it a new series high.

TV Broadcast NCIS (USA)

Season	Episodes	Season Premiere	Season Finale	Rank	Viewers (in millions)
1	23	Sep 23, 2003	May 25, 2004	26th	11,84
2	23	Sep 28, 2004	May 24, 2005	22nd	13,57
3	24	Sep 20, 2005	May 16, 2006	16th	15,27
4	24	Sep 19, 2006	May 22, 2007	20th	14,54
5	19	Sep 25, 2007	May 20, 2008	14th	14,41
6	25	Sep 23, 2008	May 19, 2009	5th	17,77
7	24	Sep 22, 2009	May 25, 2010	4th	19,33
8	24	Sep 21, 2010	May 17, 2011	5th	19,46
9	24	Sep 20, 2011	May 15, 2012	3rd	19,49
10	24	Sep 25, 2012	May 14, 2013	1st	21,34
11	24	Sep 24, 2013	May 13, 2014	3rd	19,77
12	24	Sep 23, 2014	May 12, 2015	TBA	TBA

Quelle: [15]

Awards and Nominations

ALMA Award
Nominated – Outstanding Actress in a Drama Television Series – Cote de Pablo (2008)
Won – Outstanding Actress in a Drama Television Series – Cote de Pablo (2011)
Nominated – Favorite TV Actress-Drama – Cote de Pablo (2012)

ASCAP Award
Won – Top TV Series – Matt Hawkins, Maurice Jackson, Neil Martin (2012)
Won – Top TV Series – Matt Hawkins, Maurice Jackson, Neil Martin (2011)
Won – Top TV Series – Matt Hawkins, Maurice Jackson, Neil Martin (2010)
Won – Top TV Series – Matt Hawkins, Maurice Jackson, Neil Martin (2009)
Won – Top TV Series – Matt Hawkins, Maurice Jackson, Neil Martin (2008)
Won – Top TV Series – Matt Hawkins, Maurice Jackson, Neil Martin (2007)
Won – Top TV Series – Matt Hawkins, Maurice Jackson, Neil Martin (2006)
Won – Top TV Series – Matt Hawkins, Maurice Jackson, Neil Martin (2004)
Won – Top TV Series – Steven Bramson (2004)

BMI Film & TV Awards
Won – BMI TV Music Award – Brian Kirk (2009)
Won – BMI TV Music Award – Brian Kirk (2008)
Won – BMI TV Music Award – Joseph Conlan (2005)

California on Location Awards
Won – Location Team of the Year (Episodic Television) – Emily Kirylo, Jim McClafferty, Joel Sinderman, Michael Soleau (2008)

Emmy Awards
Nominated – Outstanding Stunt Coordination – Diamond Farnsworth, "Requiem" (2008)
Nominated – Outstanding Guest Actor in a Drama Series – Charles Durning (2005)
Nominated – Outstanding Stunt Coordination for a Drama Series, Miniseries, or Movie – Diamond Farnsworth, "Revenge" (2013)

NAACP Image Awards
Nominated – Outstanding Supporting Actor in a Drama Series – Rocky Carroll (2010)

People's Choice Awards
Nominated – Favorite TV Drama (2009) - Favorite TV Drama Actor – Mark Harmon (2009)
Nominated – Favorite TV Drama (2010)
Nominated – Favorite TV Crime Drama (2011)
Nominated – Favorite TV Crime Drama (2012)
Nominated – Favorite TV Drama Actor – Mark Harmon (2013)
Nominated – Favorite TV Crime Drama (2014) - TV Drama Actor: M.Harmon - TV Drama Actress: P.Paurette
Nominated – Favorite TV Drama (2015)

Imagen Foundation Awards
Nominated – Best Actress/Television – Cote de Pablo (2011)
Nominated – Best Supporting Actress/Television – Cote de Pablo (2009)
Won – Best Supporting Actress/Television – Cote de Pablo (2006)

Young Artist Awards
Nominated – Best Performance in a TV Series – Guest Starring Young Actor – Dominic Scott Kay, "Lost & Found" (2008)
Nominated – Best Performance in a TV Series – Guest Starring Young Actress 11–15 – Sadie Calvano (2011)
Won – Best Performance in a TV Series – Guest Starring Young Actress 11–15 – Madisen Beaty (2011)
Nominated – Best Performance in a TV Series – Guest Starring Young Actress Ten and Under – Melody Angel (2012)

Quelle: [16]

Home Video (DVD) Releases

The first nine seasons of NCIS have been released in Regions 1, 2 and 4. In Germany (Region 2), seasons 1–4 and 6–8 were released in two separate sets for each season. The first season DVD omits the two introductory episodes from season eight of JAG, though they are featured on the JAG season eight DVD.

Latest release USA (DVD Region 1): Season 11 with 24 Episodes (6 discs) on Aug 19, 2014

Quelle: [17]

Other Releases

In 2010, CBS Interactive and GameHouse released a mobile video game, NCIS: The Game for iOS, Android, BlackBerry, Windows Mobile, and BREW/J2ME. The game features five different cases written by the show's writers.

On November 1, 2011, Ubisoft released NCIS, a video game for the PC, Xbox 360, PlayStation 3, and Wii. A Nintendo 3DS version was released on March 6, 2012. The video game was deemed as a mockery to the show by reviewers and players alike, and received a 2/10 rating on GameSpot.

Quelle: [20]

Soundtrack

CBS Records released the show's first soundtrack on February 10, 2009. The Official TV Soundtrack is a two-disc, 22-track set that includes brand new songs from top artists featured prominently in upcoming episodes of the series as well as the show's original theme by Numeriklab (available commercially for the first time) and a remix of the theme by Ministry. The set also includes songs performed by series regulars Pauley Perrette and Cote de Pablo.

A sequel to the soundtrack was released on November 3, 2009. NCIS: The Official TV Soundtrack; Vol. 2 is a single disc, 12 track set that covers songs (many previously unreleased) featured throughout the seventh season of the show, including one recording titled "Bitter and Blue" by Weatherly, as well as two songs used in previous seasons.

Quelle: [18]

The NCIS Authority: Naval Criminal Investigative Service

The United States Naval Criminal Investigative Service (NCIS) is the primary security, counter-intelligence, counter-terrorism, and law enforcement agency of the United States Department of the Navy. It is the successor organization to the former Naval Investigative Service (NIS).

Roughly half of the 2,500 NCIS employees are civilian special agents who are trained to carry out a wide variety of assignments at locations across the globe. NCIS special agents are armed federal law enforcement investigators, who frequently coordinate with other U.S. government agencies. NCIS special agents are supported by analysts and other experts skilled in disciplines such as forensics, surveillance, surveillance countermeasures, computer investigations, physical security, and polygraph examinations.

NCIS traces its roots to Navy Department General Order 292 of 1882, signed by William H. Hunt, Secretary of the Navy, which established the Office of Naval Intelligence (ONI). Initially, the ONI was tasked with collecting information on the characteristics and weaponry of foreign vessels, charting foreign passages, rivers, or other bodies of water, and touring overseas fortifications, industrial plants, and shipyards.

In anticipation of the United States' entry into World War I, the ONI's responsibilities expanded to include espionage, sabotage, and all manner of information on the Navy's potential adversaries; and in World War II the ONI became responsible for the investigation of sabotage, espionage and subversive activities that posed any kind of threat to the Navy.

The major buildup of civilian special agents began with the Korean War in 1950, and continued through the Cold War years. In 1966 the name Naval Investigative Service (NIS) was adopted to distinguish the organization from the rest of ONI, and in 1969 NIS special agents were reclassified from contract employees and became Excepted Civil Service.

The early 1970s saw an NIS special agent stationed on the USS Intrepid (CV-11) for six months which was the beginning of the "Deployment Afloat" program, (now called the Special Agent Afloat program). In 1972, background investigations were transferred from NIS to the newly formed Defense Investigative Service (DIS), allowing NIS to give more attention to criminal investigations and counter-intelligence. The first female agent was stationed at Naval Air Station Miramar, California, in 1975.

In 1982, NIS assumed responsibility for managing the Navy's Law Enforcement and Physical Security Program and the Navy's Information and Personnel Security Program. Additionally, in 1982 two classes of NIS Special Agents were trained at the Federal Law Enforcement Training Center (FLETC), Glynco, GA, in an assessment of FLETC's capability to train military investigators. Prior to this and subsequently until 1984 NIS Special Agent Training was in ONI Headquarters, Suitland, MD.

Two months after the October 1983 bombing of the Marine Barracks in Beirut, the agency opened the Navy Antiterrorist Alert Center (ATAC). The ATAC was a 24-hour-a-day operational intelligence center that issued indications and warnings on terrorist activity to Navy and Marine Corps commands. ATAC was the facility at which Jonathan Pollard was working when he committed the acts of espionage for which he was convicted in 1987. In 2002 the ATAC became the Multiple Threat Alert Center (MTAC).

In 1984, special agents began training at the Federal Law Enforcement Training Center (FLETC) in Georgia, the training facility for most other federal investigative agencies except the FBI, the DEA, and the United States Postal Inspection Service.

In 1985, Cathal L. Flynn became the first admiral to lead NIS. The command took on the additional responsibility of Information and Personnel Security. In 1986, the Department of the Navy Central Adjudication Facility (DoN CAF) was established and placed under the agency, as the agency was now once again responsible for adjudicating security clearances (although not the actual investigations). DoN CAF renders approximately 200,000 eligibility determinations annually for the Department of the Navy.

In 1991, the NIS was responsible for investigating the Tailhook scandal, involving sexual misconduct and harassment by Naval and Marine Corps officers in Las Vegas, Nevada.

In 1992, the NCIS mission was again clarified and became a mostly civilian agency. Roy D. Nedrow, a former United States Secret Service (USSS) executive, was appointed as the first civilian director and the name changed from Naval Investigative Service to Naval Criminal Investigative Service. Nedrow oversaw the restructuring of NCIS into a Federal law enforcement agency with 14 field offices controlling field operations in 140 locations worldwide. In 1995, NCIS introduced the Cold Case Homicide Unit.

In May 1997, David L. Brant was appointed Director of NCIS by Secretary of the Navy John Howard Dalton. Director Brant retired in December 2005. He was succeeded by Director Thomas A. Betro who was appointed Director of NCIS in January 2006, by Secretary of the Navy Donald C. Winter. Betro retired in September 2009. On September 13, 2009, Deputy Director of Operations Gregory A. Scovel was appointed Acting Director by Under Secretary of the Navy Robert Work. He served concurrently as Deputy Director for Operations until the new Director was selected.

In 1999, NCIS and the Marine Corps Criminal Investigation Division (CID) signed a memorandum of understanding calling for an integration of Marine Corps CID into NCIS. (USMC CID continues to exist to investigate misdemeanors and felonies and other criminal offenses not under NCIS investigative jurisdiction.)

In 2000, Congress granted NCIS civilian special agents authority to execute warrants and make arrests. Virtually all NCIS investigators, criminal, counterintelligence, and force protection personnel are now sworn civilian personnel with powers of arrest and warrant service. The exceptions are a small number of reserve military elements engaged in counter-intelligence support.

A growing appreciation of the changing threat facing the Department of the Navy in the 21st century, culminating with the terrorist bombing of the USS Cole (DDG-67) in Yemen and the attacks on September 11, 2001, led NCIS to transform the Anti-terrorist Alert Center into the Multiple Threat Alert Center (MTAC) in 2002.

NCIS agents were the first U.S. law enforcement personnel on the scene at the USS Cole bombing, the Limburg bombing and the terrorist attack in Mombasa, Kenya. NCIS's Cold Case unit has solved 50 homicides since 1995 — one of which was 33 years old.

NCIS has conducted fraud investigations resulting in over half a billion dollars in recoveries and restitution to the U.S. government and the U.S. Navy since 1997. NCIS investigates any death occurring on a Navy vessel or Navy or Marine Corps aircraft or installation (except when the cause of death is medically attributable to disease or natural causes). NCIS oversees the Master at Arms programs for the Navy, overseeing 8800 Masters-At-Arms and the Military Working Dog program. NCIS's three strategic priorities are to prevent terrorism, protect secrets, and reduce crime.

Current missions for NCIS include criminal investigations, force protection, cross-border drug enforcement, anti-terrorism, counter-terrorism, major procurement fraud, computer crime and counter-intelligence.

NCIS Special Agent Peter Garza conducted the first court-ordered Internet wiretap in the United States. Jonathan Jay Pollard was an NCIS analyst who was convicted of spying for Israel after being caught by NCIS and FBI. He received a life sentence in 1987.

On February 14, 2010, Mark D. Clookie became the fourth civilian Director of NCIS, having been appointed to the position by the Secretary of the Navy Ray Mabus. Clookie leads an agency composed of some 2,500 civilian and military personnel that has a presence in over 150 locations world-wide. He is responsible for executing an annual operating budget of approximately $460 million.

In December 2012, the FBI released redacted documents regarding operations against Occupy Wall Street. In one FBI report, the NCIS is quoted as looking into links between Occupy and "organized labor actions" in December 2011.

The Special Agent Afloat Program of NCIS sends NCIS Special Agents aboard U.S. aircraft carriers and other ships (for example, hospital ships and amphibious assault ships). The purpose of the program is to provide professional investigative, counterintelligence, and force protection support to deployed Navy and Marine Corps commanders. These special agents are assigned to aircraft carriers and other deployed major combatants. Their environment can best be described as a "floating city." The assignment offers many of the same investigative challenges found by any criminal investigator working in a metropolitan city. A special agent assigned to a carrier must be skilled in general criminal investigations including: crime scene examination, expert interview techniques, and use of proactive law enforcement procedures to stop criminal activity before it occurs. The special agent afloat also provides guidance on foreign counterintelligence matters, including terrorism. It is also the mission of the special agent afloat to offer Navy and Marine Corps leadership advice and operational support on security issues which might threaten the safety of ships, personnel and resources.

NCIS's former standard issue sidearm was the 9×19mm SIG Sauer P228. Their current standard issue pistol is the SIG Sauer P229R DAK or SIG Sauer P239 DAK in .40 S&W.

Quelle: [19]

The NCIS TV-Show

NCIS, formerly known as NCIS: Naval Criminal Investigative Service, is an American police procedural drama television series revolving around a fictional team of special agents from the Naval Criminal Investigative Service, which conducts criminal investigations involving the U.S. Navy and Marine Corps. The concept and characters were initially introduced in a two-part episode of the CBS series JAG (JAG episodes 8.20 and 8.21). The show, a spin-off from JAG, premiered on September 23, 2003 on CBS and, to date, has aired eight full seasons and has gone into syndicated reruns on USA Network, Cloo (formerly Sleuth) and Ion Television. Donald Bellisario, who created JAG as well as the well-known series Airwolf, Magnum, P.I. and Quantum Leap, is co-creator and executive producer of NCIS.
NCIS was originally referred to as Navy NCIS during Season 1; however, "Navy" was later dropped from the title as it was redundant. NCIS was joined in its seventh season by a spin-off series, NCIS: Los Angeles, starring Chris O'Donnell and LL Cool J.

NCIS follows a fictional team of Naval Criminal Investigative Service Major Case Response Team (MCRT) special agents headquartered at the Washington Navy Yard in Washington, D.C. It is described by the actors and producers (on special features on DVD releases in the United States) as being distinguished by its comic elements, ensemble acting and character-driven plots.

NCIS is the primary law enforcement and counter-intelligence arm of the United States Department of the Navy, which includes the United States Marine Corps. NCIS investigates all major criminal offenses (felonies)—crimes punishable under the Uniform Code of Military Justice by confinement of more than one year—within the Department of the Navy. The MCRT is frequently assigned to high profile cases such as the death of the U.S. president's military aide, a bomb situation on a U.S. Navy warship, the death of a celebrity on a reality show set on a USMC base, terrorist threats, and kidnappings.

The MCRT is led by Supervisory Special Agent Leroy Jethro Gibbs (Mark Harmon). Gibbs's team is composed of Special Agent and Senior Field Agent Anthony "Tony" DiNozzo (Michael Weatherly), Special Agent Timothy McGee (Sean Murray) and Special Agent (formerly Mossad liaison officer) Ziva David (Cote de Pablo), who replaced Caitlin "Kate" Todd (Sasha Alexander) when she was shot and killed by rogue Mossad agent Ari Haswari (Rudolf Martin) at the end of season two. The team is assisted in their investigations by Chief Medical Examiner Donald "Ducky" Mallard (David McCallum), his assistant Jimmy Palmer (Brian Dietzen), who replaced Gerald Jackson (Pancho Demmings), and Forensic Specialist Abigail "Abby" Sciuto (Pauley Perrette).

It has been revealed through flashbacks that the 'original' head of the MCRT was Special Agent Mike Franks (Muse Watson), who led the unit when it was part of the Naval Investigative Service (NIS), the predecessor agency of the NCIS. He recruited Gibbs shortly after Gibbs' retirement from the Marine Corps, eventually retiring himself some years later. After Franks' departure, Gibbs recruited DiNozzo from the Baltimore Police Department's Homicide Section. The two were briefly joined by Vivian Blackadder (Robyn Lively), whom Gibbs recruited from the FBI. In the second part of the NCIS pilot, Blackadder allowed her emotions to nearly derail an anti-terror operation in Spain. Gibbs is noticeably disappointed; Blackadder is not present in the series' first regular episode, replaced by Caitlin Todd, a Secret Service agent who joins Gibbs' team after resigning from the Secret Service. McGee first appears as a Field Agent assigned to the Norfolk Field Office. He uses his computer skills to aid the

MCRT in subsequent investigations through the rest of the first season, until he is officially promoted with his own desk at the Navy Yard in the beginning of the second season.

NCIS is currently led by Director Leon Vance (Rocky Carroll). The first director seen in the series, Thomas Morrow (Alan Dale), left after being promoted to Deputy Director of the Department of Homeland Security. Jenny Shepard (Lauren Holly) was appointed director after Morrow in the first episode of season three. After Shepard was killed in a shootout at the end of the fifth season Vance, who was Assistant Director of NCIS before her death, was seen as Acting Director after her death and was promoted to take her place.

Source: [1]

Main Cast

Name	Portrayed by	Episodes Main	Seasons Main	Episodes Recurring	Seasons Recurring
Special Agent Leroy Jethro **Gibbs**	Mark Harmon	001–	1–		
Special Agent Anthony „**Tony**" DiNozzo	Michael Weatherly	001–	1–		
Abigail „**Abby**" Sciuto	Pauley Perrette	001–	1–		
Dr. Donald „**Ducky**" Mallard	David McCallum	001–	1–		
Special Agent Caitlin „**Kate**" Todd	Sasha Alexander	001–46	1–2	047–48	3
Special Agent Timothy „Tim" **McGee**	Sean Murray	024–	2–	007, 11, 18–23	1
Special Agent **Ziva** David	Cote de Pablo	050–236	3–11	047–48	3
Director Jennifer „**Jenny**" Shepard	Lauren Holly	055–113	3–5	047–54	3
Director Leon **Vance**	Rocky Carroll	114–	6–	108–109, 111, 113	5
Jimmy **Palmer**	Brian Dietzen	114–	6–	021–113	1–5
Special Agent Eleanor „**Elli**" **Bishop**	Emily Wickersham	246–	11–	243-246	11

Source: [1]

Recurring Cast

From Season 1:

- Joe Spano asTobias Fornell (1–)
- Alan Dale as Thomas Morrow (1–3)
- Rudolf Martin as Ari Haswari (1–3)
- Jessica Steen as Paula Cassidy (1–4)
- Pancho Demmings as Gerald Jackson (1, 3)

From Season 2:

- Troian Bellisario as Sarah McGee (2, 4)
- Tamara Taylor as Cassie Yates (2–3)

From Season 3:

- Michael Bellisario as Charles „Chip" Sterling (3)
- Muse Watson as Mike Franks (3–)
- Don Franklin as Ron Sacks (3–4)

From Season 4:

- Liza Lapira as Michelle Lee (4–6)
- Scottie Thompson as Jeanne Benoit (4–5)
- Susanna Thompson as Hollis Mann (4–5)
- David Dayan Fisher as Trent Kort (4–)
- Armand Assante as René Benoit (4–5)

From Season 5:

- Susan Kelechi Watson as Nicki Jardine (5)
- Paul Telfer as Damon Werth (5, 7)
- Jonathan LaPaglia as Brent Langer (5–6)

From Season 6:

- Merik Tadros as Michael Rivkin (6)
- Michael Nouri as Eli David (6–)
- Ralph Waite as Jackson Gibbs (6–)
- Jude Ciccolella as SecNav Phillip Davenport (6, 8)

From Season 7:

- Robert Wagner as Anthony D. DiNozzo Sr. (7–)
- Rena Sofer as M. Allison Hart (7)
- Dina Meyer as Holly Snow (7)
- Marco Sanchez as Alejandro Rivera (7–8)
- Diane Neal as Abigail Borin (7–)
- T.J. Ramini as Malachi Ben-Gidon (7–)
- Jacqueline Obradors as Paloma Reynosa (7–8)

From Season 8:

- David Sullivan as Larry Krone (8)
- Annie Wersching as Gail Walsh (8)
- Sarah Jane Morris as Erica Jane „E.J." Barrett (8–)
- Enrique Murciano as Ray Cruz (8–)
- Wendy Makkena as Dr. Rachel Cranston (8–)
- Matthew Willig as Simon Cade (8–9)
- Matt Craven as SecNav Clayton Jarvis (8–)

From Season 9:

- Matt L. Jones as Ned Dorneget (9–)
- Jamie Lee Curtis as Dr. Samantha Ryan (9–)
- Scott Wolf as Jonathan Cole ak Casey Stratton (9)

Source: [1]

Name: Leroy Jethro Gibbs

Occupation: Supervisory/Senior Special Agent in Charge (NCIS), Former Gunnery Sergeant (Marine sniper and Military Police)(USMC)

Gender: Male

Family: Jackson Gibbs (Father)

Spouse(s): Shannon Gibbs (deceased)
Diane Sterling (divorced)
Unknown (divorced)
Stephanie Flynn (divorced)

Children: Kelly Gibbs (deceased)

Supervisory Special Agent Leroy Jethro Gibbs, portrayed by Mark Harmon, was born in Stillwater, Pennsylvania to Jackson Gibbs and an unnamed mother. He joined the United States Marine Corps in 1976 and became a Scout Sniper instead of attending college. After serving tours of duty in Panama and Iraq, he retired from the Marine Corps with the rank of Gunnery Sergeant. He joined NIS, which later became NCIS, after his wife Shannon and only daughter Kelly were murdered in 1991. Gibbs later travelled to Mexico and murdered the drug dealer responsible, a crime he kept concealed for twenty years. Since then, he has been married and divorced three times, and is currently single.

He currently leads a team consisting of Anthony DiNozzo, Timothy McGee, Abigail Sciuto, and Ziva David. In the episode "Bête Noire" Gibbs comes face to face with terrorist Ari Haswari and puts a bullet through Ari's left shoulder. Finding Ari later becomes an obsession for Gibbs when he and DiNozzo witness original team member Agent Kate Todd get shot dead in front of them in the season 2 finale, "Twilight".

He is often shown in his basement building boats, at least one of which he named after his daughter; another was named after one of his ex-wives. In the episode "Blowback", when confronting "Goliath" on the plane about "ARES", Gibbs revealed he is a Virgo. He is a deadshot marksman, as evidenced in "Hiatus" with flashbacks of him hitting a long-distance headshot of his family's murderer, who was driving a moving vehicle, a 1200-yard killshot, from a file read by Director Leon Vance in the episode "Deliverance" and in "Jeopardy" he hits a kidnapper with a very swift killshot in the forehead – he takes this shot while kneeling from inside a car trunk, with his left hand. In "Truth or Consequences", Gibbs saved his entire team by shooting the leader of a terrorist cell with a killshot after DiNozzo and McGee get captured looking for Ziva after she quits NCIS. Gibbs is one of three characters to have appeared in every episode.

Source: [1]

Gibbs' Rules

Rule #1:   Never let suspects stay together.

Rule #2:   Always wear gloves at a crime scene.

Rule #3:   Don't believe what you're told. Double check.

Rule #3:   Never be unreachable. (Rule #3 double-used)

Rule #4:   If you have a secret, the best thing is to keep it to yourself. The second-best
                is to tell one other person if you must. There is no third best.

Rule #5:   You don't waste good.

Rule #6:   Never say you're sorry. It's a sign of weakness.

Rule #7:   Always be specific when you lie.

Rule #8:   Never take anything for granted.

Rule #9:   Never go anywhere without a knife.

Rule #10:   Never get personally involved in a case.

Rule #11:   When the job is done, walk away.

Rule #12:   Never date a coworker.

Rule #13:   Never, ever involve lawyers.

Rule #15:   Always work as a team.

Rule #16:   If someone thinks they have the upper hand, break it.

Rule #18:   It's better to ask forgiveness than ask permission.

Rule #22:   Never, ever interrupt Gibbs in interrogation.

Rule #23:   Never mess with a Marine's coffee if you want to live.

Rule #27:   There are two ways to follow someone: 1st way - they never notice you
              2nd way - they only notice you.

Rule #35:   Always watch the watchers.

Rule #36:   If it feels like you're being played, you probably are.

Rule #38:   Your case, your lead.

Rule #39:   There is no such thing as coincidence.

Rule #40:   If it seems like someone's out to get you, they are.

Rule #42:   Don't ever accept an apology from someone that just sucker-punched you.

Rule #44:   First things first, hide the women and children.

Rule #45:   Clean up your messes.

Rule #51:   Sometimes - you're wrong.

Rule #69:   Never trust a woman who doesn't trust her man.

Source: 2

Name: **Anthony D. DiNozzo**

Occupation:	Special agent, Major Case Response Team Senior Field Agent, NCIS, Former Detective (BPD)
Gender:	Male
Nationality:	American, Italian descent
Family:	Anthony D. DiNozzo Sr. (father) Unnamed mother

Source: 1

Senior Special Agent Anthony "Tony" D. DiNozzo, portrayed by Michael Weatherly, is a former homicide detective for the Baltimore Police Department. Prior to Baltimore, he worked for Philadelphia PD and Peoria PD. Like Gibbs, has a limited patience for the scientific method and technical terms. DiNozzo is perhaps best known for his seemingly-endless film references; Ziva insists that his dying words will be "I've seen this film".

He attended Ohio State University as a physical education major and was a member of the "Alpha Chi Delta" fraternity, class of 1989. DiNozzo is said to have played college basketball, "running the point for Ohio State" according to Abby Sciuto in a discussion with her assistant, Chip.

It is mentioned that he comes from a wealthy family but was disowned by his father, Anthony DiNozzo Sr, played by Robert Wagner who in turn was played by Weatherly in a TV movie. DiNozzo's mother was over-protective, and she "dressed him like a sailor until he was ten."

He is a flirt, and has had his fair share of success in that department. He has a fondness for playing pranks on his co-workers and little respect for their boundaries.

During the course of the fourth season, he was on an undercover assignment that Director Jenny Shepard led, the key mission being to find arms dealer La Grenouille by posing as La Grenouille's daughter's boyfriend, but ended up falling in love with her.

In the episode "Knockout", he revealed that he was not doing well with women and that he was still hurting from his relationship with Jeanne Benoit. There is a great deal of romantic tension between Tony and Ziva.

Despite his playboy manner and light-hearted nature, DiNozzo is frequently shown to be very sharp; he is able to coax Mossad Director Eli David into admitting that he ordered Rivkin and Ziva to spy on NCIS.

Reassigned as an Agent Afloat in Season 5 ("Judgment Day")

Transferred back to the Major Case Response Team in Season 6 ("Agent Afloat").

Tony DiNozzo is one of three characters to have appeared in every episode.

Source: 1

Name: **Caitlin Todd (†)**

Occupation: Special Agent, Major Case Response
Team Field Agent, (NCIS)
Former Special Agent, (USSS)

Gender: Female

Family: Rachel Cranston (older sister)
Three Unnamed brothers

Caitlin Todd, portrayed by Sasha Alexander, first appeared in the episode "Yankee White". Todd was a former Secret Service agent, recruited by Gibbs after she successfully helped him solve a murder aboard Air Force One.

She worked well with everyone on the team, becoming particularly close with Ducky and Abby, who convinced her to get a tattoo (referenced in the episode "Kill Ari (Part 1)"). Her relationship with Gibbs is unique, as there appeared to be a real friendship between the two characters; which is unusual considering Gibbs is not a close friend with anyone.

Her relationship with Tony, however, was more adversarial and appeared to be more of siblings than anything else. Tony frequently flirted with her and went through her personal belongings, no matter how many times she pointed out that his behavior was grossly unprofessional. At the same time, Kate is willing to risk her life for DiNozzo and admits that life would be considerably less interesting without him around.

Todd was killed in the line of duty at the end of the episode "Twilight" by Ari Haswari, collateral damage in the terrorist's obsession with Gibbs. She received a fatal gunshot wound to the head from a sniper rifle fired by Ari Haswari. Todd also made appearances in "Kill Ari" parts 1 and 2 as a hallucination, remembered by her teammates.

She was replaced at NCIS by Israeli Mossad Liaison Officer Ziva David.

Source: 1

Name:	**Ziva David**

Occupation:	2009-present, Special agent, Major Case Response Team Field Agent, NCIS (Season 7–present), 2005-2009 Mossad Liaison Officer (with NCIS) (seasons 3–7, 2003–2005) Mossad operative, Control officer, 2001–2003 Soldier in the Israeli Army

Gender:	Female

Family:	Eli David (father) Rivka David (deceased) (Mother, deceased) Ari Haswari paternal half brother (deceased) Tali David (sister, deceased)

Ziva David, portrayed by Cote de Pablo, formerly held the post of Mossad Liaison Officer to NCIS, to which she was appointed following the murder of Special Agent Caitlin Todd by a rogue Mossad operative named Ari Haswari. Ziva was Ari's control officer and half-sister. After Agent Todd's death, she requested a liaison assignment to NCIS, where she subsequently joined Special Agent Leroy Jethro Gibbs' team. At the end of Season 6, Ziva falls under suspicion as a spy for the Mossad.

Her specialty with the Mossad was espionage, assassination and terrorism and is highly trained in the martial arts. She speaks Hebrew, English, Arabic, Spanish, French, Italian, German Title, Russian and Turkish. Despite being fluent in English, she sometimes misinterprets idioms and phrases that have different meanings in other languages if translated directly; this is a running joke within the series.

Ziva is very skilled with a knife and has been shown teaching her colleagues how to throw it properly. She is the one person Gibbs trusts with any type of firearm in difficult, potentially hazardous, situations.

In her career, she has traveled extensively to countries including Egypt (where she met Jenny Shepard), Iraq, the United Kingdom and Morocco.

In the episode "Good Cop, Bad Cop" Ziva became a probationary NCIS Special Agent after she terminated her links with Mossad for good. Since then, Tony has referred to her (as with McGee) as "Probie". As of "Rule Fifty-One", she is a citizen of the United States and able to become a full agent which is made official in Season 9's "Nature of the Beast".

Ziva rarely speaks of her personal life. Her father Eli David was the director of Mossad (killed in Season 10). The show rarely mentions Ziva's mother, Rivka, who taught her to drive; all that is known is that she does not have the same mother as Ari.

Her younger sister, Talia "Tali" David, was killed in a Hamas terrorist attack against Israel at the age of sixteen. She also has an Aunt Nettie who likes to play mahjong.

Ziva's hobbies include playing the piano, singing, dancing (she took ballet when she was young), cooking, reading, and boxing. She enjoys the fictional drink Berry Mango Madness.

She drives a red Mini Cooper, likes listening to the Israeli band Hadag Nachash and the Latin American band Kinky. She does not own a television but her favorite film is The Sound of Music.

De Pablo describes the character as someone who is "completely different from anyone else on the show" and that because "she's been around men all her life; she's used to men in authority. She's not afraid of men."

On July 10, 2013, CBS television studios announced that Cote de Pablo would be leaving NCIS in Season 11. She would appear in the beginning of the eleventh season to close out Ziva's storyline, but would not be cast as a series regular.

Source: [1]

Name:	**Timothy McGee**

Occupation:	Special agent, Major Case Response Team Field Agent, NCIS (Seasons 2-Present) Norfolk Case Agent and Major Case Response Team TAD Field Agent, NCIS (Season 1)
	Gender: Male
Family:	Sarah McGee (Sister) Penelope Langston (Grandmother)

Timothy McGee, portrayed by Sean Murray, first appeared in the episode "Sub Rosa" as a Case Agent stationed at Norfolk, and was promoted to Field Agent and assigned to Agent Gibbs' team in the second season, becoming a regular character, where he became a Junior Special Agent with NCIS. He serves as a field computer consultant and occasionally assists Abby Sciuto in the lab.

He clashes with DiNozzo, though after the two became partners (following Ziva's departure from the team at the end of season six), they are frequently shown to form an effective team; however, once Ziva returns, their relationship reverts to its original state. McGee's methods are often indecipherable to the other team members, have earned him the pejorative nickname "McGeek" and "McGoo" (along with other derisive nicknames based on his surname), as well as "Probie", and "Elf Lord", the latter used by multiple characters due to his elf character in an online role playing computer game. He was trained in biomedical engineering at Johns Hopkins University, and computer forensics at Massachusetts Institute of Technology (MIT). He also graduated the top of his class at the Federal Law Enforcement Training Center.

McGee is also a writer, writing mystery crime novels including a national best seller, Deep Six, under the pseudonym Thom E. Gemcity (an anagram of his name), featuring characters based on his fellow co-workers and others from his everyday life. He also drives a silver Porsche Boxster as seen in the episode "Twisted Sister". He has Apple's iPhone smartphone, and uses it frequently on investigation. He owns a dog named Jethro. Jethro was in a prior episode where he had been falsely accused of killing his police handler. Abby proved his innocence, named him Jethro and had to convince McGee to take Jethro because her landlord wouldn't let her keep the dog.

McGee was transferred to Cybercrimes Division in Season 5 ("Judgment Day") and back to the Major Case Response Team in Season 6 ("Last Man Standing").

Source: [1]

Name: **Abigail Sciuto**

Occupation: Forensic Specialist, NCIS

Gender: Female

Religion: Catholic

Abigail "Abby" Sciuto, portrayed by Pauley Perrette, is a forensic specialist with NCIS. As indicated in the episode "Seadog", she is the child of deaf parents. She is known for her gothic style of dress and addiction to the fictional, high-caffeine beverage "Caf-Pow". Abby had a brief sexual relationship with Special Agent McGee, as seen in the episode "Reveille" in season one, which ended with the two remaining friends.

She is the most active and affectionate person of the team, often hugging everyone and talking fast, though she can be easily distracted. She is one of the few who can talk to Gibbs freely, and he often buys her Caf-Pow. She and Gibbs are both fluent in sign language. She has a stuffed farting hippopotamus named Bert that often appears in the show.

Abby developed a fondness for a Navy sniffer dog in the season 5 episode "Dog Tags". Originally named "Butch", she renamed it "Jethro" (after Gibbs) for being "handsome and quiet". The dog was framed for the murder of a petty officer, but Abby proves Jethro's innocence. Afterwards, Abby forces McGee to adopt him, much to his dismay (as Jethro had attacked him earlier in the episode). Abby would have preferred to adopt Jethro herself, but was prohibited from doing so by her landlord.

Abby's hobbies include a bowling league with nuns, helping build homes for the needy, and playing computer games. She also sleeps in a coffin and is, according to DiNozzo, "the happiest goth you will ever meet."

Abby is one of three characters to have appeared in every episode and like Director Leon Vance, also appears on the spin-off series, NCIS Los Angeles.

Source: [1]

Name: Dr. Donald Mallard

Occupation: Chief Medical Examiner

Gender: Male

Dr. Donald "Ducky" Mallard, portrayed by David McCallum, is the Chief Medical Examiner at NCIS. Dr. Mallard is a Scottish-born doctor, who has been long-time friends with Gibbs, and underwent medical education at the University of Edinburgh Medical School, and served in the Royal Army Medical Corps. He has a "second talent", as Gibbs calls it, to be able to read people, which he expands in Season 4 by studying psychology. In cases without actual bodies, he assists by using his psychological training to decipher the clues left by the perpetrators. Dr. Mallard is an eccentric character who often talks to the deceased and rambles to the living with many long personal remembrances or historical accounts, but is a kind man at heart. He also calls co-workers by their full first names (ex: Abigail instead of Abby)—with the exceptions of Gibbs and medical assistant Jimmy Palmer, whom he addresses as Jethro and Mr. Palmer, respectively (although he does refer to Palmer by his first name, Jimmy, when concerned for him, as revealed in About Face).

Although most of his time is spent in autopsy and going to crime scenes to examine bodies, he was sent on a highly important undercover mission in the episode "Blowback". He also spent some time in Afghanistan during the Soviet invasion, and in Bosnia during the Balkan conflict.

Ducky and Gibbs have worked together for many years. When Gibbs was asked, "What did Ducky look like when he was younger?" he replied, "Illya Kuryakin"—the Russian spy played by McCallum in the 1960s television show The Man From U.N.C.L.E. Ducky drives a Morgan that he restored himself. In the episode "Hung Out to Dry," it is revealed that he has a nephew, though no further information follows. The ring tone on his cell phone features bagpipes playing "Scotland the Brave".

He lived with his aging mother and her corgi dogs until season 6. In the episode "Broken Bird", Ducky revealed his mother had moved out and had Alzheimer's disease. Nina Foch, the actress who played Ducky's mother, died on December 5, 2008, necessitating the change.
In the episode "Double Identity", it was revealed Ducky's mother had died. Her headstone indicated 1912-2010.
The rest of the team only learns of Victoria Mallard's passing when Abby follows Ducky to her gravesite. Later Gibbs pays him a condolence call in the autopsy room, but Ducky seems relieved at her death rather than sad (probably that she was no longer suffering from Alzheimer's), and grateful to have been her son.
He expresses to Gibbs his pride at the fact that she had almost lived to the age of 100.

Source: ¹

Name: **Jimmy Palmer**

Occupation: Medical Examiner Assistant

Gender: Male

Jim (Jimmy) Palmer, portrayed by Brian Dietzen, and sometimes referred to by Tony as "Autopsy Gremlin", first appeared in the episode "Split Decision".

After Gerald Jackson was incapacitated, Palmer became Mallard's medical assistant both in the field and in the morgue. In the episode "About Face", Jimmy became a central character of the episode who must recover his memory to find a suspect to the murder case and his attempted killer. He self-identifies as a sufferer of a "mild" case of diabetes mellitus in the episode "In The Dark". He is terrified of Gibbs.

Part of the reason that Doctor Mallard and he are often not at the crime scene until well after Gibbs and his team arrive is related to Dr. Mallard's emphasis on Jimmy being a horrible driver and always getting lost, although Jimmy tries to defend himself by pointing out that Ducky is the one with the map. He was named after former Baltimore Orioles pitcher Jim Palmer, but does not like baseball.

In many of the episodes, Jimmy is seen fraternizing with Michelle Lee. Often they make excuses for working late and are seen entering and exiting the underside of the autopsy table. In the episode "Last Man Standing", Palmer admits to Gibbs and Vance that he and Agent Lee had been "doing it" for a while. In the episode "The Good Wives Club" it is revealed that Jimmy is claustrophobic; when he is entering the enclosed hallway he is seen sweating profusely and when he has to go get the body bag he gets freaked out about having to go back through it.

In the episode "About Face", as Jimmy was being hypnotized by Abby, it can be inferred that he has a foot/shoe fetish as he dreamily states in great detail about Ziva and Abby's footwear, instead of recalling information about the current case. The episode also leads us to believe that his mother's name is Eunice. In the episode "Bounce" it is shown that Palmer regularly helped Tony when he was in charge. Jimmy Palmer is also shown to have severe tinnitus.

In season 7 it was revealed that Jimmy was in love with a girl named Breena Slater, who appeared in the episode "Mother's Day". In the season 8 finale "Pyramid", NCIS special agent E.J. Barrett congratulates Jimmy with his engagement.

Source: [1]

Name: **Jennifer Shepard (†)**

Occupation: NCIS Director

Gender: Female

Jenny Shepard, portrayed by Lauren Holly, first appeared in the episode "Kill Ari (Part 1)". She replaced former NCIS director Thomas Morrow, at the start of the third season after Morrow took a Deputy Director's position with the Department of Homeland Security. She is also a "military brat" as her father Colonel Jasper Shepard was an Army officer.

She was Gibbs' former partner and former lover. While she and Gibbs were stationed in Europe, Gibbs was ordered back to the States and she was offered her own section in Europe. When Gibbs asked Jenny to go with him, she refused. They were reunited in "Kill Ari (Part 1)" which stirred Gibbs' heart, and opened a constant flirtation between her and Gibbs. Jenny was killed in the episode "Judgment Day (Part 1)". At the time of her death she was already dying from a terminal illness that was never specified. Only she, Ducky, and Mike Franks ever knew, and Ducky broke the truth to Gibbs after her passing.

Shepard had a close relationship with Ziva David and occasionally provided her with key information on a case without going through regular channels or telling Gibbs, as in the Season 3 episode "Head Case." They made it a point to keep these dealings confidential; "What Gibbs doesn't know can't hurt us," Shepard quipped. Later in the episode, though, Gibbs' remarks revealed that he knew about her assistance. Shepard and Ziva had a working relationship prior Shepard being appointed Director of NCIS.

During season 4, Director Shepard places Tony DiNozzo on an undercover assignment to get close to notorious international arms dealer René Benoit, otherwise known as La Grenouille. The sub-plot comes to a head late in the season when it is revealed that she blames Benoit for the death of her father and that Benoit is now central to a major CIA deep-cover operation.

Gibbs confronts her over the operation, suggesting that Shepard is letting her emotions dictate her actions and that she has knowingly placed DiNozzo in danger and jeopardized a major CIA operation for the purposes of getting revenge, while hiding behind her position as NCIS director to justify her actions.

During the episode "Internal Affairs", it is strongly implied that Shepard was responsible for the murder of La Grenouille, something reiterated when Gibbs looks through the FBI's file on the death of La Grenouille in "Judgement Day (Part 1)".

In several episodes during season five, before her death in the episode "Judgement Day (Part 1)", her failing health becomes a plot issue, as for example when Ducky is shown to be ordering a test on a blood sample to Abby, telling her that it is from a John Doe. However, when Abby talks to Jimmy Palmer, he says that they have no John Does. Gibbs deduces, correctly, that the only person Ducky would act this way for would be the Director, at the end of the episode "Stakeout". In the next episode "Dog Tags", Gibbs questions Jenny about her illness and she lies to him, saying she is fine. It is never revealed as to what was killing her.

Mike Franks also discovers her illness by going through her purse and finding her medication. In the episode "Judgment Day (Part 1)", Franks and Jenny are talking in an abandoned diner in the California desert and she indicates that she is dying and reveals that she regrets her decision to leave Gibbs in Paris and that she is still in love with him. It is revealed that she botched an operation ten years prior where she and Gibbs had been ordered to assassinate Russian lovers who were crime lords.

Gibbs shot the man, but Jenny faced the woman, Natasha (AKA Svetlana), down and let her live. As a result, Natasha sends assassins who kill Jenny in the diner but only after Jenny manages to kill all of them. Franks, who had been outside at the time of the shooting, returns to Jenny's house where Natasha is trying to kill Gibbs and Franks shoots her.

Gibbs and Franks decide to cover Jenny's mistake and death by burning down her Georgetown mansion and her cause of death is reported as "death in home fire". Her death rattles the crew and makes them all depressed. Abby regrets that she never told Jenny she was a snappy dresser, and says that would have made her smile.

After Director Shepard's death, she was replaced by Assistant Director Leon Vance.

Source: [1]

Name: Leon Vance

Occupation: NCIS Director

Gender: Male

Leon Vance, portrayed by Rocky Carroll, first appeared in the episode "Internal Affairs" as Assistant Director in Season 5. He is named Director after the death of Jenny Shepard. It has been revealed in the episode "Knockout" that he was originally from Ohio, but grew up in Chicago where he trained to be a boxer. In this episode, his wife stated that Vance attended the United States Naval Academy and was commissioned as a 2nd Lieutenant in the Marine Corps, but was forced to take a medical discharge before ever serving due to having undergone surgery to repair a detached retina suffered during his boxing career.

However, at the end of the episode, Ducky reveals to Gibbs that Vance's close, childhood friend who had died just prior to the start of the episode also suffered a detached retina. In the course of this episode, Vance also revealed that it was this friend who decided that Vance should leave Chicago while the friend stayed behind. Vance said this despite his insistence to Gibbs that his friend was a Marine though there was no record of his friend's service in the military.

In 1991, just prior to joining NCIS, Vance was a student at the United States Naval War College in Rhode Island. His coursework at this time included Combat Philosophy and Advanced Cryptography. It was during his time at the War College that he began to take an interest in black operations and even imagined one himself: Operation Frankenstein, which would later play a big part in the season 8 finale.

NIS took an interest in him and he was hired for an operation by Special Agent Whitney Sharp for an operation in Amsterdam codenamed Trident. Vance was trained by Sharp and left after a six-week training course for Amsterdam where he met his handler, Riley McAllister. McAllister told him that the target of the operation was a Russian intelligence operative who was known to Vance only as the Russian. NIS believed that he was bribing sailors in return for intelligence. Vance later met Eli David, a promising agent of the Mossad, who told him that he knew of the operation and that the Russian would kill him. Later, Eli betrayed Vance to the Russian but it was revealed that it was so that he would try to kill Vance sooner so that he could kill him himself. Eli also told Vance that he had been chosen because he was expendable and that he wasn't someone who would be missed.

Eli and Vance kill the Russian's hit team but the Russian manages to escape and Eli is unable to find him or who he was for that matter. Vance was credited for the elimination of the hit team and he started to rise swiftly through the ranks at NCIS. He kept believing along with Eli, that Amsterdam was not what it had seemed and they came to the conclusion that there was a dirty agent in NCIS, the one who had really tipped off the Russian of Vance's mission. It was later revealed that McAllister had masterminded the entire operation: being an expert in Russia, he had seen that the Soviet Union's collapse had laid attention away from Russia and onto the Middle East. Knowing that new attention to a potential Russian threat would throw him in the spotlight for Director of NIS, he had planned to have Vance killed by a Russian operative so as to show that Russia still posed a threat and so that he could satisfy his ambitions.

Notably, Vance took over for Jenny Shepard during her leave of absence between "Internal Affairs" and "Judgment Day," establishing himself as a formidable presence with Gibbs and his team. He and Gibbs clash during this span, prompting a cold
war between them which ends with a détente between the two of them in "Agent Afloat" at the start of the sixth season; however, the two of them clash later on, as Gibbs feels he cannot fully trust Vance, though he cannot identify a specific reason why.

Vance spearheads the investigation into Jenny Shepard's death, and is angered greatly when he is not kept in the loop by Gibbs and Mike Franks, who ultimately manipulate the situation to exonerate Shepard from her past failure, not what Vance had in mind. After Shepard's death, and possibly before, he lobbies the Secretary of the Navy hard to take over NCIS, as told in "Cloak," but in "Semper Fidelis" the Secretary of the Navy informs Gibbs of a major operation which will require Vance to serve as its head, and that NCIS and the Navy will need Gibbs and Vance to get along, to which Gibbs is not comfortable but appreciates the situation.

Things come to a head in "Aliyah," when Gibbs accuses Vance of selling out his team to Mossad Director Eli David, to which Vance responds that Ziva was a plant, used to get Mossad a foothole in NCIS through Gibbs. After this, the two of them realize that circumstances will prove one of them right.

At the start of the seventh season, Vance approves Ziva's transfer to NCIS, proving that Gibbs was right, and Ziva was loyal to NCIS. Despite his professional attitude towards Gibbs's team, he shows that he does care about them at least once when Alejandro Rivera threatens Abby in "Spider and The Fly". He tells Alejandro to leave before he gets hurt and when Alejandro asks by who, he replies angrily: "By me."

Even after the events of "Aliyah," Vance has been shown to still be in official contact with Eli David in David's capacity as Director of Mossad. This is shown when he receives a text message on his phone from Eli which says only: "I found him". Vance also refuses to discuss an Eli-phone call with Gibbs, despite knowing how dangerous Eli is, and his precarious relationship with Gibbs and his team.

Upon being promoted to the director's position at the end of Season 5, Vance immediately goes to former Director Shepard's office, and is seen to shred a single mysterious document from his own personnel file. It is later revealed in season 6 ("Semper Fidelis") that the document was written by his supervising agent at the time. The Secretary of the Navy tells Gibbs that the file is a fabrication and that he thought all copies had been destroyed. It is further revealed in the season 8 episode, "Enemies Domestic", that the head of the San Diego field office, when Vance was assigned there, had begun creating a legend for Vance that incorporated fictitious information about Vance in order to backstop a deep cover assignment, including the false information that Vance had been a pilot and director of a field office.

Leon Vance's wife, Jackie, was killed in season 10. He has two children, a daughter, Kayla, and a son, Jared. He met his wife while attending a University of Maryland basketball game while Len Bias was playing.

Vance is also a recurring character on the NCIS spin-off, NCIS Los Angeles.

Source: [1]

Name: Eleanor „Ellie" Bishop

Occupation: Special Agent

Gender: Female

Eleanor "Ellie" Bishop is an NSA analyst who debuted in the season 11 episode "Gut Check." Bishop is from Oklahoma and has three older brothers.

She wears a wedding band, but is coy to DiNozzo's question about her marital status. It is eventually revealed that she is married and her husband's name is Jake.

Described by her boss at the NSA as a "reclusive data freak", Bishop claims she "remembers almost everything she reads."

She applied at NCIS before taking the job with the NSA, and Gibbs has invited her to a "joint duty assignment."

Gibbs later offers her a probationary position as a Special Agent in "Monsters and Men", affectionately referring to her as "probie" for the first time.

She is a "country girl" from Oklahoma.

When first introduced, DiNozzo and McGee quickly noticed her wedding band but she remained coy when asked about her marital status. It is eventually revealed that she is married and her husband's name is Jake Malloy (Jamie Bamber), an attorney for the NSA. He is frequently mentioned and only introduced in the episode "Grounded". They met during their first week at NSA.

Source: [1]

Spin-off

The concept and characters were initially introduced in a two-part episode of the CBS series JAG (JAG episodes 8.20 and 8.21). The show, a spin-off from JAG, premiered on September 23, 2003 on CBS and, to date, has aired eight full seasons and has gone into syndicated reruns on USA Network, Cloo (formerly Sleuth) and Ion Television. Donald Bellisario, who created JAG as well as the well-known series Airwolf, Magnum, P.I. and Quantum Leap, is co-creator and executive producer of NCIS.

Source: [1]

Season 1 (Episodes 1.1- 1.23)

Originally broadcast between September 23, 2003 and May 25, 2004, the first season essentially dealt with introducing the characters and their strengths, skills and weaknesses. It also introduced the main foe for the first two seasons, Ari Haswari, two recurring characters in the form of Timothy McGee and Jimmy Palmer after Gerald Jackson, Ducky's assistant, was shot, and Special Agent Caitlin Todd as Special Agent Vivian Blackadder's replacement.

Source: [1]

Original Air Date USA   September 23, 2003 – May 25, 2004 on CBS

Original Air Date German Language   March 17, 2005 – August 25, 2005 on Sat 1

Episodes Season 1

No.	German Title	US Title	Air Date USA	Air Date GER	Directed by	Written by
1.1	Air Force One	**Yankee White**	Sep 23, 2003	Mar 17, 2005	D.Bellisario	D.Bellisario & D.McGill

While on Air Force One, a Navy Commander tasked with carrying the "football" dies under mysterious circumstances, forcing an emergency landing in Wichita, Kansas but while his death is originally thought be to a tragic accident, NCIS eventually uncovers evidence suggesting the Commander was murdered and that it might be connected to a possible assassination attempt on the President. *Source:* [1]

Gibbs Rule #1: Never let suspects stay together.
Gibbs Rule #2: Always wear gloves at a crime scene.
Gibbs Rule #3: Never believe what your told always double check.

Kate: I can't give him Air Force One's floor plans, they're top secret!
Gibbs: Come on, Agent Todd. I saw all this in a Harrison Ford movie.
Gibbs: NCIS does not leak. These plans get out... you can shoot DiNozzo.
Kate: No, I think I'm destined to shoot you.

Gibbs: Please
Abby: Wow! Gibbs said "Please".

Gibbs: Don't believe what you're told. Always double check.
Kate: Should I write these on my Palm Pilot, or crochet them on pillows?

Gibbs: I heard you quit, Agent Todd.
Kate: Happy news gets around fast. Yes, I resigned. It was the right thing to do.
Gibbs: Yep. Pull that crap at NCIS, I won't give you a chance to resign.
Kate: Is that a job offer?

(Tony is in an FBI van in a body bag, pretending to be a dead body)
Tony: Hello?
Gibbs: We're in the clear.You can get out of the body bag.
Tony: I never thought I'd say this, but I'm not sure I want to.
Gibbs: What? You gotta search Commander Trapp's apartment tonight.
Tony: Aw, Gibbs, come'on.It's one am.
Gibbs: Agent Axelrod is tailing you to pick up the bag when the FBI tosses it.
Tony: That's funny, Gibbs, real funny.....Gah!
Gibbs: I guess they found him.

Kate: I may not know the finer points of investigating, like sticking needles in liver and measuring swimsuit models, but I do know enough to hold the stewards who prepared and served the President's lunch.
Gibbs: Hum. Okay.
Kate: You want to question them?
Gibbs: No, they're not going anywhere, and we've got a crime scene to investigate. Rule Number One. Never let suspects stay together.
Kate: Well, I didn't consider them suspects.
Gibbs: Then why'd you hold them?

Tony: Tell me her measurements.
Kate: You're pathetic.
Tony: No, I'm serious. Can you tell if she's five foot four and a thirty-four C, or five foot seven and a thirty-six D? You can't. Not from a photo. That's why we do sketches and take measurements. Thank you.

Source: [3]

Episodes Season 1

No.	German Title	US Title	Air Date USA	Air Date GER	Directed by	Written by
1.2	Sprung in den Tod	**Hung Out to Dry**	Sep 30, 2003	Mar 31, 2005	A.Levi	D.McGill

A Marine dies during a night-time training jump. The culprit seems to be a faulty parachute, but the standard investigation reveals that the death might not have been an accident after all. Gibbs begins to believe that the supposed accident which resulted in the Marine's death may actually be murder and he, Tony and Kate set out to find out who tampered with the dead Marine's faulty parachute and eventually sent him unknowingly to his death.
Source: [1]

Tony: Ducky, why would Gibbs rip his hard line out and dunk his cell phone in a jar of paint thinner?
Ducky: Oh, dear.
Tony: What?
Ducky: Oh, I should have realized the time of year. It's his anniversary.
Tony: Which marriage?
Ducky: Well, the last one, of course.
Tony: Ducky. I'm not following.
Ducky: Every year, ex-wife number three gets drunk on their anniversary and calls him repeatedly.
Tony: Why doesn't he, ah, change his number?
Ducky: No idea. In case you haven't noticed, Gibbs is a man of more questions than answers.

Gibbs: Only thing you can use the DNA registry for is to identify a body.
Kate: Well, there has to be a way around that.
Gibbs: See? Now you're thinking like an NCIS agent.

Gibbs: *(referring to the boots)* Put 'em on. Can't work a field in high heels.
Tony: Depends on the kind of work you're doing.
Kate: Your mind, DiNozzo, runs the gamut from X to XXX.
Tony: Yeah?

Tony: Very electric Kool-Aid, Abby.
Abby: I was thinking more Blue Man Group.
Tony: Wow, why didn't you take to me this fast?
Abby: You're like a piercing, Tony. It takes a while for the throbbing to stop and the skin to grow back.
Tony: That's more than I wanted to know.

Kate: How did you get into NCIS?
Tony: I smiled.
Kate: How'd you get into this?
Abby: Filled out an application.

Tony: Do you jump?
Gibbs: Only when I get an electric shock.
Tony: That explains the lack of power tools.
Gibbs: So you gonna do it?
Tony: What?
Gibbs: Spend $180 to defy gravity?
Tony: *(grinning)* Yeah, I think I am.
Gibbs: Y'know, some of these guys freeze on their first jump. Have to be kicked in the ass to get them out.
Tony: Not me.
Gibbs: Nope. You fall in the category of want to get kicked in the ass on the ground.
Source: [3]

Episodes Season 1

No.	German Title	US Title	Air Date USA	Air Date GER	Directed by	Written by
1.3	Seadog	**Seadog**	Oct 7, 2003	Apr 7, 2005	B.May	D.Bellisario & J.Kelley

When a Naval Commander is murdered, seemingly during a freelance drugs deal gone sour, the media is quick to link him to drug trafficking and the evidence stacks up. Being a former Marine himself, Gibbs refuses to believe that a good officer could be so corrupt, and in his efforts to clear the Commander's record and good name, uncovers a turf war between two rival drug gangs, and a terrorist's scheme to knock out the national power grid. The NCIS team is aided in its investigation by the DEA, and FBI Special Agent Tobias Fornell. *Source:* [1]

Gerald: You shoved a French cop over a cliff?
Ducky: There was a lake below.
Gibbs: Sixty feet below!

Kate: I did work for the Secret Service. We tend to get all hot and bothered over large sums of $100 bills.
Tony: Is that what does it for you?
Kate: What does it for me, Tony, is a mystery that you will never solve.

Source: [3]

No.	German Title	US Title	Air Date USA	Air Date GER	Directed by	Written by
1.4	Die Unsterblichen	**The Immortals**	Oct 14, 2003	Apr 14, 2005	A.Levi	D.Meyers

The discovery of a drowned sailor in dress whites, with an officer's ceremonial sword and weights chained to his waist, sparks a suicide investigation and eventually sends the team to the USS Foster so that they can dig into the deceased officer's life and find out what his colleagues thought of him. Kate refuses to believe that the deceased sailor committed suicide, as like her, he came from a Catholic family where suicide is a mortal sin. Meanwhile Abby discovers a link between the crew of the USS Foster and an MMORPG known as 'The Immortals', and begins searching the game for clues and evidence in order to assist Gibbs in solving the case and saving the ship from possible destruction. *Source:* [1]

Tony: Aren't you guys interested at all in what I brought you back from Puerto Rico?
Gibbs/Kate: *(sighing)* Sure. Fine. *(Tony grins and hands them a couple bags, Kate looks in hers)*
Kate: You gotta be kidding.
Tony: A bikini. Two-piece.
Kate: A bottom. And a hat?
Tony: Puerto Rican!
Gibbs: Any chance you're going to try that on?
Kate: *(tosses it at Gibbs)* You first.
Gibbs: *(looks over the bikini bottom)* Trust me. It's not gonna fit.
Kate: Pigs. I work with pigs.
Tony: *(as Gibbs is opening his gift)* It's a fantasy RPG book. Complete with character sheets and dice. Baby steps, Gibbs. Baby steps.
Gibbs: It's in Spanish.

Tony: There's just no pleasing you, is there?

Source: [3]

Episodes Season 1

No.	German Title	US Title	Air Date USA	Air Date GER	Directed by	Written by
1.5	Der Fluch der Mumie	**The Curse**	Oct 28, 2003	Apr 21, 2005	T.O'Hara	Bellisario,McGill&Vlaming

Gibbs and the team are called in when a mummified lieutenant, who was believed to have absconded with 1.2 million dollars of stolen Navy funds ten years previously, is found in a half-buried cargo pod with Navy markings on it. Two former shipmates who serve with the deceased come under suspicion for both the murder and the theft. Gibbs and Tony work at investigating the murder, while Kate is charged with tracking down the missing funds. Abby uses a computer reconstruction to work a confession out of a possible suspect. *Source:* [1]

```
Gibbs: Tony you gas the truck
Tony: Uh Gibbs you know most agencies have people who do that sort of thing.
Gibbs: Uh huh...so do we.

Tony: I didn't become an NCIS agent yesterday Kate. As a matter of fact tomorrow...
Gibbs: ...is going to be two years.
Tony: That's kind of touching Gibbs. Remembering the day you hired me.
Gibbs: Yeah, well it seemed like a good idea at the time.

Gibbs: That tank came off a Tomcat. Somebody filed a TFOA report.
Kate: TFOA?
Tony: Things Falling Off Aircraft.
Kate: You're kidding.
Gibbs: Nope, that's what they're called.
```

Source: [3]

No.	German Title	US Title	Air Date USA	Air Date GER	Directed by	Written by
1.6	Speed	**High Seas**	Nov 4, 2003	Apr 28, 2005	D.Smith	L.Moskowitz & J.Vlaming

One of Gibbs's former team members, NCIS Special Agent Stan Burley (Joel Gretsch) who is Agent Afloat on the USS Enterprise calls for assistance when a sailor suffers a meth overdose while on leave, despite the sailor in question claiming that he's never taken the drug. When another sailor is admitted to sickbay under the same circumstances, Tony and Kate investigate the source of the drugs within the crew while Gibbs begins to suspect that a senior officer on the ship may secretly be doping the crew with performance-enhancing drugs. *Source:* [1]

```
Tony: Five years with Gibbs? Amazed the guy didn't end up in a straitjacket.
Gibbs: What was that?
Tony: Uh, nothing, Boss, just praising your communication skills.

Gibbs: Above his mattress, below his mattress, inside his mattress. If there's such a thing as a
fourth mattress dimension, go over that, too.

Tony: Is this going to turn into one of those guy-girl things where you insist we stop and ask for
directions?

Abby: Smart money says that that is not a Tic-Tac.

Gibbs: That pouch may be clear, but my gut is still in living color.

Tony: I say it's time we turn out the lights and play in the dark.
```

Source: [3]

Episodes Season 1

No.	German Title	US Title	Air Date USA	Air Date GER	Directed by	Written by
1.7	Unter Wasser	**Sub Rosa**	Nov 18, 2003	Mar 24, 2005	M.Zinberg	F.Cardea & G.Schenck

NCIS Norfolk Case Agent Timothy McGee works on a case of a partially dissolved corpse found in a barrel of acid at the Norfolk Naval Base, and calls in the Major Case Response Team to help him. As the investigation continues, it soon becomes apparent that the killer took steps to prevent the body from being identified. Gibbs quickly comes to believe that the motive for the brutal murder was identity theft and his suspicions are further confirmed when it's revealed that although a submariner is dead, no-one has been reported missing, leading Gibbs to believe that an imposter is on one of the submarines. Tony, Abby, and McGee are tasked with identifying the deceased, while Gibbs and Kate are sent underwater on a submarine to vet five possible suspects, one of whom might have been responsible for the murder and also prevent a chemical attack from happening. *Source:* [1]

McGee: I've heard stories about Special Agent Gibbs.
Tony: Only half of them are true. Trick is figuring out which half.

Abby: There's good news and bad news.
Ducky: I hate it when you play this game, Abby. All right, let's get it over with.
Abby: His last meal was a Big Mac and fries.
Ducky: Well, probably half the base had that for lunch. I was hoping you'd come up with something more exotic. Tandoori, perhaps. And the good news?
Abby: I know what's in the special sauce.

Gibbs: Drink.
Kate: What's with all the water?
Gibbs: Oh, you gotta hydrate on a sub marine.
Kate: All you've had me doing is hydrating.
Gibbs: Drink it. *(she takes a drink)* So how's your bladder?
Kate: What?
Gibbs: The COB's at the end of the passageway are trying to keep an eye on us.You gotta distract 'em. *(Kate looks at him)* You're gonna need help working the toliet.
Kate: Gibbs....
Gibbs: Trust me, Kate, on a Sub Marine it's a very complicated mechanism.
Kate: Is that why you've been shoving water down my throat for the past hour?
Gibbs: I wan to check out Petty Officer Thompson.
Kate: Well, you don't have to drown me.You could just ask.
Gibbs: Hydrating good for ya'.Go, unhydrate.
Kate: Never heard it called that before.
Gibbs: Go on.

Tony: Nice hat. Did they make you the boat mascot?
Kate: That's your way of saying you missed me, isn't it?
Tony: No.

Kate: Do people react that way because we're NCIS, or do you just have that effect on them?
Gibbs: I like to think it's me.

Source: [3]

Episodes Season 1

No.	German Title	US Title	Air Date USA	Air Date GER	Directed by	Written by
1.8	Schlimmer als der Tod	**Minimum Security**	Nov 25, 2003	May 12, 2005	I.Toynton	D.Bellisario&P.DeGuere

The team heads for Cuba when Ducky and Gerald discover that a dead Guantanamo Bay translator they've been working on has a stomach full of emeralds. NCIS Special Agent Paula Cassidy proves to be more than a match for Tony when he is ordered to investigate her involvement, while Gibbs and Kate try to discover where the emeralds came from, how they ended up in their translator's stomach, and prevent the assassination of an important prisoner. *Source:* [1]

Gibbs: See if you can brand the cologne.
Abby: Why, you want some?
Gibbs: Nope, don't use cologne. Women I date think the smell of sawdust is sexy. Probably why I don't date *(pause)* many women.
Abby: Perfume is the most powerful accessory a woman can wear.
Gibbs: Yeah, well, how much did all this power cost us?
Abby: Around fifteen hundred.
Gibbs: Fifteen hundred dollars?
Abby: Well, not including the tax. I stuck to the thirty most popular scents hoping we'd get lucky.
Gibbs: Ah, how fiscally responsible, Ab.

Source: [3]

No.	German Title	US Title	Air Date USA	Air Date GER	Directed by	Written by
1.9	Anruf von einem Toten	**Marine Down**	Dec 16, 2003	May 19, 2005	D.Smith	J.Kelley

When a dead Marine seemingly calls his wife on the day of his funeral, Gibbs, Tony and Kate begin investigating. The case quickly becomes complicated, as the Marine's CO apparently has two physical forms, and Tony somehow manages to meet and interrogate the victim's wife in a park without even leaving the office. As the investigation continues, the Marine turns up embalmed, having been killed two days after his funeral supposedly took place. Gibbs suspects CIA involvement, and is soon tracking a rogue operative in an attempt to rescue the deceased Marine's partner before another murder takes place. *Source:* [1.]

Kate: Gibbs can be wrong sometimes.
Tony: Name once?
Kate: Tony, the man has been married like four times.
Tony: There is that.
Gibbs: There's what, DiNozzo?

Tony, Gibbs, Kate on Military Plane:
Tony: What are you looking for Kate?
Kate: Um the ladies room? *(Gibbs and Tony look at Kate.)*
Kate: Okay, the men's room.
Gibbs: There is no men's room.
Kate: Well then where am I supposed to go to the bathroom?
(Gibbs takes out a white plastic bag and gives it to her. Kate looks disgusted, decides she can wait. Finally gives up and snatches the bag from Gibbs.)
Kate: ****. Where?
Gibbs: Well, if you want some privacy, you can go down behind those boxes.
Kate: God, I miss Air Force One.

Gibbs: Morning! Sleep well?
Kate: If by well, you mean violently throwing up all night and bouncing around like rag dolls...
Tony: Then yeah, boss, we slept very well, thanks for asking.
Gibbs: Ah, you get used to it.
Kate: That's what I'm afraid of.

Source: [3]

Episodes Season 1

No.	German Title	US Title	Air Date USA	Air Date GER	Directed by	Written by
1.10	Lebendig begraben	**Left for Dead**	Jan 6, 2004	May 26, 2005	J.Whitmore, Jr.	D.Bellisario & D.McGill

Kate immediately bonds with a woman suffering from amnesia after she wakes up and crawls from her grave following a murder attempt, claiming to remember that a bomb is present on a Navy ship and that people will die unless it's found. But unknown to Kate and the team, the anonymous Jane Doe is actually lying to Kate as she is secretly already beginning to remember who she really is and is probably planning something to strike back against her employers, something that might end in bloodshed... *Source:* [1]

Tony: Speaking of dates to work from, we've worked together for two years and, you know, I have no idea where you live.
Ducky: Well, I'd just as well we kept it that way, Tony.

Abby: I suppose you want me to tell you what chastity belt this opens?
Gibbs: Do I look like DiNozzo?
Tony: Not funny, Boss. Besides, I could open a chastity belt.
Abby: Have you ever seen one? Mine's awesome. It's eighteenth-century French.

Abby: Like when photocopiers first came out, and people were copying everything from C-notes to their butts.
Tony: You sat your naked butt on a photocopier, didn't you, Abby?
Abby: Yep.

Ducky: Jethro, I don't answer forensic questions I don't know the answers to. Why do you keep asking me?
Gibbs: *(shrugs)* Force of habit.

Tony: You remember when I stayed with you that time, when it didn't really go so well?
Gibbs: Yeah, I remember, DiNozzo.
Tony: Well, listen, I was younger then, immature, a little unfocused -
Gibbs: It was six months ago, Tony.

Tony: What is it with Germans and the alphabet thing? You know, BMW, BMG, BASF, and they're all B's.
Gibbs: I'm resisting the urge to say cut the BS.

Tony: We gotta do something, Boss.
Gibbs: Have you ever made a mistake, Tony?
Tony: According to you or to me?
Gibbs: You.
Tony: Yeah.
Gibbs: Could anyone make you feel better?
Tony: *(pause)* No.

Ducky: I don't have a body.
Gibbs: Well go find one Ducky.
Ducky: Here?
Gibbs: Sure. How many times have we had multiple victims?

Abby: Hey guys. What's you'd find?
Tony: Kate willing to give her bedroom to Jane Doe. But not me.
Abby: *(sarcastic)* Shocking.

Source: [3]

Episodes Season 1

No.	German Title	US Title	Air Date USA	Air Date GER	Directed by	Written by
1.11	Wintersonne	**Eye Spy**	Jan 13, 2004	Jun 2, 2005	A.Levi	F.Cardea, D.Coen & G.Schenck

NCIS is called in to investigate the murder of a naval officer at Little Creek Naval Base following an anonymous tip-off. McGee manages to track the tip-off to Langley, suggesting that the CIA has been spying on the base. Gibbs and Kate follow the tip-off, coming across a witness who leads the team to several possible suspects. At first the murder seems to be tied in with work the officer was involved with, but the team soon begins to suspect a more domestic motive. *Source:* [1]

Tony: I've weighed exactly the same since the day I graduated from college; never up, never down.
Kate: Certainly you would know. Do you weigh yourself a lot?
Tony: I never weigh myself.
Kate: I see.

Tony: You got me thinking, Kate; maybe I should improve my diet.
Kate: When you gonna start?
Tony: What do you call this? *(gestures with nutrition bar)*
Kate: Bad things masquerading as something good for you.

Kate: Let's see, what do we got here. High fructose corn syrup - basically, sugar. High maltose corn syrup - another sugar. Sugar! Sugar. Fractionated palm kernel oil. That sounds yummy! And contains less than two percent natural flavor. That would make it ninety-eight percent artificial flavor.
Tony: So what are you saying?

Tony: Come on, come on, McGee, you said you could do this.
McGee: But I didn't say it was gonna be easy.
Tony: Actually, that's exactly what you said, only on the phone, you ended it with a 'sir.'

Kate: With the exception of finding a decent barber, Gibbs can do pretty much anything he says he can.

Kate: You know I bet this is why number two came after you with a nine iron, isn't it? You just refused to sit down and talk things through.
Gibbs: Actually that wasn't it at all.
Kate: So what was it, then?
Gibbs: Seven iron.

Kate: We know the killer was left handed, which eliminates Commander Tyler whose service file confirms she's a rightie.
Tony: We also know the killer's a woman unless Obermaier went Norman Bates on the guy. Actually, when you think about it the MO's match. (Makes stabbing motion at Kate's back)
Gibbs: DiNozzo.
Kate: *(turns)* What'd you do?

Source: 3

Episodes Season 1

No.	German Title	US Title	Air Date USA	Air Date GER	Directed by	Written by
1.12	Ein Bein in West Virginia	**My Other Left Foot**	Feb 3, 2004	Jun 9, 2005	J.Woolnough	J.Bernstein

When the leg of a marine is discovered in a dumpster, Gibbs and the team have a problem - identifying who the leg belongs to and finding the rest of his body. Kate and Tony are ordered to find the marine's place of burial and exhume the body, only to discover that the marine to whom the leg belongs to was apparently cremated years ago. With no solid leads available, the team is stuck following red herrings, until it becomes apparent that the marine was in fact alive until recently, and another marine was killed and falsely identified in the past. This revelation prompts the NCIS team to investigate closer to home. *Source:* [1]

Tony: You really like small towns?
Kate: Peace and quiet. A place where people know you by name. No Blockbuster and Starbucks on every corner. What's not to like? Tony: Too quiet, everybody knows your name, there's no Blockbuster and Starbucks on every corner.
Kate: Big cities just can't give you what small towns can, Tony. It's a simpler way of life, a slice of Americana.
Tony: One that doesn't include fifty yard line seats to the Redskins or women with full sets of teeth.
Kate: Yeah it always comes back to that doesn't it?
Tony: See... You do get me.

Tony: I don't get the whole tattoo thing.
Kate: I'll add that to the ever-growing list of things you don't get.
Tony: Being stuck with a needle thousands of times for a piece of artwork? No thank you.
Kate: It's more than just artwork, Tony.
Tony: On a woman, maybe.
Kate: What?
Tony: You know, on a woman. Means she's up for anything.
Kate: Abby's got tattoos.
Tony: No comment.

Gibbs: Any more tattoos?
Tony: Just the rose on Kate's butt.
Gibbs: It's not a rose.

Abby: You know what they say about guys with big hands and big feet, right?
Ducky: What?
Abby: They're clowns.

Gibbs: What's wrong?
Abby: Look at it.
Gibbs: Looks like a match.
Abby: Precisely.
Gibbs: Good work, Abby.
Abby: No, it's not! You gave me 2 samples form the same tree. B matched and A didn't. I screwed up.
Gibbs: Sycamore A was from a tree down the street.
Abby: What?!
Gibbs: The idea of matching plant DNA was a bit...hinky for me.
Abby: Oh, ye of little faith!
Gibbs: Abby, c'mon! All I did was give you a blind test.
Abby: Well, you could've done that by not telling me which sample was from the suspect's sycamore!
Gibbs: I didn't think of that.

Source: [3]

Episodes Season 1

No.	German Title	US Title	Air Date USA	Air Date GER	Directed by	Written by
1.13	Todesschüsse	**One Shot, One Kill**	Feb 10, 2004	Jun 16, 2005	P.Ellis	G.Grant

When a marine recruiter is killed, the NCIS team quickly discover that a highly intelligent and skilled sniper was behind the attack. Initially, the team believes the sniper had a grudge against the recruiter, but when a second attack occurs the investigation takes on a wider scope. When Gibbs notices that the sniper left a calling card at each scene, he realizes that the sniper was meeting the recruiters before the shooting took place. Hoping to lure out the killer, Gibbs dons his old Marine uniform and takes over in the recruitment office with Kate, his new "commanding officer", co-ordinating with DiNozzo and assisted by an FBI team. *Source:* [1]

Gibbs Rule #9: Never go anywhere without a knife.

Tony: Do you think he'd let me borrow his uniform for the weekend?
Kate: I don't know. I just hope I'm there when you ask him.

Gibbs: Hey, DiNozzo, kinda reminds me of your apartment - except for that minty fresh urine smell.
Tony: For your information, I have a maid now.
Gibbs: You can afford a maid?
Tony: It's amazing what you can do when you don't have to pay three alimonies. *(pause)* Ow!

Kate: Next time drive a little faster, Tony. I think my glands have an ounce of adrenaline left.
Tony: Response to a crime scene investigation demands a timely arrival, Kate.
Kate: It would help if the investigators didn't PUKE all over the crime scene.
Gibbs: Brings back memories.
Kate: Memories of what?
Gibbs: Marriage.

Source: [3]

No.	German Title	US Title	Air Date USA	Air Date GER	Directed by	Written by
1.14	Der gute Samariter	**The Good Samaritan**	Feb 17, 2004	Jun 23, 2005	A.Levi	J.Bernstein

A local county sheriff calls in NCIS upon discovering a murdered lieutenant commander by the roadside, quickly followed by the murder of a civilian contractor two counties over. As the team struggle to find a motive or suspects for either case, another murder occurs; this time a naval aviator. Ducky points out that while the murders appear to follow the same modus operandi and seem to have been carried out by a serial killer, some elements are different, indicating that the murders were not carried out by the same individual. A DNA sample draws suspicion onto the widow of the third victim, but she has an iron-clad alibi, leaving Gibbs with a complex investigation and many loose ends to tie up. *Source:* [1]

Gibbs: Anything Abby?
Abby: This is the left rear tire off Commander Julius's car. Notice anything unusual?
Gibbs: It's inflated.
Abby: Is that a guess, or do you actually know where I'm going with this?
Gibbs: What do you think?
Abby: Well, I don't know, that's why I asked you.
Gibbs: Why don't you just tell me?
Abby: So you don't know.
Gibbs: I want to make sure you know.
Abby: Hmmmm.
Gibbs: Hmmmm.
Abby: We should play poker sometime.
Gibbs: Yeah, we should.

Source: [3]

Episodes Season 1

No.	German Title	US Title	Air Date USA	Air Date GER	Directed by	Written by
1.15	Der Colonel	**Enigma**	Feb 24, 2004	Jun 30, 2005	T.J.Wright	J.Kelley

Fornell and Gibbs clash when it is discovered that a marine colonel, William Ryan (Terry O'Quinn) who also happens to be Gibbs's former C.O has absconded from Iraq with two million dollars, and returned to the states under an assumed name. Fornell thinks he stole the money for himself while Gibbs denies the claim, believing he's innocent. Ryan later contacts Gibbs, and explains that he has discovered a conspiracy to siphon funds out of Iraq for use on black ops. Gibbs is drafted in to aid in bringing down the conspiracy, and meets the Colonel's partner - a lieutenant named Cameron who had actually died in Gibbs's arms years ago. After being arrested for "pissing off the FBI", Gibbs and Fornell set out to discover the truth behind the Colonel's claims in a tense standoff. It is soon discovered that Ryan is suffering from paranoid schizophrenia and after the standoff ends, he is put into a mental hospital so that he can be treated for his mental illness. *Source:* [1]

Gibbs Rule #12: Never date a co-worker.

Kate: Do all Marines build boats?
Tony: Only the ones who've been married a few times.
Kate: Why's that?
Tony: The rest of them can afford to buy one

Kate: So what happened?
Tony: She broke into my apartment and filled my closet with dog crap.
Kate: Ha! Really? I knew there was a reason I liked her.
Tony: I still have her number. Maybe you two can get together and boil rabbits or something.
Kate: Not my style, Tony. I would just shoot you.
Gibbs: And that would be the reason for rule number twelve.
Kate: Rule twelve?
Gibbs: Never date a co-worker.

Source: [3]

No.	German Title	US Title	Air Date USA	Air Date GER	Directed by	Written by
1.16	Alptraum im Keller	**Bête Noire**	Mar 2, 2004	Jul 7, 2005	P.Ellis	D.Bellisario

Ducky responds to an emergency call when the Israeli Embassy sends a Royal Navy officer to NCIS for autopsy, only to find a gunman (revealed in later episodes to be recurring antagonist Ari Haswari) inside the body bag. As Ducky, Gerald and eventually Kate are held hostage in the autopsy lab, the director coordinates with an FBI strike team to negotiate their release. Meanwhile, Kate hesitates when presented with an opportunity to kill her captor, while Gibbs and Tony take more pro-active measures to get their co-workers out safely, ending with a showdown during which shots are fired, one of which hits Gibbs's left shoulder, leaving both himself and Gerald who had been shot during the siege injured. *Source:* [1]

Ari: Same way I came in?
Kate: I don't know how you came in.
Ari: In a body bag.
Kate: Same way you're going out!

Gibbs: He**, I still use a notebook and a pencil, instead of a PDQ.
Tony: It's a PDA. You can call it a Palm Pilot.
Gibbs: It desn't matter what I call it if i can't use it!
Tony: I'll teach you.
Gibbs: You'll teach me? McGee teaches you! You teach me! It's backwards! I need coffee.

Source: [3]

Episodes Season 1

No.	German Title	US Title	Air Date USA	Air Date GER	Directed by	Written by
1.17	Fünf Musketiere	**The Truth is Out There**	Mar 16, 2004	Jul 14, 2005	D.Smith	J.Bernstein

During a rave party, the body of a Petty Officer falls through the ceiling. Preliminary investigation suggests that the Petty Officer was killed in the nearby parking lot, and was dressed after his death. Upon checking the victim's room, evidence surfaces that he may have been taking financial bribes. Gibbs suspects the victim's co-workers of involvement in the death when their separate versions of events are too consistent. Forensic evidence links them to the scene, and they eventually confess that the death was a prank gone wrong, but Gibbs still believes that there's more to the case than meets the eye. *Source:* [1]

Abby: Do you have any fetishes?
Gibbs: I have three ex-wives. I can't afford any fetishes.

Tony: Have you ever been in a men's room before?
Kate: No. Have you?

Kate: Never put anything on videotape that you don't want to be seen.
Tony: Just ask Paris Hilton.

Source: [3]

No.	German Title	US Title	Air Date USA	Air Date GER	Directed by	Written by
1.18	Falsche Fährten	**UnSEALed**	Apr 6, 2004	Jul 21, 2005	P.Ellis	T.Moran

A former Navy SEAL convicted of double homicide escapes from Leavenworth, resulting in Kate and McGee being assigned to protect the son and in-laws of the escaped prisoner. During the night, the SEAL breaks into the house to see his son before fleeing, leaving Todd tied to a chair and unarmed, her weapon having been taken by the SEAL. Profiling his behavior, Kate theorizes that he may actually be innocent, and had discovered the identity of the real killer while in jail. Gibbs brings in the presiding defense and prosecution attorneys, one of which is Lt. Commander Faith Coleman to go over the evidence while attempting to arrest the true killer before the fugitive finds the actual murderer and delivers his own brand of justice: revenge. *Source:* [1]

Tony: She sleeps with a gun boss...
Gibbs: Is that true?
Kate: Sort of...sometimes..yes
Gibbs: *(grins)* Good Girl

Tony: Do we know what this guy was in for?
Gibbs: Same thing I'm gonna be if you don't get your a** moving.
Tony: Right. *(whispering to Kate)* Murder.
Kate: And you didn't even use a lifeline.

Kate: For the sake of argument, lets say he's innocent.
Tony: Why?
Gibbs: Because I said so.
Tony: Inocent, sure, why not.

Gibbs: Are you thinkin' what I think you're thinkin'?
Tony: I don't know, Boss.Are you thinkin' what I think you're thinkin'?

Source: [3]

Episodes Season 1

No.	German Title	US Title	Air Date USA	Air Date GER	Directed by	Written by
1.19	Wenn Tote sprechen	**Dead Man Talking**	Apr 27, 2004	Jul 28, 2005	D.Smith	F.Cardea & G.Schenck

Special Agent Chris Pacci is brutally murdered while investigating a cold case, prompting a guilt-ridden Gibbs to step in and take over the case while attempting to find Pacci's killer. The team follows the trail of millions of dollars, and is led to a woman with ties to the thief. The agents take shifts conducting a stake-out on the woman's house, until Tony's caught raiding the mailbox. Forced to improvise, he introduces himself as a resident of the neighbourhood and strikes up a conversation based on what he had heard via surveillance. This gives him a chance to get close to the suspect in order to find out more, as he goes on a successful date with her. Meanwhile, Abby makes a shocking discovery which leaves Tony horrified and vulnerable to an onslaught of merciless taunts and teasing from Kate: the suspect they've been trailing, Amanda Reed is in fact Lt. Commander Voss, the Officer who faked his own death in a car accident and who's responsible for stealing money from the Navy. Things come to a head in a bar where Voss/Reed attempts to kill Tony in front of witnesses but Gibbs gets there just in time and shoots Voss/Reed dead, avenging Pacci's death. *Source:* [1]

Abby: Reminds me of the Crying Game.
McGee: Don't know it.
Abby: It was such a cool flick.
Tony: Abby, could you pick some other movie please.
Abby: Oh um Victor Victoria?
Tony: That was a girl pretending to be a guy pretending to be a girl?
Abby: Right.
Tony: Yeah. That one's ok.

Abby: You rule
Gibbs: I know...but remind me why?

Abby (*to McGee*): Whatever you do, do not lie. Gibbs is like Santa Claus, he knows if you've been naughty.

Gibbs: Problem?
Kate: Well, you really want to do that to McGee? Special Agent Bligh... (*gesturing to Tony*)...here is going to eat him alive.
Tony: McGee looks up to me, as a mentor.
Kate: Ugh.
Gibbs: You want to be stuck in a cramped apartment with DiNozzo? Be my guest.
Kate: On the other hand, it'll help McGee build character.

Kate: I'm warning you DiNozzo, don't even go there.
(*Kate leaves*)
Tony: We've gotta go there. Any ideas, McGee?
McGee: No.
Tony: Well, don't worry. I've got plenty.
McGee: You realize that any prank we play on Kate we'll also be pulling on Gibbs?
Tony: That's a problem.
McGee: Unless...nah.
Tony: What?
McGee: Well, I was thinking. Since she is expecting something, maybe we should do nothing.
Tony: ...That's brilliant. It'll drive her nuts trying to figure out what we did, that we didn't do. You're all right McGee.

Gibbs: (*to Tony about information*) Are you going to spit it out, or do I have to waste my coffee on your head?

Source: [3]

Episodes Season 1

No.	German Title	US Title	Air Date USA	Air Date GER	Directed by	Written by
1.20	Willkommen in der Hölle	**Missing**	May 4, 2004	Aug 4, 2005	J.Woolnough	J.Kelley

The disappearance of a marine draws NCIS in to investigate, and it's discovered that several marines from the same unit have also vanished under similar circumstances. When skeletal remains of one of the missing men is found chained to a pipe in a small sewer room, Gibbs begins to suspect the unit CO (the only team member not dead or missing) as a serial killer. However, after Tony vanishes, the investigation takes on a more frantic pace and McGee is called in from Norfolk to help as Gibbs and Kate work against the clock to find Tony before it's too late. *Source:* [1]

Gibbs Rule #9: Never go anywhere without a knife.

Tony: Admit it, you were worried about me. *(no response)* You don't have to say it, I know. *(still no response)* Okay, I want you to say it.You do care right? *(elevator doors open and Gibbs walks out)* So.....are you saying you don't care?
Gibbs: *(stops)* Tony, as far as I'm concerned *(taps his cheeks)*, you're irreplaceable.
Tony: I knew it *(laughs a little)*. I knew behind the whole marine thing you really are at heart--
Gibbs: Forget it McGee, he's still alive.

Kate: Tony, you are so lucky you didn't have sisters growing up.
Tony: Why's that?
Kate: Because youd never have reached puberty. Of course, one could argue you still haven't reached it.

Kate: You were pretty tough with her.
Gibbs: She reminds me of my ex-wife.
Tony: Which one?
Gibbs: All of them!

Source: [3]

No.	German Title	US Title	Air Date USA	Air Date GER	Directed by	Written by
1.21	Verbotene Waffen	**Split Decision**	May 11, 2004	Aug 11, 2005	T.O'Hara	B.Gookin

As Ducky meets his new assistant, Jimmy Palmer, Gibbs takes the case of a marine found impaled on a tree stump. The investigation uncovers the sale of decommissioned military weapons on the black market. Tony goes undercover and meets the buyer, only to stumble into an ATF operation. Working with ATF Special Agent Stone, Gibbs poses as a weapons supplier to complete the deal, and must double cross everyone in order to find the corrupt person at the centre of the investigation, and the one responsible for the marine's death. *Source:* [1]

Gibbs: Abs, leave a few gaps, don't make it so neat.
Abby: Please Gibbs, I've been making fake IDs since I was 15.

Abby: It's not like they have any new ideas. It's just so...
Ducky: The song remains the same?
Abby: Exactly. And bonus points for the gratuitous rock reference.

Tony: He said you could use his computer?
McGee: Uh huh.
Tony: Really? You know, when mine fried, he wouldn't let me touch his.
Gibbs: 'Cause your fingers are always greasy from fried chicken and pizza.

Source: [3]

Episodes Season 1

No.	German Title	US Title	Air Date USA	Air Date GER	Directed by	Written by
1.22	Abgestürzt	**A Weak Link**	May 18,2004	Aug 18, 2005	A.Levi	J.Bernstein

Routine training results in the death of a U.S. Navy SEAL lieutenant just days before he was due to deploy on a classified hostage rescue operation. The death is initially dismissed as an equipment malfunction, but Abby discovers that the link attaching the lieutenant to his rappelling rope was made of a weaker material than factory standard, suggesting sabotage and potentially murder. Pressure is applied by the CIA for the investigation to be wrapped up within 38 hours so the operation can continue or else the entire mission will be scrubbed. As the case goes on, Gibbs discovers that the lieutenant had a secret, and that his wife might be holding back vital information about his death. *Source:* [1]

Gibbs: Let's pretend we don't know anything.
Tony: Not much of a stretch.

Gibbs: What if I wanted to get into that account?
Kate: Get a search warrent for the servers.
Gibbs: Don't have time for a warrent. What's a quicker way?
Kate: Hack in the server.
(Gibbs smiles)
Kate: I can't believe I just said that.I would have never suggested that before I started working here.
Gibbs: You're welcome.

Gibbs: DiNozzo, was there something in my tone of voice that made that sound like a suggestion?

Source: [3]

No.	German Title	US Title	Air Date USA	Air Date GER	Directed by	Written by
1.23	Der Terrorist	**Reveille**	May 25, 2004	Aug 25, 2005	T.J.Wright	D.Bellisario

As Gibbs's obsession with tracking down the infiltrator who held Todd and Ducky hostage begins reaching new heights, the team grow more concerned about him. McGee works at identifying him with a modified FBI program, while Todd and Tony go for lunch with Ducky. As Tony leaves in pursuit of his "dream woman" who is actually a terrorist, Kate heads back to the office for a video conference with Paula Cassidy, only to be kidnapped and reunited with her captor, now revealed as a Hamas terrorist who is planning to shoot down Marine One - a transport helicopter carrying President Bush and Ariel Sharon. At first, she refuses to cooperate, but she reluctantly relents when the female terrorist threatens to kill Tony after sleeping with him. As Gibbs grows increasingly agitated, the search for the terrorist is narrowed down by McGee and Abby calculating his exact age, and Ducky concluding that he attended medical school. McGee's program locates him as a graduate of a Scottish medical school. As the terrorist tries to convince Kate to identify Marine One, McGee finally discovers his name - Ari Haswari. It is soon revealed that Marine One cannot be identified out of the other choppers and that Haswari is actually an undercover Mossad operative in Al-Qaeda. He infiltrated the Hamas cell to draw them into a trap, making them believe that Marine One could be identified. ... *Source:* [1]

Gibbs: **Rule No.7:** Always be specific when you lie.

Gibbs: He stay at your place?
Abby: Yep.
Gibbs: You sleep in the coffin, McGee?
McGee: *(looks at Abby)* Coffin? Well...you...you said it was a box sofa bed.
Abby: Well...it is...sort of.
McGee: That's why you wouldn't turn the lights on! *(scoffs)* I can't believe I slept in a coffin.
Abby: *(shrugs)* Not just slept.

Source: [3]

Season 2 (Episodes 2.24- 2.46)

Originally broadcast between September 28, 2004 and May 24, 2005, the second season shifts away from the naval setting of the show somewhat, and includes more character development than the first season. Season 2 saw Norfolk Case Agent Timothy McGee being promoted to a full-time field agent, and transferring to NCIS HQ in Washington to work with the Major Case Response Team. Tony DiNozzo nearly died of the pneumonic plague in "SWAK" while in the season finale, "Twilight," Caitlin Todd was shot and killed by Ari Haswari.

Source: [1]

Original Air Date USA   September 28, 2004 – May 24, 2005 on CBS

Original Air Date German Language   September 1, 2005 – March 9, 2006 on Sat 1

Episodes Season 2

No.	German Title	US Title	Air Date USA	Air Date GER	Directed by	Written by
2.24	Unsichtbar	**See No Evil**	Sep 28, 2004	Sep 1, 2005	T.Wright	C.Crowe

When an eight-year-old blind girl Sandy Watson (played by Abigail Breslin) and her mother, Jill are kidnapped to blackmail a Navy captain (David Keith) into transferring $2 million in government funds, Gibbs and his team are faced with a unique challenge. An unexpected twist is uncovered when Abby and McGee manage to trace the money. The twist is that Captain Watson is the one responsible for arranging the kidnapping in the first place as he wanted to steal money from the government. After helping them solve the case, Tim McGee who was on a brief transfer from Norfolk gets an unexpected surprise from Gibbs: he is promoted to a full-time field agent and as a result is transferred to the Navy Yard, becoming a permanent member of Gibbs's team in the process. *Source:* [1]

Kate: "When I'm a mother, I'm never letting my kids out of my sight."
Tony: "Yeah, how do you plan on doing that? "
Kate: "G-P-S locater strapped to the ankle. Audio and video surveillance built into their clothes."
Tony: "No, I mean the part about becoming a mother."

Kate: Can't you tell when somebody's kidding with you, McGee?
McGee: I used to and then I met you guys.

Gibbs: McGee, where are you going?
McGee: Uh, Norfolk.
Gibbs: Well, I got some good news and some bad news.You've just been promoted to a full time field agent.
McGee: Really? That's incredible! What's...
Gibbs: You belong to me now!

Abby: Face it, McGee. We are doomed.
McGee: Gibbs can't really expect us to hack into the pentagon in a single afternoon!
Abby: Yeah, he can.

McGee: You're right, we are doomed.

Source: [3]

Episodes Season 2

No.	German Title	US Title	Air Date USA	Air Date GER	Directed by	Written by
2.25	Die perfekte Frau	**The Good Wives Club**	Oct 5, 2004	Sep 8, 2005	D.Smith	G.Grant

The mummified remains of a woman wearing a single wedding dress are found in an abandoned Marine home. The fact that the room the victim was in was modelled on the 1950s leads the team to suspect that a serial killer, one who endured horrific abuse as a child is responsible for the crime. And in the search for answers, McGee uncovers a missing person's report, this one in Jacksonville regarding a Petty Officer who had vanished on her way to work months and who has been missing for four months. The team then head to the Base and begin working with the NCIS Special Agent there in the hope of finding the missing Officer before it's too late and to also stop the killer once and for all. *Source:* [1]

Gibbs: "What do you have Abby?"
Abby: "What don't I have Gibbs? Clothing fibers, carpet fibers, dust, beetle parts, soiled bedding, there's even a pamphlet called "The Good Wives Guide" what's up with that?"
Gibbs: "Ask McGee."
Abby: "McGee?"
Gibbs: "Ma-Gee"
Abby: "Really?"

Gibbs: Put someone in a wedding dress.
Kate: Tony would look cute.
Gibbs: No. He's off interviewing the victim's parents.
Kate: Well, McGee then.
Gibbs: No, he's with Tony.
Kate: Abby.
Gibbs: No, up to her tatts in forensic tests.
Kate: Well, what about you? (Gibbs gives her a look) You won't have to wear the dress.
Tony: *[at weird crime scene]* This is really sick. Stephen King would love it.

Source: [3]

No.	German Title	US Title	Air Date USA	Air Date GER	Directed by	Written by
2.26	Auge um Auge	**Vanished**	Oct 12, 2004	Sep 15, 2005	T.Wright	C.Crowe

A marine attack helicopter is discovered in the middle of a crop circle in a rural area and both the pilots who were originally thought to have been on aboard, are missing. Soon, NCIS discovers that only one of the pilots was on the flight and that there is a ten year feud going on in the town of Smokey Corners, West Virginia andas a result, the missing pilot on the run, seeking revenge for something while some of the locals are going to great lengths to hide secrets that could help solve the case. *Source:* [1]

Ducky: "DNA doesn't lie, Jethro. People do"

Kate: "Most people tend to their personal hygiene at home."
Tony: "This bothers you?"
Kate: "No, what bothers me is that it doesn't bother me anymore."
Tony: "I'm an acquired taste."
McGee: "Actually, it's more like the Stockholm Syndrome. The emotional attachment to a captor formed by a hostage as a result of continuous stress and a need to cooperate for survival."
[after telling McGee about a movie which depict the parents as aliens]
Tony: Whew! Scared of my parents for years after that.
McGee: I'm sure the feeling was mutual.

Source: [3]

Episodes Season 2

No.	German Title	US Title	Air Date USA	Air Date GER	Directed by	Written by
2.27	Neptuns Zeichen	**Lt. Jane Doe**	Oct 19, 2004	Sep 22, 2005	D.Smith	G.Grant

While on leave, two sailors discover the body of a young woman dressed in a Navy uniform and due to the fact that she has no ID on her is given the name, Lt. Jane Doe. However, the case becomes very personal for Ducky when he realizes that it bears a striking resemblance to a similar case that he investigated ten years ago... *Source:* [1]

Jimmy: Ducky went to Norfolk, I think he drove.
Gibbs: Why?
Jimmy: Why did he drive?
Gibbs: No, why did he go to Norfolk!!!
Ducky: Unlike the living, when the dead speak, they do not lie.

McGee: If I said that to Gibbs, I would be seeing stars.
Abby: Well that's the advantage of being me.

Tony: Do you believe in Karma Boss?
Gibbs: I've had three wives, DiNozzo.

Source: [3]

No.	German Title	US Title	Air Date USA	Air Date GER	Directed by	Written by
2.28	Der Maulwurf	**The Bone Yard**	Oct 26, 2004	Sep 29, 2005	T.O'Hara	J.C.Kelley

The NCIS team attends a crime scene, and end up finding multiple remains among the wreckage. When one set of remains is revealed to be an undercover FBI agent, the team realises that they've stumbled upon a dumping ground which the mob have been using for eighteen years to dispose of their victims. The FBI suspect an agency mole is responsible for the exposure and subsequent death of the murdered agent, and it appears as though Fornell's being set up to take the blame for what's going on. Gibbs then sets out to find the real mole and clear Fornell's name, using tactics that shock his team. *Source:* [1]

Kate: "Maybe we don't need one. That is, if you're ready to become a father"
Tony: "I think she's talking to you, Probie"
Kate: "We go down to the lab and see if I'm carrying your baby. It'll be fun"
McGee: "Oh! And we can steal Little Rickey's DNA test"
Kate: "Photograph it for Abby"
Tony: "I'll do it"
McGee: "Why you?"
Tony: "Do you think anyone would believe you actually slept with Kate?"

Kate:" Wow, I thought you were the only one who could piss him off like that."
Tony: "You never met his second wife."

Abby: Hear Kate kicked your butt this morning, McGee.
McGee: Oh. You heard wrong. Wasn't my butt...
Abby: So she kicked you in the...?
McGee: I thought I was joining a Federal Agency, not reliving my junior year in high school.
Abby: Just remember, they torture you because they care.
McGee: So, if I make them dislike me...?
Abby: It'll get worse.

Source: [3]

Episodes Season 2

No.	German Title	US Title	Air Date USA	Air Date GER	Directed by	Written by
2.29	Schatten der Angst	**Terminal Leave**	Nov 16, 2004	Oct 6, 2005	R.Director	J.Woolnough

When an Iraq veteran is threatened and very nearly killed by a group of terrorists, the NCIS team steps in to protect her and her family from further danger. While trying to convince an FBI agent to help them, the team is convinced that they've discovered the bomber. However, things might not be what they seem when another car bomb nearly kills Tony and Kate during their protection duty of the Lieutenant Commander. In the meantime, a single family secret may pose more of a threat than even terrorists could. *Source:* [1]

Kate: "Tony."
Tony: "Yes, Kate dear."
Kate: "There's only one bathroom downstairs."
Tony: "And your point is?"
Kate: "The seat stays down."
Tony: "Unless it's up."

Kate: *(from the shower)* Tony! Out of here. Now!
Tony: What? I'm just brushing my teeth. Oh, hey, don't use up the hot water 'cause you've been in there forever.
Kate: Tony, how long have you been in here?
Tony: Long enough to know you can't sing... and haven't shaved your legs in a week.

Tony: Oh, sounds like we're goin' to need the infrared scope on this one, McGee.
McGee: The one that can see through walls at night?
Tony: Better than pay-TV.And the best part? It's free.
Kate: And that's the reason why, Tony.
Tony: Why what, Kate?

Kate: You'll never get my home address.

Source: [3]

No.	German Title	US Title	Air Date USA	Air Date GER	Directed by	Written by
2.30	Der Held von Iwo Jima	**Call of Silence**	Nov 23, 2004	13. Oct 13, 2005	T.Wright	R.Director

A former Marine, and Medal of Honor recipient who fought in World War II (played by Charles Durning), confesses to having murdered his friend in battle. Gibbs does not believe this is the whole truth and goes on to prove his innocence.The team become personally involved with the case, with Gibbs using deceptive tactics to pull the truth from the elderly man. *Source:* [1]

Kate: Coleman is going to use this to put Yost away for the rest of his life.
Tony: Do we have to tell her?
Gibbs: *(sarcastically)* No. Here at NCIS we just report the evidence we like.

Henry: "Gibbs."
Gibbs: "Hey, Morning Henry."
Henry: "That sushi place you sent me to,"
Gibbs: "What, you didn't like it?"
Henry: "I liked it fine. Only, you didn't tell me I had to speak Japaneses to order."
Gibbs: "You don't order, you eat what you're served with a smile. Just like being married."

Source: [3]

Episodes Season 2

No.	German Title	US Title	Air Date USA	Air Date GER	Directed by	Written by
2.31	Herzenssachen	**Heart Break**	Nov 30, 2004	Oct 20, 2005	D.Smith	G.Schenck & F.Cardea

A Navy Commander dies after a successful surgery. At first glance, it appears that the sudden death might have been a case of spontaneous human combustion. While researching the dead man's past, the team discovers that he had gained a lot of enemies recently, not least of all a young ensign, who makes himself the prime suspect with some bizarre behaviour. However, while analysing the evidence from the scene of the death, Abby and Tony discover the truth, and in turn find a new suspect. In the meantime, Ducky develops a soft spot for the doctor who was treating the commander. *Source:[1]*

Tony: I saw that movie!
Ducky: The silent version, or the British mini series?
Tony: They were talking.

Tony: Too bad you didn't get to bed at a sensible hour. I mean, to sleep, cause obviously, you were in bed.
Kate: I get it, Tony.

Source:[3]

No.	German Title	US Title	Air Date USA	Air Date GER	Directed by	Written by
2.32	Leere Augen	**Forced Entry**	Dec 7, 2004	Oct 27, 2005	D.Smith	J.Stern & J.C.Kelley

A Marine's wife shoots an intruder in self defense when he is about to rape her but things change when Gibbs and the team uncoverevidence suggesting that she might have lured her supposed attacker to her home under the guise of a date. *Source:[1]*

Gibbs Rule #23: Never mess with a Marine's coffee if you want to live.

Gibbs: Hey Kate, your brothers are really like that?
Kate: Sadly, yes.
Gibbs: Huh, explains a lot.

McGee: Well, there's about a 150 gigabytes of data on several hard drives.
Gibbs: Only a 150?
(Gibbs pat McGee on the shoulder)
Gibbs: Hell, that shouldn't take much time at all.
McGee: He has no idea what a gigabyte is, does he Abby?
Abby: I don't think he knows what a hard drive is McGee.

Source:[3]

No.	German Title	US Title	Air Date USA	Air Date GER	Directed by	Written by
2.33	Flucht in Ketten	**Chained**	Dec 14, 2004	Nov 3, 2005	T.Wright	F.Military

Tony goes undercover as an escaped prisoner. He is tasked with sticking to a convict who has information about stolen Iraqi antiques. During the investigation, Tony disappears, and the GPS locator that Abby placed on him is no longer working. After some startling discoveries in the case including information that the convict Tony is accompanying may in fact be a murderer with blood on his hands, the team realise that Tony's life may be in danger and race against time to find him before it's too late. *Source:[1]*

Kate: EEEK!
(over the monitor)
Abby: What's wrong?
Kate: Gibbs is driving.
Abby: I'm saying a prayer in many languages.

Source:[3]

Episodes Season 2

No.	German Title	US Title	Air Date USA	Air Date GER	Directed by	Written by
2.34	Ein Mann für unlösbare Fälle	**Black Water**	Jan 11, 2005	Nov 10, 2005	T.O'Hara	J.C.Coto & J.C.Kelley

A Navy officer's body is found in a car pulled from a lake by a celebrity private investigator. The man had been missing for two years. The PI now wants to claim the reward posted by the family, but the NCIS team must complete the investigation to find the killer before the money is awarded. The case changes from accidental death to suspected murder when McGee discovers a bullet lodged in the car. The team initially suspect that the dead man's brother may be a prime suspect, but forensic evidence suggests someone unexpected is responsible for the killing. *Source:* [1]

Ducky: Do you suspect foul play?
Gibbs: Oh, you know me, Duck... I suspect everything.
Ducky: Yes, an admirable trait in an investigator. And also the reason your three marriages ended in divorce.
Gibbs: Oh yeah? All these years I thought it was because I was a b*****.

Jimmy: Did you ever meet any of special agent Gibbs' wives?
Ducky: Actually, I presented him to the last one.
Jimmy: What went wrong?
Ducky: I don't know, she doesn't speak to me anymore.

McGee: I'm not surprised you haven't heard of it. There's no pictures in it.
Tony: Did you say something, Probie?
McGee: Yeah. I'm not a dork."
Tony: Whatever you say, Sponge Bob.

Source: [3]

No.	German Title	US Title	Air Date USA	Air Date GER	Directed by	Written by
2.35	Doppeltes Spiel	**Doppelgänger**	Jan 18, 2005	Nov 17, 2005	T.O'Hara	D.Bellisario & J.Bernstein

A telemarketer hears a murder while trying to sell a long distance call package. The team investigates with the help of a civilian law enforcement team whose personalities seem to be an exact copy of Gibbs and his team. Each team member discovers different crucial facts about the case, leading to the discovery that the murder may not have been all it seemed to be. When Abby and McGee discover that the dead man was using the Navy computer system for his own financial gain, they consult with the people he worked with to see if they can shed light on who may have wanted him dead. But the investigation becomes more intense when the missing Petty Officer is actually found dead and the team find themselves hunting down his killer. *Source:* [1]

McGee: Where are we going, Boss?
Gibbs: To talk to Petty Officer Lambert's shipmates.
McGee: He's not on a ship, Boss. Oh, sorry. You were using a military euphemism.
Gibbs: You think?
McGee: So you mean Bethesda Hospital Computer Center.
Gibbs: You speak their language.
McGee: You mean I'm going to interview them?
Gibbs: I interview, you translate. Come on!

Abby: No one gets everything right the first time, McGee. Except Gibbs.

Source: [3]

Episodes Season 2

No.	German Title	US Title	Air Date USA	Air Date GER	Directed by	Written by
2.36	Blutiges Puzzle	**The Meat Puzzle**	Feb 8, 2005	Nov 24, 2005	F.Wright	F.Military

After several months, Ducky and Jimmy finally start identifying the bodies in the meat puzzle they have been working on. It is not long before Ducky realises he testified in the court case of a would-be Medical Examiner named Vincent Hanlon who was accused of murder and was eventually jailed for eight years as a result. They soon discover that the dead men were involved in the case and it dawns on Gibbs that Ducky might be the next target. Tony and Kate are assigned to protection detail which means safeguarding Ducky and his elderly mother, but a mistake by Kate leads to Ducky being kidnapped from his home during the night. The team must race against time to find him before he ends up dead like all the other previous victims while Jimmy and Abby begin working together to uncover the truth. *Source:* [1]

Kate: Gibbs, what did Ducky look like when he was younger?
Gibbs: Illya Kuryakin.

Abby: I am one of the few people in the world who can murder you and leave no forensic evidence.

Source: [3]

No.	German Title	US Title	Air Date USA	Air Date GER	Directed by	Written by
2.37	Die Zeugin	**Witness**	Feb 15, 2005	Dec 1, 2005	J.Whitmore jr.	G.Schenck & F.Cardea

A beautiful young MIT graduate (Danica McKellar) witnesses a sailor being strangled. Local police doubt her story, but McGee asserts that her account warrants further investigation. When a sailor's body is found at another location, the story gains ground. The witness also captivates McGee who, after a sudden twist in the investigation, ends up unknowingly holding the key to solving the case. *Source:* [1]

McGee: What do you got, Abs?
Abby: *(to Gibbs)* Do I have to answer the newbie?
Gibbs: Humor him.

Gibbs: Any more food fights in here and I'm joining in. With peas.
Kate: Frozen peas?
Gibbs: Nope. In a can.

Source: [3]

No.	German Title	US Title	Air Date USA	Air Date GER	Directed by	Written by
2.38	Männer und Frauen	**Caught on Tape**	Feb 22, 2005	Dec 8, 2005	J.Woolnough	C.Crowe, G.Grant, J.C.Kelley

A Marine falls off a cliff, and his camera records him falling to his death. The prime suspects are his wife and his best friend with whom he was staying in the camp. Gibbs finds out they had an affair behind a dead man's back and he tries to persuade them to blame each other. In the meantime, Abby reconstructs the damaged film footage on the camera and reveals a previously dismissed suspect to have been in the vicinity at the time of death *Source:* [1]

Gibbs: What do you think?
Kate: The word disgusting comes to mind.
Gibbs: Do you smell that?
Kate: If you mean the urine's, then YEH.

Source: [3]

Episodes Season 2

No.	German Title	US Title	Air Date USA	Air Date GER	Directed by	Written by
2.39	Wege zum Ruhm	**Pop Life**	Mar 1, 2005	Dec 15, 2005	T.Wright	F.Military

A dance club bartender wakes up in bed with a dead female petty officer and claims this was not the woman he came home with, despite the fact that he was drunk at the time. DNA tests reveal that he was telling the truth, but the team must still work to figure out whether this means that he didn't kill the dead woman. The victim's sister and a local corrupt businessman may know more than they are telling. Guest Starring Mýa. *Source:* [1]

Tony: I knew this girl once. She squeaked. She made this little squeaking...
Kate: Tony! You want to tell Ducky that story?
Gibbs: He's heard it. We all have.

Gibbs: Are you done?
Tony: Almost.
Gibbs: Done or fired. Those are your options.
Tony: Done.

Source: [3]

No.	German Title	US Title	Air Date USA	Air Date GER	Directed by	Written by
2.40	Blau wie Kobalt	**An Eye for an Eye**	Mar 22, 2005	Jan 12, 2006	D.Smith	S.Kane

When a Petty Officer working in Intelligence receives a pair of cobalt blue eyeballs in the mail, the NCIS team starts investigating the case. The sailor commits suicide during the investigation and after Abby matches the eyes to a South American girl in a photo with the dead man's lecturer, Kate and Tony must travel to the Triple Frontier destination of Paraguay to discover the truth.. *Source:* [1]

McGee: Hey, you know what this reminds me of? Pacci's suspect that we were staking out last year.
Kate: That's right! The beautiful pre-op transsexual who seduced Tony.
Tony: She didn't seduce me. I was undercover.
Kate: Yeah, well didn't you stick your tongue down…
Tony: I took one for the team, all right? Someone had to keep her occupied.
McGee: Don't you mean him?

Source: [3]

No.	German Title	US Title	Air Date USA	Air Date GER	Directed by	Written by
2.41	Bikini Girl	**Bikini Wax**	Mar 29, 2005	Jan 19, 2006	S.Cragg	D.North

A Virginia Beach bikini contestant drowns in a public bathroom toilet. When the team discover she posed partially naked in a magazine, and was pregnant at the time of her death, clues are revealed that lead to an unlikely suspect. Tony finds a juicy secret from Kate's past. *Source:* [1]

Kate: "Gibbs would never walk in here and tells us how much he paid for his shirt."
Tony: "That's because the prices have been pretty consistent at Sears since the late seventy's."

Kate: "Give it five seconds."
McGee: "Until what?"
Kate: "Until he notices there's a..."
Tony: "Bikini contest!"

Source: [3]

Episodes Season 2

No.	German Title	US Title	Air Date USA	Air Date GER	Directed by	Written by
2.42	Stimmen	**Conspiracy Theory**	Apr 12, 2005	Jan 26, 2006	F.Military	J.Woolnough

The team investigates a suicide case, believing that the main reason of her death is a nervous breakdown, but Ducky believes that she was actually murdered. FBI Special Agent Fornell helps them in the investigation. The team discovers that the dead woman was involved in a love triangle and that this may have contributed to her death. *Source:* [1]

Abby: It's complicated.
Gibbs: You don't know do you?
Abby: Not a clue.

Source: [3]

No.	German Title	US Title	Air Date USA	Air Date GER	Directed by	Written by
2.43	Die rote Zelle	**Red Cell**	Apr 26, 2005	Feb 2, 2006	D.Smith	C.Silber

A marine is found dead on the school campus, his neck broken and the team immediately finds a suspect. However, they are forced to start again when they find the suspect has also suffered the same fate as the victim, having had his neck broken with his body being buried in a construction site. McGee and Abby discover a trace in the e-mails, a mysterious group called "Red Cell," which leads the team to believe that the marine must have been involved in a serious death game. *Source:* [1]

Kate: "I hate to say it but that was actually smart, Tony"
Gibbs: "What was, Kate?"
Kate: "Tony might have figured out how to find the hacker"
Gibbs: "It's his job. You think I keep him around for his personality?"

Kate: "The place needs a lot of work McGee."
Tony: "At least you're not building a boat in your basement."

Source: [3]

No.	German Title	US Title	Air Date USA	Air Date GER	Directed by	Written by
2.44	Mit allen Ehren	**Hometown Hero**	May, 3 2005	Feb 9, 2006	J.Whitmore jr.	G.Schneck & F.Cardea

The executor of a petty officer's will discovers the skeletal remains of a missing girl in the dead man's rented storage unit. As the petty officer who died in Iraq is up for a Silver Star, it is very important that NCIS determines if he was a murderer within 24 hours or else the Silver Star will be cancelled altogether. Soil samples and further forensics lead Abby to discover that if the Marine was the killer, he could not have acted alone. Tony and McGee find CCTV footage that suggests the Marine was entirely innocent. Tony also has to deal with his car being stolen. *Source:* [1]

Kate: "Tony's car was towed. Poor baby had to take the bus to work"
Tony: "You know what kind of people take the bus?"
McGee: "Yeah, I take the bus"
Tony: "Exactly!"
Tony: "Do you realize Mother Teresa would have road rage hell out there?"
McGee: "I know it's a long shot"
Tony: "A long shot is you getting laid by Penelope Cruz, McGee!"

Source: [3]

Episodes Season 2

No.	German Title	US Title	Air Date USA	Air Date GER	Directed by	Written by
2.45	Todeskuss	**SWAK**	May 10, 2005	Mar 2, 2006	D.Smith	D.Bellisario

All hell breaks loose at the NCIS office when Tony opens a mysterious letter containing a small puff of white powder which may be a deadly bacteria. Kate calls for help and as a precaution, she and Tony are put into a bio-hazard isolation room while McGee and Gibbs are left to discover who sent the envelope and their reasons for doing so while searching for a cure to help their friends before it's too late *Source:* [1]

Gibbs: "Kate, play it safe. Go with Tony."
Kate: "That's safe?!!!"

Tony: "If I get Anthrax how would you feel?"
Gibbs: "Not as bad as you DiNozzo."

Tony: "I have allergies"
Gibbs: "Never had allergies. Never had a cold either."
Kate: "You don't get colds?"
Gibbs: "Nope. Never had the flu either."
Kate: *(whispers to DiNozzo)* "Why do I believe him?"
Tony: "If you were a bug, would you attack Gibbs?"
McGee: "I get colds all the time."
Tony: "'Course you do, Probie."

McGee: "Wish I had my PDA."
Gibbs: "Use Ducky's."
Palmer: "Ah... Agent Gibbs, sir...Dr. Mallard doesn't have...."
Gibbs: "Requisition replacement cell phones and weapons for my team. Go!"
Palmer: "Pistols?"
Gibbs: "Well, no, Palmer, crossbows, if you think they might work better."
McGee: "Boss, I can't find Ducky's PDA."
Gibbs: "McGee, it's a pad and a pencil."

Abby: "You got to get a life, Gibbs."
Gibbs: "Last thing I need is another wife."
Abby: "Life. You got to get a life."

Gibbs: "I thought these tests were fast."
Abby: "It's not a pregnancy test."

Ducky: "Where do you think you're going?"
Gibbs: "Find out who sent the letter."
Ducky: "You cannot leave autopsy! It's negative-pressured so airborne pathogens can't contaminate the the building."
Gibbs: "I've been scrubbed, sanitized for all I know, sterilized. I have an investigation to open."
Ducky: "I have a possible contagion to contain. Until your blood test clears you, I cannot permit you to leave this room."

Source: [3]

Episodes Season 2

No.	German Title	US Title	Air Date USA	Air Date GER	Directed by	Written by
2.46	Die Rückkehr	**Twilight**	May 24, 2005	Mar 9, 2006	T.Wright	J.C.Kelley

With Ari Haswari back in the country again and out to kill Gibbs, the team find themselves attempting to stop Ari from completing the task. In the meantime, they also try to find out who killed two off-duty sailors whose deaths might be linked to an upcoming terrorist attack and the theft of a drone from a company. But in the end, it might not be enough as NCIS find themselves paying a very high price for their efforts when one of their own is brutally murdered in Gibbs and Ari's battle with each other.... *Source:* [1]

Fornell: My second biggest mistake, Jethro? That's very dramatic. What was the first?
Gibbs: When you married my second wife.
Fornell: You could have warned me.
Gibbs: I did.
Fornell: In my own defense, I thought he was exaggerating. He wasn't.

McGee: Do you miss him as much as I do?
Kate: More.
McGee: I thought you said he was pig-headed.
Kate: That's part of his charm - he's like an X-rated Peter Pan.
Tony: "Me and Kate? Never happen."
McGee: "Why not?"
Tony: "She's too smart for that."

Gibbs: "Tony..."
Tony: "Yeah?"
Gibbs: "Go lie down before you pass out."
Tony: "I'm not going to pass out. I might cry a little, maybe feel sorry for myself, but DiNozzos do not pass out! I'm comin' Boss."

Tony: "You're never going to believe who's back in town."
Gibbs: "Ari."
Tony: "Maybe you will. Fornell said that he's here to..."
Gibbs: "Kill me. Yeah. I know. I just had coffee with him."
Tony: "So... what happened?"
Gibbs: "He tried to kill me."

Abby: "Hey. I had a weird dream about Tony last night."
Kate: "Ew! Not the one where you two are at the zoo and he..."
Abby: "No, he's fully clothed in this one. But he had blood all over his face. I woke up crying,
Kate: I never cry. Never ever ever."

Gibbs: "Protection detail's over, Kate."
Tony: "You did good."
Gibbs: "For once, DiNozzo's right."
Kate: "Wow...I thought I'd die before I ever heard a comp...." *(Kate is shot through the head and killed)*

McGee: You don't look so hot.
Tony: Well, at least that's an improvement.
McGee: Over what?

Tony: According to Gibbs, I look like crap.

Source: [3]

Season 3 (Episodes 3.47- 3.70)

Originally broadcast between September 20, 2005 and May 16, 2006, the third season opens in the aftermath of "Twilight", with the entire team in shock and Gibbs on a vendetta to seek revenge for Kate's murder. Matters are complicated by the intervention of Gibbs' former lover and new NCIS Director Jenny Shepard, and Mossad Officer Ziva David.

Source: [1]

Original Air Date USA   September 20, 2005 – May 16, 2006 on CBS

Original Air Date German Language   March 16, 2006 – January 7, 2007 on Sat 1

Episodes Season 3

No.	German Title	US Title	Air Date USA	Air Date GER	Directed by	Written by
3.47	Das Duell – Teil 1	**Kill Ari (Part I)**	Sep 20, 2005	Mar 16, 2006	D.Smith	D.Bellisario

As the team struggles to come to terms with Kate Todd's brutal murder, Gibbs clashes with the new NCIS Director Jenny Shepard, who believes that Ari Haswari was not the one responsible for firing the bullet that killed Agent Todd due to the fact that there's no proof linking him to the crime. Ziva David, Ari's Mossad control officer, sides with the director, and causes problems when she arrives at the office, claiming that Ari is completely innocent. However, Ziva's motives for defending Ari become murky when she communicates with him and does not tell anyone in the NCIS office although Gibbs is aware and orders DiNozzo to tail her. Ari later returns and holding Gerald Jackson hostage yet again, kidnaps Ducky to divert the team's attention away from Ziva as he attempts to force Ducky into a meet. *Source:* [1]

Jenny: Jethro... I know it has been a difficult day for both of us...
Gibbs: That's what my DI used to say. Never believed him.

Tony: I don't want you to get pissed...
Gibbs: I thought you wanted me pissed.
Tony: I did...It was kind-of weird when you were being nice, not that your not nice... I mean, ah...

Ziva: She wasn't attractive?
Tony: She was... but not to me...
Ziva: Then why did you imagine her naked?

Source: [3]

Episodes Season 3

No.	German Title	US Title	Air Date USA	Air Date GER	Directed by	Written by
3.48	Das Duell – Teil 2	**Kill Ari (Part 2)**	Sep 27, 2005	Mar 23, 2006	J.Whitmore, Jr.	D.Bellisario

Gibbs' determination to kill Ari increases after he mounts attacks against various members of the team in his sadistic game with Gibbs. Ari's control officer, Ziva David, begins to doubt Ari's innocence and agrees with Gibbs' plan to present Ari with the opportunity to kill him. Gibbs arrives at his house and to his surprise, Ari has been waiting for him, with Gibbs' rifle. But just before Ari can kill Gibbs, Ziva arrives and shoots Ari and killing him. It is only after the encounter between the three of them, that Gibbs discovers why Ziva was so quick to defend the murderer: she and Ari share the same father, Deputy Director Eli David of Mossad, making Ari Ziva's half-brother. After all is said and done, the team bid a sad farewell to Kate as she is laid to rest with civilian honors. Before resigning, former NCIS Director Tom Morrow approved Gibbs's request that Todd be awarded the Presidential Medal of Freedom. *Source:* [1]

Tony: Thanks for the pizza boss.
Gibbs: Thank the night shift... I swiped it from them.

Gibbs: We both can shut up.
Ziva: Espresso.Take it. It's not a bribe.
Tony: How long have you known I was......
Ziva: Following me? Since I left the Navy yard.
Tony: I don't think so.
Ziva: Blue sedan, you laid behind a white station wagon for a while, then a telephone van.You lost me at the traffic circle.
Tony: Okay, okay.You knew.
Ziva: *(offering him the coffee again)* Take it. It's chilly out here.You shouldn't feel bad, I was trained by the best.
Tony: You know, that's what I like about Mossad.
Ziva: Our training?
Tony: Your modesty.
Ziva: *(as Tony goes to throw away a pizza box)* Um, there's a slice in there! *(he gives it to her)* Todah.
Tony: Prego.
Ziva: ......I lost my little sister, Taili, in a Hamas sucide bombing.She was sixteen and the best of us.Tali had compassion.
Tony: I'm sorry.
Ziva: After Tali's death, I was like Gibbs.All I wanted was revenge.
Tony: Is that why you joined Mossad?
Ziva: I was Mossad long before Tali's death.Old....
Tony: Family tradition.
Ziva: Israeli sense of duty.
Tony: But come on.Who recruited you? Father? Uncle? Brother? Boyfriend?
Ziva: Aunt, sister, lesbian lover.
Tony: You're good.You almost got me off the question. Almost.
Ziva: I volunteered.....Laila tov.
Tony: Buonanotte.

Gibbs: From now on, we're going to use phonetics like we did in the Marines.
Abby: Golf India Bravo Bravo Sierra?
Gibbs: What is it, Abbs?
Abby: Can I please go back to my lab;I'm flipping out up here with nothing to do
Gibbs: Fine, but--
Abby: I know, no leaving the building! Bravo Yankee Echo.
Gibbs: If I ask you something, Tobias are you going to lie to me?
Fornell: Depends on the question.
Gibbs: What's Ari Haswari's real mission here?
Fornell: I'm going to lie to you.Mossad lies to the CIA, they lie to us, I lie to you.I don't know who you lie to, being the bottom of the food chain......And not married. *Source:* [3]

Episodes Season 3

No.	German Title	US Title	Air Date USA	Air Date GER	Directed by	Written by
3.49	Der Mann in der Todeszelle	**Mind Games**	Oct 4, 2005	Mar 30. 2006	W.Webb	G.Schenck & F.Cardea

Death row prisoner Kyle Boone is a serial killer whom Gibbs arrested ten years ago. Having been placed on Death Row and due to be executed in a few days time, he insists that he will disclose the location of the missing bodies of his murder victims to Gibbs alone, forcing the reluctant team leader to meet with him. When Abby and McGee locate the place where the victims had been murdered, the team, assisted by Agent Cassidy, finds that the latest four victims in Boone's scrapbook had been killed in the last three years, meaning Boone has an accomplice. When Agent Cassidy goes missing, the team is forced into a desperate race against time to prevent her from becoming victim number five of the copycat killer. *Source:* [1]

Abby: You're not listening to a word I'm saying. I'm pregnant, McGee. Twins. Haven't told the father yet. It's Gibbs. I know it's wrong, but something about his silver hair just gets me all tingly inside
Tony: Excuse me for a second. I think I'm going to vomit
Abby: I'm joking, Tony. Except for the part about Gibbs' hair. That is really hot. McGee is ignoring me again
Tony: Easily fixable
(Tony hits McGee)
McGee: What?! What'd I do?
Tony: Stop ignoring Abby. She's sensitive

Ducky: Gibbs was a very different man 10 years ago.
Tony: You mean meaner?
Ducky: No, a lot like you, Tony!

McGee: Do we actually have knee pads Tony?
DiNozzo: I don't know Probie. Inventory is Kate's responsibility. Why don't you ask...

Ducky: Do you know the difference between good and bad cholesterol Tony?
Tony: No, but I'm guessing it has something to do with taste.

McGee: Uh, you two might wanna get busy. Gibbs is headed this way and he looks pissed.
Paula: Think he caved to the Governor?
Tony: No way.
McGee: No way, if Gibbs doesn't want to do something he doesn't.
Tony: No matter who's asking. (Gibbs gets his gun and badge out and walks off) Where you going boss?
Gibbs: Sussex State Prison to interview Kyle Boone. Be gone the rest of the day.
Paula: Yep, you two sure have him pegged.
Tony: The difference between ten years ago and today, Ducky? We have Gibbs' back.
Ducky: There's another difference, Tony.Ten years ago, Gibbs was a very different man.
Tony: You mean he was actually meaner?
Ducky: No, quite the opposite.He was......he was was a lot like you.

Source: [3]

Episodes Season 3

No.	German Title	US Title	Air Date USA	Air Date GER	Directed by	Written by
3.50	Sarg aus Eisen	**Silver War**	Oct 11, 2005	Apr 6, 2006	T.O'Hara	J.Lurie

A deceased Marine is found encased in a Civil-War era tomb at the Smithsonian museum and evidence later comes to light suggesting that he was probably buried alive. In the meantime, Ziva David joins NCIS as a liaison officer for Mossad and is assigned by the new director of NCIS, Jenny Shepard to Gibbs' team without his consent much to Gibbs's anger although Jenny insists that the team needs Ziva. She is forced to prove her worth to the team as they track down the people responsible for the Staff Sergeant's death, which is linked to a Civil War treasure. When Ducky and Ziva are placed in a difficult position, Ziva shows her value by saving both their lives. *Source: [1]*

Ducky: How do you tell a woman you have no mental recolection of her what-so-ever?
Palmer: I suppose one could always lie.
Ducky: Have you been spending time with Agent DiNozzo again?

Ziva: Who's the woman with Gibbs?
Tony: Yeah, once you're here long enough you'll figure it out.
Ziva: Is that his girlfriend?
Tony: I have no idea.
Ziva: You just told me....
Tony: Well, you'll figure out there are some things you don't ask about.

Source: [3]

No.	German Title	US Title	Air Date USA	Air Date GER	Directed by	Written by
3.51	Rollentausch	**Switch**	Oct 18, 2005	Apr 13, 2006	T.J.Wright	G.Grant

The team is called to investigate the murder of a Petty Officer who was gunned down while driving on a freeway. While visiting the sailor's commander to inform him of the death, the team discovers that another man claims to be the Petty Officer and that his identity may have been stolen. Secrets in both men's lives are revealed, but it is shrewd observations by Abby that end up solving the case. *Source: [1]*

Ziva: I'll drive, Tony.
Tony: No, no, no! Not gonna make that mistake again.
Ziva: Did you really think my driving was that terrible? Aside from the high speed and near misses?
Tony: Let's just say it's an acquired taste. Like regurgitated lunch.

Gibbs: I'd hate to start smacking you like I do DiNozzo
Abby: You wouldn't. You would?
Gibbs: It won't be on the head.

Ziva: Is he always this juvenile?
McGee: Only on the days of the week ending in day.

Ziva: Just to be clear, are there any more of these rules I should be aware of?
Gibbs: About 50 of them.
Ziva: And I don't suppose they're written down anywhere that I could...
Gibbs: NO.
Ziva: Then how am I supposed to...
Gibbs: My job is to teach them to you.

Source: [3]

Episodes Season 3

No.	German Title	US Title	Air Date USA	Air Date GER	Directed by	Written by
3.52	Voyeure im Netz	**The Voyeur's Web**	Oct 25, 2005	Apr 20, 2006	D.Smith	D.J.North

Jamie Carr, a Marine Sergeant's wife, is thought to have been abducted until Gibbs and his team found evidence to suggest that she may have been murdered live on the internet. Carr and her neighbor, Leanne Roberts, had been making money by running a live internet sex site while their husbands were deployed abroad. Roberts's body is later found but the team is still unable to find any trace of Carr. With the help of her new assistant, Charles Sterling who Director Shepard has hired for her, Abby determines that the video of Jamie might not be all it seems. *Source:* [1]

Ziva: Where did all these people come from?
Tony: Didn't you see the signs? It's yard sale day.
Ziva: I see. And do Marines sell their yards often?
McGee: No, it's actually when people gather stuff they don't want anymore, and sell it in their yards.
Ziva: Why would anyone want to buy somebody else's junk?
Tony: One man's junk is another man's treasure.
Ziva: In Israel, we have a saying. "Zevel Ze Zevel."
[Tony and McGee look at her, confused]
Ziva: Crap is crap.

McGee: My girlfriend is always emailing me these internet videos. She sent me one of this room last week.
Tony: Why do I find that hard to believe?
McGee: What, you never get forwarded weird videos to your email?
Tony: All the time. I meant the part about you having a girlfriend.

Abby: Oldest you've ever been with?
Tony: 26, my dry cleaner....You have a stuffed animal that farts?
Abby: Yeah! Cool, huh?
Tony: Yeah... in a disturbing kinda way...

McGee: Good news, boss. Naughty Naughty Neighbors has a webmaster
Gibbs: Web what?
McGee: Webmaster. It's a person that is hired to design and update the page. His name is Carter Finch
Tony: Is this guy like a Super Fly cyber pimp?
McGee: Not exactly

Tony: I feel like I've just walked into page 8 of the IKEA catalogue...

Gibbs: The French wine in this particular region is terribly overrated.

Ziva: I've been meaning to ask you about that, Tony.How does a fifteen-year-old boy go about meeting a coquette?
McGee: She means rockette, boss.

Ziva: The odds of finding him off a list of that size is....
Gibbs: Better than the odd of you winning this argument.

Ziva: It could take days to search this place.
Tony: Why don't you tell Gibbs that, he loves our input.

Source: [3]

Episodes Season 3

No.	German Title	US Title	Air Date USA	Air Date GER	Directed by	Written by
3.53	Projekt „Honor"	**Honor Code**	Nov 1, 2005	Aug 13, 2006	C.Bucksey	C.Silber

Gibbs befriends a young boy after his father, a Lt. Commander, is kidnapped. The Lt. Commander had been working on a classified project named Honor and is the only person who has the code keys to the project. The release of the code keys can pose a serious threat to national security. Although the evidence gathered by Gibb's team suggests that the Lt. Commander was a part of the scheme, Gibbs believes otherwise due to the strong bond between the Lt. Commander and his son. *Source:* [1]

Jenny: Always admired your way with children. Ever think of having any of your own?
Gibbs: It that an offer Jen?
Jenny: No, it wasn't an offer, Jethro, it was merely an observation.

Gibbs: Dinner at the White House?
Jenny: A date, actually.
Gibbs: Must be an important guy for you to get all decked out.
Jenny: I would prefer it if you would just say you liked my dress.
Gibbs: I haven't decided yet.

Tony: Zach, hey. I'm Special Agent DiNozzo, you can call me Tony, okay? That's a smart thing to do, calling NCIS. Good boy. All right, I know this is really scary, but I want you to be brave. Can you do that? Okay, I want you to think back to what happened today. Try to remember the details. There's no wrong answer here.
Gibbs: What do we know?
Tony: Nothing. I think the kid's in shock.
Zach: No, I'm not. I'm waiting for Agent DiNozzo to ask me a question.
Tony: *(about Zach)* Do you see the way he's been acting around me?
Ziva: I think it's because he doesn't like you, Tony.
Tony: Kids dig me.
Ziva: No they don't. *(Tony scoffs)*
Tony: Zach. Zacharoo, buddy. Come on over here, man. I was gonna wait until tomarrow when everyone was here but considering what a brave little boy you've been and how much you've helped us, I'm gonna make you an honorary NCIS agent.
Zach: Thanks.I've gotta go to the head.
Ziva: (laughs) Yes, Tony, I was mistaken.Your way with children is only rivaled by your way with women.
Tony: He's under a lot of stress.

McGee: Have you ever considered the fact that Gibbs could be wrong this time?
Abby: *(gasps)* "Ooh! McGee! Bite your tongue. Gibbs knows what he's doing, we just have to show him The Love.
Tony: We show him the love, Abby. We just don't want the bad guys to get away while we're doing it.

Ziva: The man is spick and Spam.
Tony: The saying is 'spick and span'. Spam is lunch meat.
Ziva: Oh. What exactly is 'span' then?
Tony: Span is.....I'll get back to you on that.

McGee: How many people owe you favors?
Ziva: How many dates does Tony go on a month.

Source: [3]

Episodes Season 3

No.	German Title	US Title	Air Date USA	Air Date GER	Directed by	Written by
3.54	Goldherz	**Under Covers**	Nov 8, 2005	Aug 20, 2006	L.Lipstadt	L.D.Zlotoff

When it is discovered that two married assassins, who were fatally wounded in a car crash, were planning an assassination at the United States Marine Corps Birthday Ball, Gibbs sends Ziva and Tony to pose as the married assassins in order to find out who the couple had planned to assassinate and who had hired them. After the team finds out that the couple were expecting a baby and may have been planning to retire, they realize that the assassination plot could have been a set-up and that the married assassins were potentially the real targets. Meanwhile, an attraction between Tony and Ziva surfaces. *Source:* [1]

Tony: Sweetheart? You know what I could really use right now?
Ziva: Some deodorant?

Tony: Maybe she didn't know.
Ziva: Oh, she knew.
Tony: Then why do this job risking to lose the baby?
Ziva: Maybe she needed the money.
Tony: Yeah, kids are expensive...
Ziva: And bullets are cheap.

Ducky: Though it may be common knowledge that I talk to my patients, unfortunately to date, none of them have ever answered me back.
Gibbs: Listen harder.

Source: [3]

No.	German Title	US Title	Air Date USA	Air Date GER	Directed by	Written by
3.55	In der Falle	**Frame Up**	Nov 22, 2005	Aug 27, 2006	T.J.Wright	L.Walsh

A pair of legs are found on a Marine base, and the team is dumbfounded and shellshocked when every piece of evidence in a murder points towards Tony as the prime suspect. In an effort to help their colleague, the team compiles a list of people who may have grudges against Tony, providing them with a long list of suspects. Abby is upset that she may have incriminated Tony through the forensic evidence she provided and refuses to give up until she's proved his innocence. *Source:* [1]

Ziva: What do women try to achieve by cracking eggs on a man's car?
McGee: Most men love their cars, it's a way of saying "You broke my heart, I break yours."
Ziva: In Israel, we just shoot men who are untrue.

Ziva: She's probably passed on by now.
McGee: The term is passed out.
Ziva: Whatever, the girl is tired.

Ziva: The personnel in the evidence garage!
Tony: What about 'em?
Ziva: They hate you.
McGee: She's right; you never wait your turn to check in evidence.
Ziva: And women don't appreciate being called "baggie bunnies."

Gibbs: Ass kissing on the hill is a skill
Jenny: So is castration.
Gibbs: I wear a cup.

Abby: We have to save him Gibbs.Because if he goes to court with fingerprint and his bite mark on the leg, Tony's gonna go to prison for the rest of his life.And I'll be the one that put him there.

Source: [3]

Episodes Season 3

No.	German Title	US Title	Air Date USA	Air Date GER	Directed by	Written by
3.56	Drei Kugeln	**Probie**	Nov 29, 2005	Sep 3, 2006	T.O'Hara	G.Schenck & F.Cardea

While the team is on protective detail for the Chief of Naval Operations, McGee spots an argument taking place in an alleyway. He shoots one of the men, who he believed was aiming a gun at him. The deceased turns out to be a D.C. Metro police detective who was working undercover. When the team is unable to find any weapon or bullets left behind by anyone other than McGee, it appears that McGee may have made a probie mistake. McGee begins to doubt himself but Gibbs is suspicious of the detective's meeting, which took place that night. After speaking to the decedent's partner, the team realizes that McGee's story may be more accurate than any of them thought. *Source:*[1]

Gibbs Rule #8: Never take anything for granted.

Tony: McGee, the first time I shot at someone, I wet my pants.
McGee: Really?
Tony: Really. If you tell anyone, I will slap you silly.

Source:[3]

No.	German Title	US Title	Air Date USA	Air Date GER	Directed by	Written by
3.57	Boot Camp Babes	**Model Behavior**	Dec 13, 2005	Sep 10, 2006	S.Cragg	D.J.Nort

A supermodel is found dead after having overdosed on phencyclidine at a Marine base, where the reality TV show in which she was participating was being filmed. Her ex-boyfriend is also found dead in a motel nearby having overdosed on heroin, leading the team to believe that their deaths may have been related to their relationship. However, when it is discovered that the Marine drill instructor in charge of the TV show was romantically linked to the dead supermodel, the team look closer at the others involved in the show. When the Marine boyfriend begins to overdose on the same thing that killed his girlfriend, it appears that someone may have disapproved of the relationship, even going to extreme lengths to end it. *Source:*[1]

Supermodel: Anything else we can help you with? Like some hair tips for your girlfriend here? *(referring to Ziva)*
McGee: No, I, uh, think that about covers it. But if you can remember anything else that might help, please give us a call. *(hands her his card)*
Ziva: It's called a business card. Maybe you can have one of the Marines read it to you?

Source:[3]

No.	German Title	US Title	Air Date USA	Air Date GER	Directed by	Written by
3.58	Die Spur des Geldes	**Boxed In**	Jan 11, 2006	Sep 17, 2006	D.Smith	D.Coen

While investigating a naval stockyard for a container with illegal weapons, Tony and Ziva are ambushed and forced to take cover in a container, where they subsequently become locked in. Gibbs, McGee and Abby attempt to search for them with the help of the port security office. Meanwhile, Tony and Ziva discover that the crates of DVD movies inside the container served as a cover for hidden crates, which contain million of dollars of counterfeit money. But they both find themselves in a gunfight after the container is later taken away to a warehouse guarded by terrorists, forcing Gibbs and McGee into a race against time to find their location before Tony and Ziva end up dead. . *Source:*[1]

Gibbs: They were caught in the cross fire.
McGee: Boss you don't think......well...should we put divers in the water?
Gibbs: They're not in the water. McGee, if they were in the water they'd be dead.If they dead I'd know about it.

Source:[3]

Episodes Season 3

No.	German Title	US Title	Air Date USA	Air Date GER	Directed by	Written by
3.59	Ein langer Sonntag	**Deception**	Jan 17, 2006	Sep 24, 2006	D.Smith	D.Coen

A Navy Lt. Commander, who was in charge of a shipment of nuclear weapons, is thought to have been abducted leading to Gibbs and his team being called in on a Sunday to investigate. The team discovers that the Lt. Commander had had a meeting earlier in the day at a shopping center and that she did volunteer work at an organization which combats online pedophilia, meaning that her abductor might not have been a terrorist but a pedophile she was tracking. *Source:* [1]

Gibbs Rule #3: Never be unreachable.

Ziva: Why don't I think what she said is a good thing?
Tony: Because you're a better agent than you are a driver.

Abby: Thank you sir!
Gibbs: Don't call me sir.
Abby: Thank you ma'am!

Tony: Do you know what I like about coming to work on a Sunday?
Ziva: Relaxed dress code?
Tony: Actually no, it offers us the unique chance to get a glimpse into the private life of our co workers.
Ziva: Except I have no interest in your life.

Source: [3]

No.	German Title	US Title	Air Date USA	Air Date GER	Directed by	Written by
3.60	Schläfer	**Light Sleeper**	Jan 24, 2006	Oct 1, 2006	C.Bucksey	C.Silber

When the Korean wives of two Marines are murdered, Gibbs and his team are sent in to investigate. Since signs of domestic abuse were evident at the crime scene, they suspect that the killer is one of the women's husbands. The sudden disappearance of Yoon Dawson, a friend of the two victims, makes her husband a suspect in the case. However, the team soon discovers that Yoon is not all she seems, and that she and her two dead friends might have been in America for reasons other than having Marine husbands. *Source:* [1]

Gibbs: What did the urine tell you Abby?
Abby: Oh, all kinds of stuff, we had a really good talk.

McGee: Boss, Did you find her?
Gibbs: Yes McGee, She's hiding in my coffee cup.

Gibbs: Sign of an unhappy marriage.
Ziva: Funny. I think it looks like a hole in the wall.

Tony: It's like my father used to tell me: "Be careful who you marry, Anthony.You never know if they're gonna turn out to be a maniac serial killer.
McGee: Your father actually said that to you?
Tony: No, but I'm pretty sure he thought it.
Ziva: He probably knew your taste in women.

Gibbs: Tony, Ziva, what happened back there with that bomb.....I just want you to know....
Tony: You don't have to say it, boss, we know how you feel about us.
Ziva: We are a team, Gibbs.It's what we do.
Gibbs: I was going to say if either one of you two wing-nuts ever disobey a direct order again, I'll kill you myself.
Tony: That's our boss!

Source: [3]

Episodes Season 3

No.	German Title	US Title	Air Date USA	Air Date GER	Directed by	Written by
3.61	Kopfsache	**Head Case**	Feb 7, 2006	Oct 8, 2006	D.Smith	G.Schenck & F.Cardea

While conducting a raid on an automotive chop shop run by Marines, the team finds a severed head in one of the cars. The head belonged to a Navy Captain, who was thought to have been cremated. Their investigation leads them to the discovery of a scheme involving the illegal sale of human body parts, which came from stolen bodies. *Source: 1*

Jenny: Do you think it would be inappropriate if, as Director, I went in there and slapped that smile off her face?
Gibbs: Yeah, it would. That's what you have me for.

Tony: Sleepless in Seattle?
Ziva: That was about voodoo?
Tony: No, but the first time I saw it, scared the bejezus out of me.

Tony: You thinking what I'm thinking?
McGee: Yeah, that we've just walked into an episode of the X-files.

Source: 3

No.	German Title	US Title	Air Date USA	Air Date GER	Directed by	Written by
3.62	Familiengeheimnis	**Family Secrets**	Feb 28, 2006	Oct 15, 2006	J.Withmore jr.	S.D.Binder

An ambulance explodes and practically disintegrates the body of William Danforth, a deceased Marine it was carrying. A DNA analysis performed on a piece of body tissue informs the team that the body does not belong to Danforth. The team suspects that Danforth's best friend, who was a bomb expert, helped Danforth fake his death in order to leave the Marine Corps. When Danforth is discovered to have been a recipient of a donor organ, the team realizes that the body may in fact be Danforth's after all, and they are forced to examine reasons as to why someone may have wanted to disguise that the body was his. *Source: 1*

Gibbs: Any chance of getting the call logs?
Abby: I'd have a better chance of getting McGee to wear a a Speedo to church.

Gibbs: DiNozzo, shut up!
Tony: Shutting up, Boss!

Source: 3

No.	German Title	US Title	Air Date USA	Air Date GER	Directed by	Written by
3.63	Bärenjäger	**Ravenous**	Mar 7, 2006	Oct 22, 2006	T.Wright	R.C.Arthur

A Marine is suspected to have been eaten by a bear after a group of teenagers found his dog tags in bear feces in a national forest. However, autopsy reveals that the Marine was killed by a blade before his corpse was eaten by a bear. Evidence also shows that he was camping with a woman, who is now missing. The team's search for the woman and the Marine's killer leads them to a realization that their case may be linked to several women of similar appearance who have been found dead in the national forest. The team realizes that locals may know more than they have been telling. *Source: 1*

Abby: I was just about to call Tony and McGee.I think they were having sex.
Ziva: *(surprised)* Tony and McGee?
Abby: No!

Ziva: Not a big fan of nature huh?
Tony: Oh.. I'm a big fan of nature as long as it's on TV. *Source: 3*

Episodes Season 3

No.	German Title	US Title	Air Date USA	Air Date GER	Directed by	Written by
3.64	Der letzte Sonnenuntergang	**Bait**	Mar 14, 2006	Nov 12, 2006	T.O'Hara	L.Walsh

The teenage son of a Marine Major holds his classmates hostage inside a classroom by threatening them with a bomb strapped to his chest. Gibbs and his team arrive on scene but are unable to get audio and video of the situation inside the classroom so Gibbs puts himself in danger by offering himself as a hostage. While Tony takes charge of the team, the boy demands that his mother be brought to the classroom by sunset, but the team discovers that she has been dead for a year. Gibbs suspects that the boy is not acting alone when he sees an earwig in the boy's ear. *Source:* [1]

Tony: How long?
McGee: Depends. They could be using counter attack software. If they're using a sophicticated encryption system. It could be one hundred twenty-eight even two hundred fifty-six bit...
Tony: Probie!
McGee: On it, boss!...........Tony!
Ziva: What?
Tony: He called me boss.
Ziva: Yeah, he'll never live it down.
Tony: Nope.

Source: [3]

No.	German Title	US Title	Air Date USA	Air Date GER	Directed by	Written by
3.65	Tot im Eis	**Iced**	Apr 4, 2006	Nov 19, 2006	D.Smith	D.Coen

NCIS is called to investigate a dead Marine First Sergeant found in a frozen lake. The discovery of three more dead men in the lake leads Gibbs to the underworld of an international street gang, which may threaten the safety of the team. The team finds a link between the dead men and a one-year-old case concerning the accidental shooting of a Marine by the gang. *Source:* [1]

Ducky: Yes, I once performed an autopsy on a man who drowned in his kitchen sink. Yes, apparently, he couldn't remove the drain plug and attempted to use his teeth.

McGee: Something wrong, boss?
Gibbs: Just admiring your feminine glow.

Source: [3]

No.	German Title	US Title	Air Date USA	Air Date GER	Directed by	Written by
3.66	Das Leck	**Untouchable**	Apr 18, 2006	Nov 26, 2006	L.Libman	G.Schenck & F.Cardea

Due to suspicions of a mole working inside the Pentagon, Tony and Ziva are charged with interviewing members of the Pentagon's cryptography department. When one of their interviewees is found dead in her home, the team investigates her apparent suicide. While the cryptography department is immediately locked down, Abby uses forensic science to prove that a second person was in the room when the gun was fired.. *Source:* [1]

Abby: Rough night?
Ziva: Is there any other kind with Gibbs?

Abby: Stop being so "Palmer," Jimmy.

Source: [3]

Episodes Season 3

No.	German Title	US Title	Air Date USA	Air Date GER	Directed by	Written by
3.67	Typisch Montag	**Bloodbath**	Apr 25, 2006	Dec 3, 2006	D.Smith	S.D.Binder

After a room at a Navy lodging facility is found to have blood and fragments of flesh scattered throughout, the team is called to investigate. However, evidence suggests that it was a set-up crime scene. Meanwhile, Abby returns from court after giving testimony in an embezzlement trial and is attacked in her lab. Gibbs puts Abby into protective custody with the team while they look for the person targeting Abby, who appears to be a stalker. It was discovered that the defendant in the trial had used some of the ill-gotten money to hire a hit man to target Abby. It was Abby, who had been armed with pepper spray, brass knuckles and a taser gun, who had subdued the hit man, and helped to get the defendant arrested. *Source: [1]*

McGee: Did you request this specific room when you called the lodge?
Lillian: No we asked for the one with the eviscerated squirrels, but this was all they had.
Frank: What the h*** kind of question is that?
Gibbs: Our last one.

McGee: Or, maybe it was just a lab accident. I mean, really, who would wanna kill Abby?
Ziva: You know that's true. It's not like someone was after Tony.
McGee: Now that's a suspect list I wouldn't want to run down again.

Tony: Ya! Ha-ha! Ha-ha! I think the joke's over. We get it.

Source: [3]

No.	German Title	US Title	Air Date USA	Air Date GER	Directed by	Written by
3.68	Brüder	**Jeopardy**	May 2, 2006	Dec 10, 2006	J.Whitmore jr.	D.J.North

NCIS investigates the death of a suspect who was in Ziva's custody but the investigation turns critical when the dead man's brother kidnaps Director Shepard and threatens to kill her unless the seized evidence and his brother are returned, unaware that his brother is actually dead. While Ducky works to find the man's cause of death, the team desperately searches for their Director before it's too late. Note: The suspect dies in an elevator. In the previous week's episode, Abby tells of the low frequency of people dying in elevators. *Source: [1]*

Tony: Look, we all know that Ziva has crazy Ninja skills, but I mean, she's got some self control right? Not a lot, but some. Never mind.

Gibbs: You sure this is the stupidest thing you've ever done, DiNozzo?

Ducky: I've been traveling to crime scenes for a great many years, but I can say with complete confidence this is the shortest commute I have ever had.
Jimmy: And one of the first times I didn't get us lost.
Ducky: True.

Jenny: Gibbs thinks of me as a wife.
James: See.
Jenny: He's had three.

Abby: Oh my God. I've turned into my Uncle Larry.

Ziva: I didn't touch him... Hardly at all.

Tony: I'm afraid you'll put the Vulcan death grip on me.

Source: [3]

Episodes Season 3

No.	German Title	US Title	Air Date USA	Air Date GER	Directed by	Written by
3.69	Fünfzehn Jahre	Hiatus (Part I)	May 9, 2006	Dec 17, 2006	D.Smith	D.Bellisario

A bomb explodes as Gibbs contacts an undercover government agent on a suspicious foreign ship, killing the agent and placing Gibbs in a coma, in which he has flashbacks of the murder of his wife Shannon and daughter Kelly many years earlier, and his wounding in Desert Storm. Meanwhile, Tony becomes the temporary head of the investigation team as the group attempts to track down Pinpin Pula, a missing crew member of the ship, suspected to be an Abu Sayyaf member. Gibbs awakens from his coma at the end of the episode with no memory of Ducky, who is in the room with him. *Source:* [1]

Ducky: I sat on a bomb once. No twice. The first time I was young, the second time I was foolish.
Palmer: Why would you sit on a bomb?
Ducky: I just told you, I was young and foolish. Haven't you been listening?

Dr.Todd: How well do you know Gibbs?
Jenny: He was my mentor at NCIS; he taught me most of what I know.
Dr.Todd: Yet you're his boss.
Jenny: Jethro's a great field agent. He's a great team leader. And he deals more efficiently with difficult politicians than I do.
Dr.Todd: Then why isn't he the...
Jenny: He shoots them.

Abby: McGee said that Gibbs was in a bomb blast. He tried to sound really calm, but I could hear the fear in his voice and he should be afraid, for Gibbs to be brought to the hospital in the ambulance could not be good. I had to come see for myself and my hearse got a flat as usual so, um, I got in a cab to go to the airport and then I realised that, that by the time I got to the terminal and, and I bought a ticket and then I went through security and then I flew to Norfolk and then I got a cab here it would be better just to stay in the cab that I was in so I did that, it cost a lost of, you know what it doesn't matter what it cost because this is Gibbs we're talking about. I can't believe that he's hurt he is never hurt, not hurt enough to go to a hospital. He has to be dying to even go see a doctor. Oh my God. He isn't dying is he? I dunno what I would do. Positive thoughts, positive thoughts, positive thoughts. Ok, I know the rule is that you have to be family to go into Emergency, at least that's what they said when Uncle Charlie got his leg caught in a nurtia trap, but Gibbs and me, we're tighter than blood. I know you need ID, I have ID in here. Um, I work at NCIS, uh, forensics, and, uh, ballistics, chemical analysis and DNA typing. Uh, here, um, that's me, I promise, I just, I had to be in court that day but I swear, that is me.

Tony: Shouldn't he be awake by now?
Jenny: You know Gibbs. He keeps his own schedule. Do you know what REM is?
Tony: Sure. Rapid Eye Movement. It happens when you're asleep and dreaming.
Jenny: That's what it looks like he's doing now.
Tony: Oh well, that's gotta be a good sign right?
Jenny: If it isn't a nightmare.

Tony: This is so "Usual Suspects".
Ziva: Tony, your dying words will be, "I've seen this film".

McGee: On it boss!
Tony: I do love it when he calls me boss.
Ziva: Is that why you're being nice to him?
Tony: I'm not being nice. Lugging foot lockers is probie work.

Source: [3]

Episodes Season 3

No.	German Title	US Title	Air Date USA	Air Date GER	Directed by	Written by
3.70	Semper Fi	**Hiatus (Part II)**	May 16, 2006	Jan 7, 2007	D.Smith	D.Bellisario

Director Shepard contacts Gibbs' NCIS mentor and partner, Mike Franks in hopes of helping an amnesiac Gibbs regain his memory as only he knows the details to an impending terrorist attack. She also delves into Gibbs' past and shares with Ducky about his murdered wife and daughter. Ziva, who had appeared nonchalant about Gibbs' situation, visits Gibbs in a desperate and emotional attempt to revive his memory by telling him about their shared connection with Ari. Meanwhile, Tony and the team discover Pinpin Pula wants to blow up the ship Cape Fear. Gibbs recovers his memory and tries to stop the terrorist attack, but fails because his superiors ignore his warnings. Finally, Gibbs hands his badge to Tony and resigns before heading to Mexico to stay at Franks's house.
Source: [1]

Gibbs Rule #11: When the job is done, walk away.

Tony: My gut tells me we're missing something.
Ziva: Gibbs?
Tony: Yeah. Gibbs.

Gibbs: What can I do?
Ziva: Remember!
Gibbs: I've been trying to since I woke up in this room!
Ziva: Well try harder! ... That's a start.
Gibbs: What is?
Ziva: The old Gibbs' stare. You gave it to all of us; McGee, Tony, me!
Gibbs: What are you talking about?

Abby: Can you imagine how scray that would be? To lose the last fifteen years of your life.
McGee: Oh, man!
Abby: What?
McGee: I'd still be in highschool.
Abby: Uh, yuck! Zits, braces. rageing hormones.
McGee: Yeah, used to walk around all day with a notebook in front of my.....
Abby: In front of your what, McGee?
McGee: *(pointing to the computer)* The laundry room is off.It should actually be 3.962 meters wide, no twenty-six.
Abby: *(fixs it)* Better?
McGee: Yeah.Gotta be accurate.
Abby: Absolutly.So was it one of these tiny spiral notebooks? Or one of those big three ring binder kinda ones, Timmy?
McGee: And where were you fifteen years ago, Abby?
Abby: So where did you find Gibbs?
McGee: Afraid I'm gonna find out.... *(Abby hits him)* What was that for?
Abby: Distracting me.
McGee: I was not distracting.....
Abby: *(pointing at the computer)* Gibbs.
McGee: Between the drier and the bulkhead......Little closer to the bulkhead.Now the autopsty report indicates that Gableeb was sitting on the bomb.
Abby: Which consisted of one hundred-thirteen grands of semtex.
McGee: Wow.You can compute the amount of semtex used?
Abby: I'm a scientist, McGee.I can compute anything acurtly, including the sizr of the notebook required to.....
McGee: Stop.

Source: [3]

Season 4 (Episodes 4.71- 4.94)

The fourth season of NCIS was originally broadcast between September 19, 2006 and May 22, 2007. Special Agent Gibbs left NCIS at the end of season 3 after a terrorist attack had been successful because his superiors did not heed his warnings in time. The team is now led by DiNozzo for a short time until Gibbs' eventual return. New characters introduced in this season are Michelle Lee, who was briefly on DiNozzo's team and was transferred to the legal department upon Gibbs' return, and (already in the final episodes of season 3) Gibbs' former boss & mentor Mike Franks, both as recurring characters. Also, albeit later in the season, Army CID Lieutenant Colonel Hollis Mann is introduced as another love interest for Gibbs.

Source: [1]

Original Air Date USA	September 19, 2006 – May 22, 2007 on CBS
Original Air Date German Language	March 4, 2007 – November 18, 2007 on Sat 1

Episodes Season 4

No.	German Title	US Title	Air Date USA	Air Date GER	Directed by	Written by
4.71	Schalom	**Shalom**	Sep 19, 2006	Mar 4, 2007	W.Webb	J.C.Kelley

After witnessing a Mossad agent perform an assassination, which was not authorized by Mossad, Ziva is suspected by the FBI to be a double agent. Now a fugitive and on the run, Ziva is forced to ask for help from Gibbs, who is in Mexico after retiring from NCIS. Tony finds his leadership skills being tested to the limit as he leads the team to search for Ziva and to prove her innocence before the FBI can arrest her. *Source:* [1]

```
Tony: "Let's roll. Hey, no, this is my team now, Gibbs. My rules. And DiNozzo's Rule #1 is I don't
sit on the sidelines when my people are in trouble. You got a problem with that? Just remember
whose got a badge and who is a civilian."
Gibbs: "Done?" (He headslaps Tony)
Tony: "Yeah."
Gibbs: "I was going to say get McGee and I'll meet you there."
Tony: "You know I could arrest you for striking a Federal officer."
Gibbs: "I know that."
Tony: "Alright. Just so you know."

Tony: "You listen to Yanni. And you have an unauthorized game on your computer."
McGee: "Okay, it's your game Tony."
Tony: "You shouldn't have beaten my high score."

Tony: "That's not my point! Six months ago you were convinced that I killed a woman and chopped
off her legs!"
Sacks: "Well, I'm still not convinced that you didn't."
Tony: "Exactly."
Sacks: "So, Ziva David is being framed... by who?"
Tony: "Well, that's what I intend to find out."
Sacks: "Hah! Good luck with that."
```

Source: [3]

Episodes Season 4

No.	German Title	US Title	Air Date USA	Air Date GER	Directed by	Written by
4.72	Auf der Flucht	**Escaped**	Sep 26, 2006	Mar 11, 2007	D.Smith	S.D.Binder & C.Silber

A former Petty Officer, convicted of murder, escapes from prison and forces F.B.I. Special Agent Fornell to reopen his case in order to find the real culprit whilst claiming his own innocence. Fornell asks for Gibbs' help, who is reinstated as an NCIS agent by Director Shepard. To his former team's disappointment, Gibbs insists that the reinstatement is only temporary. The team soon finds discrepancies in the Petty Officer's case and that he may have been framed. *Source:* [1]

Ziva: You know, you used to be a nice person, McGee. I think sitting at Tonys desk is affecting your personality.
Tony: For the better! McGee picked up a girl all by himself.
Ziva: Yeah, at a funeral!

Tony: You didnt tell me that.

Source: [3]

No.	German Title	US Title	Air Date USA	Air Date GER	Directed by	Written by
4.73	Schnelle Liebe	**Singled Out**	Oct 3, 2006	Mar 18, 2007	T.O'Hara	D.J.North

Gibbs returns to NCIS and leads his team to investigate the kidnapping of a Navy Lieutenant, who is a computer specialist. They discover that the Lieutenant had used her military knowledge to profile potential husbands and was attending speed dating events. When they suspect that the kidnapper may continue attending the event in order to avoid suspicion, Ziva goes undercover at a speed-dating event to identify him. In addition, Tony is offered a promotion - his own team, as a reward for his performance as team leader while Gibbs was retired - but declines, and remains in Gibbs' team.. *Source:* [1]

Ziva: "I look like a dork."
Tony: "Yeah, that's the idea."

Gibbs: "You're a geek, Ziva David. Not mentally deranged."

Ziva: Ninety-second dates? I thought you were kidding me, Gibbs.
Gibbs: Youll do fine, Ziva. I had marriages shorter than that.
Ziva: Ha! Im beginning to understand why.

Source: [3]

No.	German Title	US Title	Air Date USA	Air Date GER	Directed by	Written by
4.74	Der größte Köder	**Faking It**	Oct 10, 2006	Mar 25, 2007	T.J.Wright	S.Brennan

A Petty Officer is found dead in his car with "NCIS" written in blood on the seat. The investigation becomes complicated when Homeland Security claims that the Russian Spy suspected of killing the officer is working for them. *Source:* [1]

Tony: *(looking at McGee asleep on the table)* "Do you have any superglue Abbs?"
Gibbs: "What did I tell you about that DiNozzo?"
Tony: "That, next time, the skin might not grow back?!"

Abby: So I have a pirstine bullet sample fired from our suspect's Thirty-eight.All I need is the bullet you pulled from him, I'll make a match and we'll send the bad guys wherever the bad guys go when we catch 'em! Where do the bad guys go when we catch

'em?

Source: [3]

Episodes Season 4

No.	German Title	US Title	Air Date USA	Air Date GER	Directed by	Written by
4.75	Die Verlobten	**Dead and Unburied**	Oct 17, 2006	Apr 1, 2007	C.Bucksey	N.Scovell

When a missing Lance Corporal is found dead in a vacant house, the NCIS team discovers that he was buried in the backyard and then exhumed. They learn about his identity and that he was to be deployed to Iraq, but he never showed up for duty. The investigation leads them to a new clue - he had two fiancées. Abby runs the DNA samples from the two women to find out if the DNA is a match to the soil found on the dead man's body. *Source:* [1]

Abby: "You know what they say about guys with big hands and big feet right."
Ducky: "What?"
Abby: "They're clowns."

Ziva: "McGee. Give me your flashlight."
McGee: "Why? You didn't bring your own?"
Ziva: "It's too heavy. It pulls my pants down."

Abby: "Aww, you shaved your moustache! I liked you with a little hair on your face."
Gibbs: "I still have my eyebrows."
Abby: "Good point."

Abby: And his underwear are boxer breifs like you wear Gibbs.
Gibbs: Youre fishing, Abbs.
Abby: So are they regular boxers? Trunks? Nothing?

Source: [3]

No.	German Title	US Title	Air Date USA	Air Date GER	Directed by	Written by
4.76	Halloween	**Witch Hunt**	Oct 31, 2006	Apr 8, 2007	J.Whitmore jr.	S.Kriozere

It's Halloween and the NCIS team is busy investigating a ransom case. A Marine's daughter has been kidnapped after the kidnapper attacked the Marine in his home. The investigation leads them to a fact that the couple has been separated. They decide to focus on the wife's ex-boyfriend, after learning that the woman is the one who destroyed their marriage. Meanwhile, McGee and Tony are stunned by Abby's Halloween costume. *Source:* [1]

Tony: Last time I did Halloween I was an astronaut. The neighborhood I grew up in, well it wasn't really a neighborhood; there were these estates with mansions smack dab in the middle of them. And really long driveways. Made Halloween very tricky. It's a lot of walking. My feet were tired that night. Dogs were barking.
McGee: Yeah, I gotta imagine it really sucks growing up rich like that.
Tony: My costume was fantastic though. Wicked awesome. I was a spaceman. No ventilation though. I was sweating like Roger Federer after a five-set tie breaker. And stinky. Stinky like cheese. But man what a haul. I made off with more candy than I could carry.
McGee: I hope this story's coming to an end soon.
Tony: But when I got home, my old man made me throw it all away. Even the apples.
McGee: He was concerned about your teeth.
Tony: Oh... no. I made my astronaut suit out of one of this $3000 designer ski suits.
McGee: Ouch.

Tony: I don't think I sat down again 'til Christmas.

Source: [3]

Episodes Season 4

No.	German Title	US Title	Air Date USA	Air Date GER	Directed by	Written by
4.77	Der Hintermann	**Sandblast**	Nov 7, 2006	Apr 15, 2007	D.Smith	R.Palm

When a Marine Colonel dies in an explosion at a military golf course, the NCIS team must investigate a suspected terrorist attack with the help from the Army Criminal Investigative Division (CID). The CIA gives them a lead to an abandoned warehouse, but it turns out to be a trap - the warehouse is set to explode. McGee uses his computer skills to break into the secret government files to uncover the terrorist cell while Tony attempts to stop the Marine Colonel's son from joining the Marines to avenge his father's death. *Source:* [1]

```
Lt.Col.Mann: If this is gonna be a pissing match you'd better bring an umbrella.
Tony: Got something boss. What'd I miss?
Ziva: Gibbs just found his fourth ex-wife.

McGee: "That's pretty clever, Boss. How did you figure that out?"
Gibbs: "Too much time around you."
```

Source: [3]

No.	German Title	US Title	Air Date USA	Air Date GER	Directed by	Written by
4.78	Einmal ein Held	**Once a Hero**	Nov 14, 2006	Apr 22, 2007	T.J.Wright	S.Brennan

When an honored Marine veteran is found dead in a hotel, the NCIS team must find out what happened to him. Soon they realize that the Marine didn't commit suicide and that he was homeless. After going through his personal belongings, they find compromising evidence against him, and Gibbs is determined to prove the man's innocence. *Source:* [1]

```
Gibbs: There's more than one reason to kiss a girl.
Tony: There is?
Jeanne: Has anyone ever told you, you're an idiot.

Tony: Yeah, my boss, all the time.
```

Source: [3]

No.	German Title	US Title	Air Date USA	Air Date GER	Directed by	Written by
4.79	Die kleine Schwester	**Twisted Sister**	Nov 21, 2006	Apr 29, 2007	T.J.Wright	S.Brennan

When McGee's younger sister Sarah (played by Troian Bellisario) shows up disoriented and bloodied, believing that she might have killed someone at his door in the middle of the night, McGee takes matters into his hands, beginning his own independent investigation but Sarah claims she's innocent although her memory of the last few hours is blank. While McGee works on figuring out what happened to his sister, the NCIS team is investigating a case of a Navy sailor, who is somehow connected to McGee's sister. Both Tony and Abby are busy with love problems, while McGee turns out to have another secret. *Source:* [1]

No.	German Title	US Title	Air Date USA	Air Date GER	Directed by	Written by
4.80	Die Mumie	**Smoked**	Nov 28, 2006	May 6, 2007	B.Webb	J.C.Kelley

A dead man in a chimney chute on a marine base leads the team to discover a serial killer's burial ground. They believe that the dead man was the serial killer until Abby uncovers something which proves he may actually be a victim. Meanwhile, Tony helps the director with a special project and makes time for his girlfriend as well while Ducky talks to Gibbs about how he felt betrayed when Gibbs left and after a heart-to-heart the two eventually repair their friendship. *Source:* [1]

```
Gibbs Rule #22:  Never, ever interrupt Gibbs in interrogation.
```

Source: [3]

Episodes Season 4

No.	German Title	US Title	Air Date USA	Air Date GER	Directed by	Written by
4.81	Sabotage	**Driven**	Dec 12, 2006	May 13, 2007	D.Smith	N.Scovell & J.C.Kelley

A woman is found dead in a classified robotic vehicle she was working on developing. Although it initially looks like suicide, when Abby puts the vehicle through some tests, it nearly takes her life as well. They discover that someone rigged the vehicle to kill the passenger and make it appear to be suicide. They discover that the woman who was killed was not the intended target. Meanwhile, Tony visits the hospital to see his girlfriend and continues working on special projects for the Director. Ziva notices Tony getting calls from the hospital and begins worrying that he is sick. *Source: [1]*

Tony: I think you should go and check the bedroom. That is... unless you want me to come with you and help...What?
Ziva: Just wondering if offering to take me to a bedroom constitutes sexual harassment?
Tony: Well, if you have to ask then it's not harassment.

Source: [3]

No.	German Title	US Title	Air Date USA	Air Date GER	Directed by	Written by
4.82	Verdacht	**Suspicion**	Jan 16, 2007	May 20, 2007	C.Bucksey	S.Brennan

When a Marine is murdered in a small town hotel room, NCIS is called in to investigate. However, the local Sheriff's department already cleaned up the crime scene and performed an autopsy. They also have a suspect - an Iraqi national who just moved to town a few months earlier. *Source: [1]*

Gibbs: "Give me some news, Abs"
Abby: "I'm not pregnant"
Gibbs: "Too much information"

Tony: Probie, i have a pimple on my left buttox that is a better writer than you.

Source: [3]

No.	German Title	US Title	Air Date USA	Air Date GER	Directed by	Written by
4.83	Giftgas	**Sharif Returns**	Jan 23, 2007	May 27, 2007	T.O'Hara	S.D.Binder

When the NCIS team learns that the missing 10 kilograms of highly toxic chemical weapons are now in the hands of Mamoun Sharif, a wanted terrorist, they will have to find a way to find the man and stop him before it's too late with the aid from Army Lt. Col. Hollis Mann and constant phone calls from Sharif himself. *Source: [1]*

McGee: So this is the guy Ziva was drooling over.
Ziva: I wasn't drooling!
Tony: Please, I saw you undressing him with your bedroom eyes.
Ziva: At least I'm not the one asking him if he waxed his eyebrows!
Tony: It's important to appreciate the competition.

Abby: *(about getting a tattoo)* What'd you think?
Gibbs: I don't think I'm the one to ask about this.
Abby: But Gibbs, you know me better than anyone else and when you're gonna make decision that's gonna effect the rest of your life you need the person around you who knows you the best for guidence. Please?
Gibbs: Where do you want to put the tattoo?
Abby: Okay, you're right. You're not the one to ask.

Source: [3]

Episodes Season 4

No.	German Title	US Title	Air Date USA	Air Date GER	Directed by	Written by
4.84	Der Frosch	**Blowback**	Feb 6, 2007	Jun 3, 2007	T.Wright	C.Silber

After catching an international arms dealer, the NCIS team learns that Navy's highly classified weapons system will be sold to "La Grenouille," an important arms dealer. To stop the transaction from happening, the team sends Ducky undercover. Meanwhile, another government agency appears to be working on the same case, with different plans. *Source:* [1]

Gibbs Rule No.4: If you have a secret, the best thing is to keep it to yourself. The second-best is to tell one other person if you must. There is no third best.

Ziva: *(about Tony's girlfriend)* Will you tell me her name if I find the pirate's copy of ARES?
Tony: Pirated copy.
Ziva: That's what I said.
Tony: No, you said pirate's copy.Pirate is a person, like Captan Jack Sparrow. A pirated copy.......
Ziva: Who is Jack Sparrow?
Tony: Johnny Depp.
Ziva: He's a pirate?
Tony: No, he's an actor.
Ziva: Oh.
Tony: *(meaning their conversation)* How did we get here?
Ziva: I drove.

Ziva: I told you I couldn't program the navigator. I'm a driver!
McGee: Ziva, I've driven with you before. I'd rather be lost than dead.

Source: [3]

No.	German Title	US Title	Air Date USA	Air Date GER	Directed by	Written by
4.85	Das letzte Lebewohl	**Friends & Lovers**	Feb 13, 2007	Sep 16, 2007	D.Smith	J.C.Kelly

A man proposing to his girlfriend finds the body of a sailor. NCIS works with local officers believing that the man died of an unintentional drug overdose. However, Abby discovers a message written in blood on a laminated card found at the crime scene. Meanwhile, Jimmy continues his relationship with Agent Michelle Lee. *Source:* [1]

Palmer: Not to mention a great source of protein.
Ducky: Ah, as I was saying, they should prove helpful in determining the time of death unless, of course, my assistant decides to eat them first.

Tony: I really need to write a book.
Gibbs: You should read one first...

Ziva: This is going to be like looking for a needle in a needlestack.
Tony: Needle in a haystack.
Ziva: I like my description better.

Ducky: However women normally hide poison in food not drinks.
Gibbs: That would explain why my last ex wife spent so much time in the kitchen.

McGee: Well, Gibbs is more interested in this. Find anything yet?
Abby: When, McGee? If you haven't noticed, I'm the only one here......Which may be the reason I started talking to my machines in the first place.
McGee: Well, Abbs, I gotta tell him something.

Abby: Tell him you love him, McGee.It works for me.

Source: [3]

Episodes Season 4

No.	German Title	US Title	Air Date USA	Air Date GER	Directed by	Written by
4.86	Wettlauf mit dem Tod	**Dead Man Walking**	Feb 20, 2007	Sep 23, 2007	C.Bucksey	N.Scovell

A Navy Lieutenant arrives at NCIS with radiation poisoning requesting that the team investigate his murder. The Navy Lieutenant is an inspector for the International Atomic Energy Agency, so the team tries to figure out who would want to make sure he didn't make it to the next inspection. However, only his two closest colleagues knew where the next inspection was to take place. Meanwhile, Ziva sympathizes with the Lieutenant, in whom she sees a reflection of her own most strongly held beliefs and develops feelings for him. It is revealed in the next episode that the Lieutenant had passed away. *Source:* [1]

```
Ziva: This is killing me, I feel like I know him.
Tony: Mossad?
Ziva: Maybe.
Tony: Internet dateing?
Ziva: I will kill you eighteen different ways with this paperclip.

Tony: If clothes make the man, what does that make McGee?
Ziva: Male Nurse?
Tony: No. Aqua Smurf.
```
Source: [3]

No.	German Title	US Title	Air Date USA	Air Date GER	Directed by	Written by
4.87	Skelette	**Skeletons**	Feb 27, 2007	Sep 30, 2007	C.Bucksey	N.Scovell

An explosion at a military cemetery mausoleum turns up a skeleton. As they investigate, Ducky discovers that they have turned up the skeleton of more than one body. The team talks to the families to try to find some link between the victims. Meanwhile, Abby is having personal problems. *Source:* [1]

```
Ziva: Last one to the party.

Tony: It's not really a party till the bomb squad says it is.
```
Source: [3]

No.	German Title	US Title	Air Date USA	Air Date GER	Directed by	Written by
4.88	Der verlorene Sohn	**Iceman**	Mar 30, 2007	Oct 7, 2007	T.Wright	S.Brennan

When the man on Ducky's table turns out to still be alive the unit must track the young Marine's actions prior to his arrival in the morgue. They discover that the marine had been on leave and used his time off for a secret trip to Baghdad. The case takes a turn when Mike Franks - Gibbs' old boss shows up revealing that the young marine is in fact his son. *Source:* [1]

```
Tony: Ever tell your dad what you were up to Probie?
McGee: Everyday!

Tony: ... wrong person to ask.
```
Source: [3]

No.	German Title	US Title	Air Date USA	Air Date GER	Directed by	Written by
4.89	Hinterhalt	**Grace Period**	Apr 3, 2007	Oct 14, 2007	J.Withmore jr.	J.C.Kelly

An NCIS team, led by Paula Cassidy, discovers a tip about terrorist activity but it turns out to be a trap, resulting in the death of two agents and Cassidy, grief-stricken begins blaming herself for what happened. Gibbs and his team are sent to investigate the deaths with Cassidy joining them during the investigation. While Ducky is sure that the man who Cassidy received the tip from was dead at least one day before the explosion, Cassidy insists otherwise. At the end, Paula Cassidy dies in an explosion, much to Tony's sadness. *Source:* [1]

Episodes Season 4

No.	German Title	US Title	Air Date USA	Air Date GER	Directed by	Written by
4.90	Das Buch zum Mord	**Cover Story**	Apr 10, 2007	Oct 21, 2007	D.Smith	D.North

During the murder investigation of a Petty Officer, McGee is unsettled when elements of the crime scene resemble the descriptions in his new novel, which is half-finished. The only person who had access to McGee's book, other than McGee himself, is his publisher. The killer promises two more kills and when the second body is found, McGee is pressured to determine who the killer plans to kill next. *Source:* [1]

Gibbs: Nice of you to join us, DiNozzo.
Tony: I thought I was gaining ground.He has a very unorthadox running style.But it's effective.
Gibbs: Not effective enough.

Abby: I will not reveal my sorcess even if you torture me.
Tony: Ducky?
Abby: Yes!
Source: [3]

No.	German Title	US Title	Air Date USA	Air Date GER	Directed by	Written by
4.91	Zum Greifen nah	**Brothers in Arms**	Apr 24, 2007	Oct 28, 2007	M.Mitchell	S.D.Binder

Director Shepard meets an informant named Troy Webster who has information on international arms dealer La Grenouille but Webster is killed. Shepard later becomes convinced that La Grenouille ordered the kill but the team are all doubting her judgement, believing she might be on a personal revenge trip which is further increased when she manages to lead the team into a trap, leaving them with no clues to La Grenouille's whereabouts after days of investigations. *Source:* [1]

Gibbs: Director of NCIS.
Jenny: Yes?
Gibbs: That's a job I wouldn't want.
Jenny: Don't worry, no one's offering.
Gibbs: You know why?
Jenny: You mean besides your impatience, total lack of respect to authority, and the fact that you still haven't learned how to play nice with others?
Gibbs: Yeah, besides all that.
Source: [3]

No.	German Title	US Title	Air Date USA	Air Date GER	Directed by	Written by
4.92	Der blinde Fotograf	**In The Dark**	May 1, 2007	Nov 4, 2007	T.Wright	S.D.Binder

The assistant of a blind photographer notices a dead Petty Officer in one of the photographs and calls NCIS. Gibbs and his team respond to the case and use the photographer's help to re-construct the crime scene through his heightened senses of hearing and scent to find out who killed the victim. Meanwhile, both Gibbs and Tony are having love troubles. *Source:* [1]

Tony: It's complicated.
Ziva: Complicated. Complicated. Complicated. You know, in America I have noticed they use that word as a code for, "If I explain it, uh, you would not agree with me. Therefore, I will use the word complicated and hopefully you will stop asking."
Tony: Yeah, that's pretty much it in a nutshell. I'm gonna go see what Abby wants.

McGee: Cant imagine what I'd do if I lost my eyesight.
Ziva: Youd adapt.
McGee: What if I didnt?
Ziva: Youd fall into a deep depression and eventually you'd die.
Source: [3]

Episodes Season 4

No.	German Title	US Title	Air Date USA	Air Date GER	Directed by	Written by
4.93	Das trojanische Pferd	**Trojan Horse**	May 8, 2007	Nov 11, 2007	T.O'Hara	D.Bellisario & S.Brennan

A man is found dead in a taxi headed to the NCIS headquarters but his body shows no signs of external injuries. Gibbs decides to lead the investigation into the man's death in preference to performing his duties as the Acting Director of NCIS while Jenny is in Paris attending an Interpol conference. When the team discovers that the people whose names were found on a list belonging to the dead man are all dead, Gibbs suspects that the list is a decoy used to distract them. *Source:* [1]

Gibbs: I had a wife like you, once, Cynthia. I divorced her.
Cynthia: Beat her to it, did you?

Ziva: Our cabbie did not take the most direct route from the Embassy.
Tony: This is America, Ziva, the land of opportunity. No cabbie ever takes the quickest route.

Gibbs: I thought you were supposed to solve these riddles Duck?
Ducky: Abby and I like to share.

Source: [3]

No.	German Title	US Title	Air Date USA	Air Date GER	Directed by	Written by
4.94	Der Todesengel	**Angel of Death**	May 22, 2007	Nov 18, 2007	T.O'Hara	D.Bellisario

Jenny returns from her European trip and discovers that she had an unannounced visitor at her home who she suspects is her supposedly dead father. All NCIS agents are scheduled to take a Homeland Security polygraph test, which Gibbs finds out to have been arranged by the CIA. An unarmed Tony and Jeanne are held hostage in the hospital morgue by a drug dealer, who is desperate to remove his shipment of drugs from the dead body packer. Tony eventually meets the man he's been trying to find all these months - René Benoit, also known as La Grenouille who is revealed to be Jeanne's father. *Source:* [1]

Jenny: In polite society one usually calls before a visit. Bourbon?
Gibbs: I've kicked in too many doors to be polite. Yes.
Jenny: I appreciate the restraint you showed by using the bell. I've been rather fond of that door since I was a child.

Ziva: I have a funny feeling doctor.
Ducky: It's teh tequilla, my dear.You've had three Shooters just in the time I've been here.
Ziva: *(looking at her phone)* Straight to voicemail just like always when he's with her.
Ducky: Tony?
Ziva: What?
Ducky: *(pause)* Nothing.
Ziva: Oh, no, no, no. That was definetly something.
Ducky: Well, why do you moniter Tony?
Ziva: I don't moniter Tony.
Ducky: Yes, you do, my dear. Like a mother with a toddler.
Ziva: That's a good description.
Ducky: Or a woman with a wayward lover.

Ducky: Ziva it's friday night, Tony is with his girlfriend and you are worried about him what does that tell you?
Ziva: He is my partner and my partner said he would be here, and......and I have this not so good feeling.

Source: [3]

Season 5 (Episodes 5.95- 5.113)

The fifth season premiered on September 25, 2007 and marks the end of Donald Bellisario's involvement as show runner. It concludes the La Grenouille storyline which ended with a cliffhanger in season four's finale, "Angel of Death". The fifth season also reveals more background information about Gibbs' past before NCIS. The strike-shortened season ended with its 19th episode on May 20, 2008; the strike-caused gap is between episodes 11 and 12. The season ended with a two-part season finale called "Judgment Day". The season featured the departure of recurring characters Colonel Hollis Mann and Jeanne Benoit, as well as the death of Jenny Shepard, one of the main characters.The Writer Guild strike limited episode production and the DVD set had only five discs instead of six. From this season on, the opening sequence was shorted to an even 30 second duration instead of the normal 37-44 second duration in the previous seasons.

Source: [1]

Original Air Date USA	September 25, 2007 – May 20, 2008 on CBS
Original Air Date German Language	March 2, 2008 – October 19, 2008 on Sat 1

Episodes Season 5

No.	German Title	US Title	Air Date USA	Air Date GER	Directed by	Written by
5.95	Meine Freundin, ihr Vater und ich	**Bury Your Dead**	Sep 25, 2007	Mar 2, 2008	T.Wright	S.Brennan

Directly following the events from the previous episode, "Angel of Death", Tony is still undercover as Anthony DiNardo and meets Jeanne's father, La Grenouille, who is aware of Tony's true identity. The team are also led to the assumption that Tony is dead, as while watching the security cameras, Tony's car explodes and Ducky's analysis indicates the body could be that of Tony. Director Shepard reveals to Agent Gibbs and his team that she had given Tony an undercover mission to build a relationship with Jeanne in hopes of capturing La Grenouille after spending nearly ten years searching for him. La Grenouille approaches Director Shepard for protection after deciding to quit the arms smuggling business against the CIA's wishes. However, Shepard refuses his plea for asylum out of pure spite. The team tries to track down La Grenouille again and find his boat, but not the man himself. They believe he made his escape and leave, until the camera pans to the water to show La Grenouille's floating corpse while also revealing that he has sustained a single gunshot wound to his forehead. *Source: [1]*

Abby: Everybody else gave you up for dead, even Ziva.
Ziva: OK, so I may have acted a little hastily.
Tony: That's my letter opener.
Ziva: Excellent balance and weight. The edge is a little dull, but I've always admired it.
Tony: Where's my American Pie coffee mug?
Abby: Palmer.
Tony: Mighty Mouse stapler?
Abby: Ducky... Hey, Ducky.
(Ducky reaches over Tony's cubicle wall)
Ducky: My dear fellow, I never believed it for a moment. Welcome home.
(Ducky hands Tony the stapler)
Gibbs: It's not every day people think you're dead, DiNozzo.

Source: [3]

Episodes Season 5

No.	German Title	US Title	Air Date USA	Air Date GER	Directed by	Written by
5.96	Familiensache	**Family**	Oct 2, 2007	Mar 16, 2008	M.Mitchell	S.D.Binder

A Petty Officer is thought to have died in a car accident until inconsistencies at the scene indicate that the Petty Officer was murdered and was not the driver of the crashed car. When the car's driver is later found, Ducky conducts the autopsy and discovers that she had been beaten to death and had given birth not long beforehand, leading the team to believe that the killer has taken her child. *Source:* [1]

McGee: Alright I think I know what happened here.
Tony: Twenty bucks says McGee's about to say something nobody can understand again!
McGee: The GPS coordinates came bundled in a proprietary packet.Since it was a beta, I thought......
Gibbs: I'm starting to think you can't help yourself, McGee.

Ziva: It was a simple question, McGee.
McGee: Yeah, one I would expect from Tony, not you.
Ziva: I'm just being curious.
McGee: About when I lost my virginity.
Ziva: No, you misunderstood.I'm not asking when you lost your virginity, but if you lost it.
Source: [3]

No.	German Title	US Title	Air Date USA	Air Date GER	Directed by	Written by
5.97	Dreieck	**Ex-File**	Oct 9, 2007	Mar 16, 2008	D.Smith	A.H.Moreno

Two women find a dead Marine Captain on an Army base, one of whom is his wife, the other is Gibbs' third ex-wife. As Special Agent Gibbs and Lt. Colonel Mann conduct a joint investigation between NCIS and the Army into the murder, a DIA agent is sent to overlook Abby's handling of the Captain's laptop, which contains highly classified information. Gibbs becomes uncomfortable when he is forced into a confrontation amongst his ex-wife, Colonel Mann, and Director Shepard. *Source:* [1]

Abby: These things hold over 145GB of music. That's over 45 000 songs, Gibbs.
Gibbs: I only listen to 5.
Abby: 5000?
Gibbs: No five.

Mann: We have a little issue.
Jenny: We?
Mann: You wanna tell her, Agent Gibbs?
Gibbs: No, not particularly.
Jenny: Is this issue going to involve lawyers?
Mann: It already did. It's his ex-wife. She's a material witness.
Jenny: And which ex would that be?
Gibbs: Stephanie.
Jenny: What number is she again? Second?
Gibbs: Third.
Jenny: Oh, right. You lived in Europe with her for a while. Frankfurt.
Gibbs: Moscow.
Jenny: Two years?
Gibbs: One.
Jenny: Well, it's hard to live in Moscow... with anyone.
Jenny: Do you think he should divorce himself from this case, Col. Mann?
Mann: No, no no...
Jenny: Nor do I, I don't see a problem if you conduct the interview. Do you have a problem with Col. Mann interviewing your ex-wife, Agent Gibbs?
Gibbs: Do I have a choice?
Jenny and Mann (Together): No.
Source: [3]

Episodes Season 5

No.	German Title	US Title	Air Date USA	Air Date GER	Directed by	Written by
5.98	Eine falsche Identität	**Identity Crisis**	Oct 16, 2007	Mar 23, 2008	T.J.Wright	J.Stern

Ducky is angered when one of his research cadavers is revealed to have been a murder victim and was mistakenly tagged as a "John Doe" and donated to science. The deceased man is identified by the team as a career felon, who was working with the FBI to track down a man suspected of supplying people with new identities. NCIS works with the FBI to capture him and find the killer. *Source:* [1]

Tony: Tell me you aren't looking for a man for Ziva.
Ziva: Not for me.
Tony: Something you want to tell me, McGoo?

Tony: Do people really like boats that much?
Gibbs: You work for the Navy, DiNozzo.

Gibbs: Check out the brunette at the table.
Tony: Good find boss! I'll tell you, my radar is totally shot. She's smoking! ..that's not what you meant.. you were suggesting that she seems interested in our investigation. A little too interested and I should question her... not a problem!

Ducky: I hope your opinion of me doesn't waver after I've given this fellow a piece of my mind.
Gibbs: Never!
Ducky: I warn you... this might get ugly!

Source: [3]

No.	German Title	US Title	Air Date USA	Air Date GER	Directed by	Written by
5.99	Der Mann auf dem Dach	**Leap of Faith**	Oct 23, 2007	Mar 30, 2008	D.Smith	G.Schenck & F.Cardea

When a Navy Lieutenant who worked at the Pentagon as an intelligence officer attempts to commit suicide by jumping off a rooftop, NCIS is called in to consult the officer. After Gibbs is able to persuade the officer to step down from the ledge, the officer is shot dead, falling to his death from the rooftop. Each member of Gibbs' team has a different theory on the murder, one of which includes the officer being a mole. *Source:* [1]

Gibbs Rule #15: Always work as a team.

Abby: I can't believe you would say that to me Gibbs? How could you think that I would be leaving? Because I got a little mad? So what?! We're family, that's allowed. I get three or four job offers every year. I have never considered any of them."
Tony: Then why did you have dinner with that headhunter?
Abby: Have you ever had the Beluga Caviar at the Ritz Carlton?
Nikki: Oh God yeah...
Abby: Besides, it was nice to feel wanted.

McGee: Oh that's a long way up.
Tony: It's a long way down.

Tony: Color back, now that you're on terra firma there, Probalicious?
McGee: I would'a done it!
Tony: Only, ah, you didn't.
Ziva: *(talking about Tony)* I think he's more afraid of heights then you are.
Tony: Please, I rock climbed!
Ziva: *(Laughing)* Yeah, twenty feet, with a harness, to impress a girl.
Tony: Well, it worked.

Source: [3]

Episodes Season 5

No.	German Title	US Title	Air Date USA	Air Date GER	Directed by	Written by
5.100	Das Geisterschiff	**Chimera**	Oct 30, 2007	Apr 6, 2008	T.O'Hara	D.E.Fesman

Gibbs' team is sent to investigate a death aboard USNS Chimera, a top-secret naval research ship sailing in the middle of the ocean. After boarding the ship, they find it abandoned except for a dead U.S. Navy scientist, who died from viral hemorrhagic fever. However, they suspect that they are not alone. Their investigation is further complicated by the Navy's reluctance to share information regarding the research which took place on Chimera. However, they quickly discover that the Chimera is not a research ship, but is in fact transporting a salvaged Russian nuclear warhead. A mole in the crew staged a viral outbreak to get the crew to abandon ship in preparation for the Russian strike team. The team sabotages the Chimera and steals the Russian strike team's boat, taking the warhead with them. As the team leaves, Navy jets destroy the Chimera to cover up any evidence of Navy involvement. *Source:* [1]

Ziva: Don't you have any paperwork to do, Dinozzo?
Tony: What do you think I'm doing? I take the paper and make it work.

Ducky: You were right, Ziva. There is someone on board.
Ziva: Not him. There's someone alive. I can feel it.
Tony: A lion-headed dragon goat?
Ziva: Maybe.

McGee: Every room is empty.
Ziva: It's like the entire crew disappeared.
Tony: Welcome aboard the U.S. N.S. Houdini.
McGee: Could be a rat.
Ziva: Would have to be an awfully big one.
Tony: Or a ghost.
Gibbs: Are you done?
Tony: Done... searching the ship? We could always search it again.

Tony: Abby, where's the gas chromata-thinga?
Abby: It's the box looking thing, with the circular door-like thing on the front.

Ziva: How did they know that we were off the ship?
Gibbs: I don't think they did.

Tony: Oh, I get it, boss.It's a black ship.
Ziva: Black sheep.
Tony: No.They don't exist.
Ziva: Oh, I've seen black sheep.
Tony: No.I said black ship not sheep.Clearly the U.S. Navy is still intent on pulling the wool over the eyes of the American people.

Tony: You ever see Run Silent, Run Deep?
Gibbs: The run silent part sounds good.

McGee: I'm dealing with my boat-phobia, Tony's dealing with his rat-phobia, and Ziva's dealing with her ghost-phobia.
Abby: So, what's Gibbs dealing with?
Gibbs: Them.

Ducky: Where's my blood analysis, DiNozzo?
Tony: I'm working on it, Ducky.It may be the last thing I do.
Ducky: Let's hope not.

Source: [3]

Episodes Season 5

No.	German Title	US Title	Air Date USA	Air Date GER	Directed by	Written by
5.101	Alte Wunden	**Requiem**	Nov 6, 2007	Apr 13, 2008	T.Wharmby	S.Brennan

The episode begins with Tony retrieving Gibbs from the water and trying to revive him. It is revealed that Maddie, a childhood friend of Gibbs' deceased daughter Kelly, comes to him for help after being stalked which leads to the events of Gibbs' car driving into water. While unconscious Gibbs hallucinates that he is visited by his dead wife and daughter and is reassured that everything is fine. *Source:* [1]

Tony: This is ground control to Major McThom. This is ground control to Major Thom. Is anybody out there?
McGee: What?
Tony: Oh. I was just checking. You've been staring into space for the last hour. Even on the McGeekle scale that is cause for concern.

Source: [3]

No.	German Title	US Title	Air Date USA	Air Date GER	Directed by	Written by
5.102	Mord im Taxi	**Designated Target**	Nov 13, 2007	Apr 20, 2008	C.Bucksey	R.Steiner

Gibbs and his team investigate the assassination of a Navy Admiral and meet a woman whose search for her husband, a political refugee from Africa, is related to the case. It turns out that a death squad by an African dictatorship who fear that the missing husband (who they only have a vague description of) will return to lead the opposition in the country. They discover the identity of the assassin and arrest him before he can finish the job. *Source:* [1]

Ziva: *(on the phone)* No, no, no, it's not you, it's just.....Well, you know, these things run their course, and well, ah, you, you must accpet.....
Tony: Personal call, David?
Ziva: *(covering the phone)* Yes! Go away!
Tony: Somebody being dumped?
Ziva: Oh, how do you tell someone you no longer wish to see them?
Tony: Easy. *(grabs the phone)* Listen dirt bag, this is Ziva's husband.I have your number now, I can find your address.If you ever try to contact her again I will reach down your throat, grab your intestines, rip them out and drive over your head! Lose this number or lose your life! *(hangs up, gives it to Ziva)* Your welcome.
Ziva: That was Aunt Neddi, from Tel Aviv. She was trying to stop seeing her eighty-six year old, mah jong partner.
Tony: Why didn't you stop me?
Ziva: Too stunned.
Tony: Where do I send flowers?
Ziva: If you communicate with her again, I will kill you!

Source: [3]

No.	German Title	US Title	Air Date USA	Air Date GER	Directed by	Written by
5.103	Gesucht und gefunden	**Lost & Found**	Nov 20, 2007	Apr 27 2008	M.Mitchell	D.North

While a group of boy scouts are on a visit to NCIS, Abby discovers that one of the boys was reported to have been abducted in 1998, leading the team to search for his father who is running from a murder he was accused of committing in 1998. The team launches a manhunt for the father, but are hindered by the son who warns his father in advance. *Source:* [1]

Playing Pictionary on a whiteboard, Carson draws a mansion
Carson: A mansion.
Palmer draws a girl
Carson: OK... I got it... I got it... The Playboy Mansion!
Palmer: A... A... Playboy...it's a school, Carson...are you sure you don't know Tony DiNozzo?

Source: [3]

Episodes Season 5

No.	German Title	US Title	Air Date USA	Air Date GER	Directed by	Written by
5.104	Wie ein wilder Stier	**Corporal Punishment**	Nov 27, 2007	May 4, 2008	A.Brown	J.Stern

The NCIS team pays a heavy price when they try to track down a Marine who believes he is still in Iraq. After a violent confrontation in which DiNozzo, McGee and Ziva are injured, the team realizes the Marine is the subject of a secret experiment. Things are further complicated when a Senator's aide begins interfering with the investigation, since the Marine was due to be awarded a medal by the Senator and such an incident would be bad for his public image. The team suspects that the Marine was an unknowing subject of a secret super soldier experiment, until they discover that he had been secretly taking steroids in order to qualify for the Marines. Due to drug use, the Marine is bound to be discharged and his medal withheld. Gibbs, sympathetic for the young Marine, gives him one of his own unused medals instead. *Source:* [1]

No.	German Title	US Title	Air Date USA	Air Date GER	Directed by	Written by
5.105	Beweise	**Tribes**	Jan 15, 2008	May 11, 2008	C.Bucksey	R.Steiner

The NCIS team investigates when a Muslim Marine is found dead near a mosque that is suspected by the FBI of terrorist recruitment. Their search is delayed when Ducky refuses to autopsy the Marine in deference to the Marine's family's religious beliefs. *Source:* [1]

Tony: Am I the only normal one here?
Gibbs: No!
Tony: "Morning Boss!

Tony: Nobody likes a know-it-all.
McGee: Gibbs does.

Source: [3]

No.	German Title	US Title	Air Date USA	Air Date GER	Directed by	Written by
5.106	Auf der Lauer	**Stakeout**	Apr 8, 2008	Aug 31, 2008	T.Wharmby	F.Cardea & G.Schenck

When a high-tech naval radar goes missing but is found again, the team stakes an abandoned warehouse to catch the thief - using the radar as bait. But the plan goes wrong and the radar is stolen - and a man is murdered nearby. In the end, the team manages to connect both cases - and reveal the truth behind the reason of the theft. The true culprit was the designer of the radar, because he knew that the radar was not complete and if the Navy found out, he would lose his contract. *Source:* [1]

No.	German Title	US Title	Air Date USA	Air Date GER	Directed by	Written by
5.107	Hundeleben	**Dog Tags**	Apr 15, 2008	Sep 7, 2008	O.Scott	D.E.Fesman, A.H.Moreno

When the NCIS team investigates a fatal dog mauling of a suspected drug smuggler within the K-9, Abby risks her career in hopes of proving the victim dog's innocence to save him from being put down. The team struggles with the case, with the director threatening to end their case, when they find a new victim and finally manage to track down the drug trafficker. The trafficker was one of the K-9 trainers, who secretly replaced her drug sniffing dog with an attack dog in order to smuggle drugs. Meanwhile, Abby befriends the "killer" dog, names him "Jethro", and works to keep him from being put down as she attempts to prove the dog is not guilty. However, her landlord doesn't allow pets, so she instead forces McGee to adopt him which he grudgingly agrees to do despite the fact that the dog attacked him at the beginning of the episode. *Source:* [1]

Episodes Season 5

No.	German Title	US Title	Air Date USA	Air Date GER	Directed by	Written by
5.108	Lang lebe die Königin	**Internal Affairs**	Apr 22, 2008	Sep 14, 2008	T.Wharmby	J.Stern & R.Steiner

The dead body of La Grenouille finally surfaces and the Washington office of NCIS is investigated by the FBI, with Jenny as the prime suspect for his murder. The team assembles discreetly at Gibbs' house and investigate for themselves and confirm that he was indeed murdered. After evidence comes to light exonerating Jenny, Jeanne reappears and blames Tony for the murder, but Trent Kort (who has since, with the blessing of the CIA, taken over La Grenouille's business) arrives and claims responsibility. At the conclusion of the episode, Gibbs tells Jenny that the story she told wasn't accurate, and it is inferred that Jenny killed La Grenouille, although Gibbs does not take any action, simply stating, "Long live the queen." *Source: [1]*

McGee: Backing up three years of files: the bulk of our lives are in these cables right now flying back and forth in zeros and ones.
Tony: You do understand that I'm the ones and you're the zeros?

Tony: Gibbs gave you a mission. Everyone's counting on you. Just do what you do best.
Abby: Dance?!
Tony: Talk.

Gibbs: Questions?
McGee: Yeah, how do you get the boat out?
Gibbs: Just break the bottle.

Source: [3]

No.	German Title	US Title	Air Date USA	Air Date GER	Directed by	Written by
5.109	Grüne Zone	**In the Zone**	Apr 29, 2008	Sep 21, 2008	T.O'Hara	L.Barstyn

When a Marine Captain is killed during a mortar attack, it turns out that he was shot. Tony and Intel Analyst Nikki Jardine are sent to Baghdad to investigate, while the rest of the team assists by investigating stateside. The team uncovers that the man he contracted to provide soil testing hired a civilian contractor in Iraq to murder him when the captain discovers the soil sample was faked. While in Baghdad, Nikki tries to make up for a Marine mistake that led to the death of the man who helped her brother when he was wounded. *Source: [1]*

Ziva: *(leans in to see what he's looking at on screen and gasps)* That is quite a kiss, McGee!
McGee: *(grins)* Not bad for a wallpaper, huh?
Ziva: *(chuckles)* Well, you seem to be enjoying yourself. *(muses)* I have never seen a tongue quite so... long.
Tony: *(walks in, looking at them curiously)* McGee has a long tongue?
Ziva: No, but the cutie-pie he's kissing does.
Tony: McGee's kissing a girl?
McGee: You can't see it, Tony.
Tony: Why not?
Ziva: This is McGee's private photograph. And if he does not want you to see it here, then you have to respect his wishes... Or.... *(hits a key to bring up a very sweet picture of McGee kneeling next to the dog Jethro, who is licking him, on the squadroom plasma screen)* ...see it elsewhere.
McGee: Hey!
Tony: *(laughs)* Oh, McRomeo... You should save that stuff for the bedroom.
McGee: You're just jealous.
Tony: Jealous? I don't think so. What you're doing there could be illegal in some states.

Source: [3]

Episodes Season 5

No.	German Title	US Title	Air Date USA	Air Date GER	Directed by	Written by
5.110	Mann ohne Gesicht	**Recoil**	May 6, 2008	Sep 28, 2008	J.Whitmore Jr.	Schenck, Cardea & Fesman

Ziva is working undercover to find a murderer who killed five women and cut off their fingers after they died. She leaves with the killer, when Tony finds the fifth victim and the killer, having found out about Ziva, directs her to an abandoned warehouse. Before he can kill her, she manages to get into a fight with him and then shoot him with his own gun. The team is happy with the killer dead but some things are still unclear. A partial fingerprint from his weapon finally leads to a Marine who killed his wife copying the killer. Meanwhile Ziva has an affair with one of the men suspected to be the accomplice of the killer. *Source:* [1]

Gibbs: Always suspect the spouse!
Ducky: Speaking from experience, Jethro?
Abby: That's why I'm never getting married.

Ziva: Uno mas, Si'l vous plait.
Michael: You're mixing your languages.
Ziva: And my liquors.

Source: [3]

No.	German Title	US Title	Air Date USA	Air Date GER	Directed by	Written by
5.111	Falsche Baustelle	**About Face**	May 13, 2008	Oct 5, 2008	D.Smith	Moreno, Stern & Steiner

When investigating the death of a man at a building site, Jimmy Palmer follows a suspicious man who is snooping around, only for the man to shoot at him. Left shellshocked, Jimmy struggles to remember the man's face and thus identify him. In the end, the team finds him but the shooter tries to flee but Jimmy manages to stop him in his car. *Source:* [1]

Abby: One time I got my lip stuck in a vacuum cleaner display at the department store. I lost, like, a quart of saliva before my cousin pulled the plug. I still have nightmares about it. Can't be alone with a HEPA filter.
Palmer: How old were you?
Abby: 22. It was like Fat Tuesday or Arbor Day...

Palmer: Did we catch him? Did we learn anything about this guy?
McGee: No ... but we certainly learned something about you...
Palmer: Whatever it is ... it's not what you think!
McGee: If the shoe fits...
Palmer: Wait! Where are you going?
McGee: These boots were made for walking.

Source: [3]

No.	German Title	US Title	Air Date USA	Air Date GER	Directed by	Written by
5.112	Der Oshimaida-Code	**Judgment Day (1)**	May 20, 2008	Oct 12, 2008	T.J.Wright	Binder, North & Waild

Two boys discover a dead man, which is later identified as former NCIS Special Agent William Decker. Director Shepard attends his funeral in LA, with Tony and Ziva tagging along as protection. Agent Decker's death was ruled a heart attack, but an encounter at the funeral leads Jenny to suspect it was murder. Jenny sends Tony and Ziva away. The Director secretly brings in Mike Franks to help her investigate, believing the murder is related to a covert mission in Paris 9 years ago, involving herself, Decker, and Gibbs. While searching an abandoned diner, four hitmen track Shepard and Franks down and a shootout ensues inside. Jenny and Franks manage to kill all of the men, but Jenny dies from injuries she receives during the gunfight and her body is found by Tony and Ziva. *Source:* [1]

Tony: She died alone.
Ziva: We are all alone.

Source: [3]

Episodes Season 5

No.	German Title	US Title	Air Date USA	Air Date GER	Directed by	Written by
5.113	Schlimme Tage	**Judgment Day (2)**	May 20 2008	Oct 19, 2008	T.J.Wright	Binder, North & Waild

In the aftermath of Jenny's death, Assistant Director Vance searches for Franks, who escaped the diner after killing the fourth gunman. Meanwhile, Tony and Ziva try to locate the one responsible, while dealing with the fallout of failing in their assignment to protect the Director. The trail points to a former hitman called Natasha, who Jenny failed to assassinate in Paris nine years previously while on an assignment that she and Gibbs were working on together. Since Gibbs killed Natasha's lover, Natasha has returned to the U.S seeking revenge. Natasha, who never saw it coming, is killed by Franks, after Gibbs set a trap for her at Jenny's house. Gibbs burns down the house to cover up Jenny's death, making the public believe she died of smoke inhalation. In the fallout of Jenny's funeral, newly appointed Director Vance shreds a page from his personnel file in the Director's office and terminates Ziva's liaison status (sending her back to Israel), reassigns McGee to the cyber crime division, and sends Tony to the USS Ronald Reagan. Vance then gives Gibbs personnel files for his new team members. *Source: [1]*

Tony: Status, McGee.
McGee: Gibbs out there. Vance out there. Natasha out there. Us here.
Tony: What are we doing?
Ziva: Waiting for the fireworks.

Ducky: Am I interrupting something?
McGee: Just Abby's nervous breakdown.

Source: [3]

Season 6 (Episodes 6.114- 6.138)

The sixth season of NCIS started on September 23, 2008. The new NCIS Director Leon Vance (played by Rocky Carroll) became a regular cast character and Agent Gibbs' new team members were introduced: NCIS Agents Michelle Lee from Legal, Daniel Keating from Cybercrime, and Special Agent Brent Langer from the FBI. After the end of the second episode, McGee, Ziva and Tony had returned to the team, while Lee and Keating were transferred back to Legal and Cybercrime respectively. Langer was killed in the first episode of the season.

Source: [1]

Original Air Date USA	September 23, 2008 – May 19, 2009 on CBS
Original Air Date German Language	March 1, 2009 – November 15, 2009 on Sat1

Episodes Season 6

No.	German Title	US Title	Air Date USA	Air Date GER	Directed by	Written by
6.114	Aus den Augen ...	**Last Man Standing**	Sep 23, 2008	Mar 1, 2009	T.Wharmby	S.Brennan

Gibbs is given the task of finding a mole inside his newly formed team. With the help of Agent McGee, Gibbs is able to trace phone calls between Lee and a dead Petty Officer the team had discovered earlier. After verifying Agent Lee's logs of the calls she is cleared. Daniel Keating is focused on next and he is interrogated. During Keating's interrogation, shots are fired, and Lee is found to have shot Agent Langer, who Gibbs and Vance agree to have been the mole. At the end of the episode, McGee and Ziva rejoin Gibbs in the squad room. Agent Lee is in the elevator, leaving, when she receives a text message saying, "Do they suspect?", to which she replies "NO", revealing to the audience that she is in fact the real NCIS mole. *Source:* [1]

Gibbs: Got work to do.
Tony: I'm on it boss. What am I on, McGee?

McGee: What do you see?

Tony: A short life. Yours, if I get caught.

Source: [3]

No.	German Title	US Title	Air Date USA	Air Date GER	Directed by	Written by
6.115	Agent zur See	**Agent Afloat**	Sep 30, 2008	Mar 8, 2009	T.Wright	D.Fesman & D.J.North

Now stationed on the aircraft carrier USS Seahawk(fictional), DiNozzo finds that a Navy Lieutenant's apparent suicide may be connected to a larger, deadly scheme. The deceased's wife is discovered in D.C to be the victim of a fatal beating, before the Lieutenant boarded. Yet it turns out that the Lieutenant was murdered in Cartagena, Colombia within 24 hours of his wife's death, and several days before he was scheduled to board his ship. It seems that someone else took his place, and may have the intention, it is initially believed, of exposing the ship's crew to anthrax. Gibbs and Officer Ziva David take off for Cartagena to help Tony with the investigation, and in the end DiNozzo is allowed to return to Washington D.C. despite Director Vance's apparent wishes to the contrary. *Source:* [1]

Ziva: It's freezing in here.
McGee: After four months in the sub-basement, this is cozy. It's like march of the Penguins down there.

Tony: Let me guess. You guys caught a bad case of DiNozzo-itis and had Vance send you down south.
Ziva: DiNozzo-itis, sounds venereal.

Tony: Okay, don't admit it. I know you missed me. I missed you Boss.

Source: [3]

No.	German Title	US Title	Air Date USA	Air Date GER	Directed by	Written by
6.116	Ein ehrenwerter Mann	**Capitol Offense**	Oct 7, 2008	Mar 15, 2009	D.Smith	G.Schenck & F.Cardea

The NCIS team is investigating a murder, about which Gibbs is acting strange. It turns out that the murdered Lieutenant Commander was having an affair with Senator Patrick Kiley, a former Marine officer who served with Gibbs. Sen. Kiley tells Gibbs to suspect a lobbyist of the oil companies for the murder, but a remark from the Senator's wife leads Gibbs to deduce that they are the murderers, and they are both subsequently arrested. Meanwhile Abby is making an investigation of her own, trying to find out who stole her cupcake, a gift from Ziva, for her hospitality after the former's house is fumigated with McGee eventually being revealed as the cupcake thief. *Source:* [1]

Episodes Season 6

No.	German Title	US Title	Air Date USA	Air Date GER	Directed by	Written by
6.117	Vater und Sohn	**Heartland**	Oct 14, 2008	Mar 22, 2009	T.Wharmby	J.Stern

A pair of Marines are ambushed outside a nightclub, leaving one dead and the other in critical condition. The NCIS team's investigation leads them to Stillwater, PA, the hometown of one of the Marines—and of Leroy Jethro Gibbs. The search leads them to a mining director and his family; his daughter is the ex-girlfriend of the wounded Marine. When the team finds out that the wounded Marine is actually the son of the director, investigation turns to his son-in-law who is discovered to have ordered the attack on the Marines. While in his hometown, the team is introduced to Gibbs' father (Ralph Waite), explores his past and the origins of his relationship with Shannon (his first wife).
Source: [1]

Tony: It might give us more than that. Stillwater High School.
McGee: That's supposed to mean something to us?
Tony: Stillwater High School. In all the time you two spend staring at computer screens you never once peeked in the man's file? Come on!
Abby: (giving Tony weird look) Who's file?
Tony: Stillwater is a small town in Pennsylvania. Coal country. Primarily known for the mine, but only slightly less well known as the birthplace of one Leroy Jethro Gibbs. This guy is from Gibbs home town.

McGee: I'm impressed with your Internet savvy Tony. How'd you find that?
Tony: I used Google.
McGee: Not so impressed. Gibbs probably could have done that.

McGee: Printed out directions, Boss.
Gibbs: Yeah? I know how to get there, McGee.
McGee: So...when was the last time that you went home?
Gibbs: I make it a point to go home every night.
McGee: I mean, when was the last time you went to Stillwater?
Gibbs: I just joined to Corps...Summer...76.
Ziva: What was it like when you left?
Gibbs: Ohhh...a whole lot of fanfare....fireworks....parades...might have been the Bicentennial.

Tony: So many questions. My mind is spinning with questions, I mean have you ever thought about it? He actually came somewhere, he didn't just appear you know? He didn't just start Gibbs, he was a boy and then he grew...
Ziva: I thought he was moulded from clay. Had life breathed into him by a group of mystics.
McGee: That's funny I thought he fell to earth in a capsule after his home planet exploded.
Ziva: No, he burst forth full-grown from the mind of Zeus.
McGee: Nice.
Tony: He's the avatar of Vishnu. He was sent to be the left hand of Yahweh. He was grown in a cabbage patch. I'm trying to pose a serious metaphysical question here. You wan't to be clever? I can be clever.
Gibbs: (walks in) Just a matter of time, DiNozzo.

Tony: Jack, I've gotta know some things. I've got a lot of questions.
Gibbs: You can have two DiNozzo.
Tony: Where do I start?
Gibbs: You've got one left.
Tony: Well that doesn't count...okay. The rules? Did he learn him from you? Did you teach him the rules?
Jackson: Sorry son, I didn't teach him much of anything.

Source: [3]

Episodes Season 6

No.	German Title	US Title	Air Date USA	Air Date GER	Directed by	Written by
6.118	Der falsche Zeuge	**Nine Lives**	Oct 21, 2008	Mar 29, 2009	D.Smith	Burstyn, Fesman & North

Gibbs and Fornell reluctantly join forces in a murder investigation. The FBI is prosecuting a Mafia Boss. One key witness is a Marine, a man suspected to have been involved in another murder. Evidence from moldy rope used in the two murders links the crimes to the Mafia Boss. The Marine escapes from FBI protection to seek revenge, finds the Mafia Boss and shoots and kills him as Gibbs and Fornell try to stop him. Meanwhile Ziva plans for a vacation in Tel Aviv and Tony snoops around and finds a picture of a shirtless man on Ziva's desk (Ziva's partner with Mossad, although Tony does not know this), piquing his interest. *Source:* [1]

Ziva: I am normal people!
Tony: You're normal people like the people from "Ordinary People" are normal people.
Tony: Why would one friend withhold information from another?
Ziva: Maybe that friend felt it was the best thing for everyone.
Tony: Best for everyone or best for herself? *(Ziva looks at him)*
McGee: Her?
Tony: Or him

Tony: I don't speak Hebrew, but I'm pretty sure you just swore. What happened? Your Men of Mossad calendar get lost in the mail?...Women of Mossad calendar get lost in the mail?

Tony: Gibbs versus Fornell. It's like Frazier-Ali or Rocky versus...everyone

Tony: What are you McDoing, McGee?
McGee: Working on Kale's phone records.
Tony: Thought you already McDid that.

Tony: See that prefix right in front of your face? That is Boynton Beach,Florida, my friend.You know what they got there? Sun, sand, old people.

Tony: I like to get to the bottom of things.It's my specialty.

McGee: You lose something there, Tony?
Tony: Just my ability to snoop around Ziva's desk without anyone noticing anything.

McGee: Think Fornell would lie to Gibbs?
Ziva: If he felt he must.
Tony: Says the woman who's being evasive to her friends about her vacation to Israel.
Ziva: I am intrigued be how intrigued you are by this Tony.
Tony: And I am curious that you are curious that I am intrigued. What's his name?
Ziva: I do not believe I said I was actually seeing anyone. Although it would be very difficult to go to Israel and not see anyone at all. It is quite populated you know.
Tony: Ah, that's cute. I don't see why you're having trouble admitting this. You know, you were in Israel for four months, plenty of time to hook up with someone.
McGee: That amount of time, Tony would've hooked up with several someones.
Tony: Hey.
Ziva: What is it you really want to know Tony?
Tony: Depends, Ziva.
Ziva: On?
Tony: On what it is you don't want me know.

Source: [3]

Episodes Season 6

No.	German Title	US Title	Air Date USA	Air Date GER	Directed by	Written by
6.119	Der Traum vom Ruhm	**Murder 2.0**	Oct 28, 2008	Apr 5, 2009	A.Brown	S.D.Binder

On the week of Halloween NCIS is targeted to investigate a series of murders by a serial killer who posts videos of the crimes on the internet. The first two victims have scrolls with links to websites of videos of their murders along with cryptic pictures spliced in. After a third video is posted, a live stream from inside NCIS, a suspect is brought in but dies in Interrogation. Video of the death ends up on the web linking the crimes to a female singer. NCIS storms a garage but Gibbs realizes that it was a setup for them to kill the singer and a man who she appears to have captive at gunpoint is actually the real killer. Gibbs is given a Civil Service Award but is a no-show and Tony stands in to accept the award on his behalf. *Source:* [1]

Tony: Run for your life Probie. Run.
McGee: What are you doing?
Tony: Just trying to save your life.
McGee: What did you do?
Tony: Why is it always me? Well that's a good point, but in this case.
Ziva: McGee!
Tony: Too late.
McGee: Why is she sitting at my…
Tony: You're on your own Probie.
Ziva: McGee, get in here.
Tony: Plea temporary insanity. It's your best bet.
Ziva: What did I tell you McGee?
McGee: Uh…about what?
(Ziva gets up and drags him over to his computer screen where there are the pictures of her in a bathing suit, from Judgment Day)
McGee: Uh…
Ziva: I told you to destroy those. Twice!
McGee: I did. No I did. I...I…um…Tony! Tony must have.
Ziva: You did not erase those photos did you? Admit it and I will spare you one of your eyes.
McGee: I did not erase those photos.
Ziva: Give me your hand.
Gibbs: Better than losing your eye McGee.

Source: [3]

No.	German Title	US Title	Air Date USA	Air Date GER	Directed by	Written by
6.120	Kollateralschaden	**Collateral Damage**	Nov 11, 2008	12. Apr 12, 2009	T.O'Hara	A.H.Moreno

Gibbs and team are assigned a Probie to help investigate a bank robbery at Quantico. The security guard is shot and killed in the heist but only $27,000 was stolen and all of it was burned in the getaway vehicle. The Probie suggests looking into other similar cases and with DiNozzo's help finds a connection. It leads to the guard's son, a former convict, and his cell mate. Gibbs believe all parties will be at the guard's funeral, and with the Probie's help the team captures them both. Gibbs starts to believe that Agent Langer wasn't the mole in his unit and places Langer's old FBI ID at a bar wall dedicated to fallen officers and agents. *Source:* [1]

Gibbs Rule #13: Never, ever involve lawyers.

Ziva: You are fortunate recruits aren't allowed to carry guns.
Tony: I don't know if you noticed Ziva but she and they don't exactly want to shoot me.
Ziva: Give them time.

Source: [3]

Episodes Season 6

No.	German Title	US Title	Air Date USA	Air Date GER	Directed by	Written by
6.121	Verraten	**Cloak**	Nov 18, 2008	Apr 19, 2009	J.Withmore Jr.	J.Stern

Gibbs sends DiNozzo and Ziva to try to break into a top secret military facility, telling them that it is a test of the facility's defenses. After being caught halfway through the act, it is revealed that the facility is in fact all a hoax, and that halfway through their attempt to break in, the mole set off the fire alarm and managed to gain access to the main computer, which had its keyboard laced with a radioactive substance. After returning from the operation, the director explains to the team that one of them is the mole, and explains about the radioactive trace. He scans the hands of Tony, Ziva, Gibbs, and Ducky, and then goes to scan the hands of Abby. When he does the counter ticks, and Abby is placed into custody. Subsequently, Abby is revealed (though not to Lee) to have been in on the plan to catch the mole from the beginning. The team is monitoring Agent Lee to see if she contacts anyone, believing that the team no longer suspects her. After Lee makes a mark on a newspaper dispenser, she is brought into custody. Lee reveals that she was forced to trade secrets, because her daughter had been kidnapped. They let her go, and the episode ends with Gibbs concealed in the back of Lee's car saying "Looks like we're working together." *Source: 1*

Gibbs: Just killing time.
Ducky: Would you like me to perform an autopsy on your watch?

Source: 3

No.	German Title	US Title	Air Date USA	Air Date GER	Directed by	Written by
6.122	Domino	**Dagger**	Nov 25, 2008	Apr 26, 2009	D.Smith	R.Steiner & C.J.Waild

Agent Lee becomes a reluctant participant in helping the NCIS team stop a top secret defense plan from being stolen. Lee is used as bait to capture her contact, Ted Bankston, who also tells of having a family member held captive. Bankston turns out to be the mastermind in the caper and takes Lee hostage, as Gibbs corners them on a bus. Gibbs receives minor wounds in the ensuing exchange. Lee gives a signal to shoot and is shot and killed along with Bankston. Gibbs takes Lee's badge and gives it to her step sister who was found alive, as the team sorts out Lee's ultimate role in the plot. *Source: 1*

Tony: Maybe that's the plan.
Ziva: What plan?
Tony: Exactly.

Tony: Don't worry, McScout, we got our Mossad hunting dog. Bark once for yes.

Source: 3

No.	German Title	US Title	Air Date USA	Air Date GER	Directed by	Written by
6.123	Fight Club	**Road Kill**	Dec 2, 2008	May 3, 2009	T.J.Wright	S.Kriozere

The team investigates the death of a petty officer, who was killed in a car accident, but the agents suspect foul play. The petty officer's death was thought to be connected to a fight club. He was killed instead by a man who was blackmailed by a criminal using a female online profile to lure married men. When the man is found dead at the petty officer's home a fight club partner is the prime suspect, but it turns out that the next-door neighbor was behind the scheme and married man's murder. Tony engages in an on-line air guitar contest that Ziva finds childish, but she takes to heart Tony's words of having choices and the episode ends with Ziva playing air guitar. *Source: 1*

Tony: Sorry Ziva, we don't talk about Fight Club.

Tony: I smell road rage.
Ziva: And I smell Big Wong.

Source: 3

Episodes Season 6

No.	German Title	US Title	Air Date USA	Air Date GER	Directed by	Written by
6.124	Stille Nacht	**Silent Night**	Dec 16, 2008	May 10, 2009	A.Brown	S.D.Binder

The fingerprints of a presumed dead petty officer, Ned Quinn, turn up at the scene of a double homicide. Claiming innocence, Quinn explains he was in the garage working for the victims when they were murdered. While fighting with metro police who want Quinn prosecuted immediately, the team discovers evidence linking a security guard to an emptied safe at the crime scene. Having been exposed, the guard shoots McGee with a taser and unsuccessfully tries to escape. Quinn, explaining that he went "undercover" after his apartment burnt down believing his wife and daughter would be better off with the service benefits from his presumed death, is convinced by Gibbs to rejoin his family for Christmas. *Source:* [1]

No.	German Title	US Title	Air Date USA	Air Date GER	Directed by	Written by
6.125	Hinter Gittern	**Caged**	Jan 6, 2009	May 17, 2009	L.Libman	A.H.Moreno

While investigating the murder of a dead marine whose skeleton was found, McGee heads to a women's prison, hoping to retrieve a written confession from her, but all hell breaks loose when the inmates riot and take over the prison. A guard is killed during the riot and the inmates want only the murderer, not all of them to be brought to justice, holding McGee and two guards as hostages. The warden issues a deadline of before sundown during which he'll retake the prison by any means possible, forcing Gibbs and his team to race against the clock to not uncover the true identity of the murderer but to also save McGee's life. *Source:* [1]

```
Tony: Ziva, some men can hit a baseball at 400 feet, other build rocket ships that sail to the
stars; I can spot a woman's smile at 20 yards.
Ziva: Her name is Hannah and she's asked me out to lunch twice.
Tony: You?!
Ziva: Did your rocket ship just take a nosedive?
Tony: No it just landed on a different planet.

Ziva: Get anything?
Tony: Yeah. An offer. Maybe his tech advisor on his next film. It's about a psycho sex-crazed cop.
McGee: Life and Times of Special Agent Anthony DiNozzo.
```
Source: [3]

No.	German Title	US Title	Air Date USA	Air Date GER	Directed by	Written by
6.126	Schatten der Vergangenheit	**Broken Bird**	Jan 13, 2009	May 24, 2009	J.Withmore Jr.	J.Stern

When investigating the death of a sailor, a female bystander attacks Ducky and he is stabbed in the hand with the same murder weapon used to committ the first crime. Gibbs and the team delve into his past to find clues and in the process, begin uncovering some disturbing secrets about his time as a doctor while serving in Afghanistan while dealing with the revelation that the woman who attacked Ducky in the beginning claims that he killed her brother. *Source:* [1]

```
Abby: Wanna talk knives?
Ziva: Always.

Gibbs: I need a favor.
Kort: Gibbs, I don't like you.
Gibbs: That's okay, I don't like you either.
```
Source: [3]

Episodes Season 6

No.	German Title	US Title	Air Date USA	Air Date GER	Directed by	Written by
6.127	Der verschwundene Ring	**Love & War**	Jan 27, 2009	May 31, 2009	T.O'Hara	D.North & S.D.Binder

The team investigates the murder of a Navy captain and uncovers possible treasonous acts he committed that may have led to his death. Meanwhile, McGee meets a new love interest named Claire online but unbeknown to him, it's actually DiNozzo. *Source:* 1

```
Gibbs: What do you got Abs?
Abby: 1989's Christmas nightmare for every parent.The unattainable....
Gibbs: Beary Smyles.
Abby: My dad waited in line two hours for one on Black Friday.
Gibbs: Six......Christmas Eve.
```
Source: 3

No.	German Title	US Title	Air Date USA	Air Date GER	Directed by	Written by
6.128	Abschreckung	**Deliverance**	Feb 10, 2009	Aug 30, 2009	D.Smith	R.Steiner & D.E.Fesman

While investigating the death of a Marine, the team finds Gibbs' Marine ID at the crime scene. It is revealed that he helped a Colombian woman 18 years ago and that her son (whose father Gibbs killed while on the mission there) tried to contact him about a major blackmailing, involving the theft of several crates of assault rifles from a Marine base. *Source:* 1

```
Tony: Oh, it could have been that girl I met at the concession stand while my date was in the
bathroom.
Ziva: You need a secretary.
McGee: Or a therapist.

Gibbs: Or both!
```
Source: 3

No.	German Title	US Title	Air Date USA	Air Date GER	Directed by	Written by
6.129	Der Sündenbock	**Bounce**	Feb 17, 2009	Sep 6, 2009	A.Brown	S.D.Binder & D.North

A Marine imprisoned for embezzlement because of a case DiNozzo worked on three years ago is released and the Navy lieutenant who was a witness against him is found dead. Tony is put in charge of the team because of Gibbs' rule #38 ("Your case, your lead") and they discover that the Marine was framed for embezzlement and now someone is trying to silence those who really did it. Gibbs' fondness of DiNozzo is shown when he tells him how proud he is of his senior field agent. *Source:* 1

```
Gibbs Rule #38: Your case, your lead.

McGee: Who'd wanna impersonate Tony?
Ziva: Perhaps Jack Nicholson. You know, impersonation revenge?
McGee: Or it's a frame-up.
Ziva: Jeanne Benoit?
McGee: Overseas. Maybe it was Trent Kort.
Ziva: Are you detecting a trend here?
McGee: Tony does have a way with people.

Tony: The burning Bed. 1984 Farrah Fawcett.
Gibbs: Torched her husband while he was sleeping. Second wife's favorite movie.
Tony: Maybe Commander Davis's wife is going for a sequel.
McGee: [he enters] Hell hath no fury...
Gibbs: Like a woman scorned. Third wife's favorite quote.
```
Source: 3

Episodes Season 6

No.	German Title	US Title	Air Date USA	Air Date GER	Directed by	Written by
6.130	Paket von einem Toten	**South by Southwest**	Feb 24, 2009	Sep 20, 2009	T.J.Wright	F.Cardea & G.Schenck

The death of an NCIS agent leads Tony and Gibbs to the desert to track down the one woman who holds the answer. *Source: 1*

Cop: Special Agent Gibbs. Got a woman who insists on talking to you. Claims she's with NCIS. Real weirdo, wearing a Dracula cape and a dog collar.
(chuckles slightly) Like she'd be with you.
(Gibbs looks over and sees Abby)
Gibbs: She is.
Cop: You serious?
Gibbs: Oh yeah, let her in.

Source: 3

No.	German Title	US Title	Air Date USA	Air Date GER	Directed by	Written by
6.131	Alleingang	**Knockout**	Mar 17, 2009	Sep 27, 2009	T.Wharmby	J.Stern

Gibbs digs into Vance's past after the Director borrows Gibbs' team for an Investigation into a friend's murder. It is revealed that Tony has been in a slump with women since his break-up with Jeanne Benoit. *Source: 1*

Ziva: You can't make an omelet without breaking some legs.
Tony: You're never making me breakfast.

Source: 3

No.	German Title	US Title	Air Date USA	Air Date GER	Directed by	Written by
6.132	Der Fluch der Waffe	**Hide and Seek**	Mar 24, 2009	Oct 4, 2009	D.Smith	D.E.Fesman

A revolver is found in the affairs of a 12-year-old son of a lieutenant commander in the Navy. Gibbs and the team are dispatched to find out the origin of the weapon. Things get complicated when Abby finds brain matter on the weapon. *Source: 1*

Ziva: This reminds me of the forests I used to have fun in as a child.
Tony: I find that hard to believe.
Ziva: What, that Isreal had forests?
Tony: No, that you had fun as a child.
Ziva: Oh, sure. My father used to blindfold us, take us to the middle of the forest, and then we had to find our way out by ourselves. Tony: I stand corrected.

Gibbs: How was the pawn shop?
Ziva: I hit a stone wall.
Tony: It's a brick wall.
Ziva: No, it was a stone wall. I backed up too quickly.

McGee: I can find an H-waffle double zigzag waffle; I can find a double zigzag H-waffle double zigzag, but not a zigzag double H-waffle zigzag.
Tony: I see a fish riding a unicorn.

Gibbs: Time of death?
Ducky: Taking a liver temp was out of the question.
Gibbs: Uh-huh. Too much time.
Ducky: Not enough liver. I suspect coyotes. You know, when I was a child I used to love liver. Mother would cook the liver of almost anything.
Gibbs: Duck?
Ducky: Well, that was her favorite. I preferred calves liver. You know, 'alla veneziana' with the onions.

Source: 3

Episodes Season 6

No.	German Title	US Title	Air Date USA	Air Date GER	Directed by	Written by
6.133	Der Schatz des Piraten	**Dead Reckoning**	Mar 31, 2009	Oct 11, 2009	T.O'Hara	D.J.North

When shady CIA agent Trent Kort calls in a favor, Gibbs agrees to meet him at an abandoned warehouse. Upon Gibbs' arrival, he finds the agent with two dead men who claims the men shot each other before his arrival. Gibbs and the team must then work with Kort to put away one of NCIS's most wanted. *Source: [1]*

Tony: Maybe he had an appointment: doctor, dentist. Check his calendar McGee
McGee: ...No. Soon as I start going through his stuff, he's gonna walk in a catch me. Forget it!
Ziva: I cannot believe it. I'll do it!
(Starts to go to Gibbs's desk, then pauses)
Ziva: Tony, watch the elevator. McGee the stairs. Now!

Source: [3]

No.	German Title	US Title	Air Date USA	Air Date GER	Directed by	Written by
6.134	Schach matt	**Toxic**	Apr 7, 2009	Oct 18, 2009	T.O'Hara	D.J.North

When a government scientist goes missing, Abby is recruited by the head of the project to carry on his work, but the team worries that she may meet the same fate as her predecessor. *Source: [1]*

Ziva: Tony, do you have to do that now?
Tony: It's spring. I'm spring-cleaning, so....yes!
Ziva: Spring-cleaning?
McGee: You don't have spring-cleaning in Isreal?
Ziva: We do not have spring. Israel is a desert.

Ziva: This is nice. Be able to work without Tony's incessant babbling. It's almost as if he cannot go on for more than 30 seconds without hearing the sound of his own voice. You know the truly amazing thing is that he fails to realize just how irritating he is to those around him.
Gibbs: Ziva.
Ziva: Yes, Gibbs?
Gibbs: Babbling.
Ziva: Oh.

Source: [3]

No.	German Title	US Title	Air Date USA	Air Date GER	Directed by	Written by
6.135	Legende – Teil 1	**Legend (Part I)**	Apr 28, 2009	Oct 25, 2009	T.Wharmby	S.Brennan

The episode introduces the team of the NCIS spin-off titled NCIS: Los Angeles. Gibbs and McGee fly to Los Angeles to work with the NCIS Office of Special Projects—Los Angeles team to solve the murder of a marine and eventually discover that the killing is linked to members of a terrorist sleeper cell. *Source: [1]*

Tony: Long distance can be hard. Tell a friend from Tel-Aviv?
Ziva: You're jealous.
Tony: I'm not jealous.
Ziva: Yes you are.
Tony: No I'm not, and I'm not arguing, boss.
McGee: Are to!
Tony: Am not!

Callen: Is there a reason we're not meeting in a bar right now?
Gibbs: Well yeah, it's 10 o'clock in the morning.
Callen: I don't know what's worse: getting older or getting wiser.

Source: [3]

Episodes Season 6

No.	German Title	US Title	Air Date USA	Air Date GER	Directed by	Written by
6.136	Legende – Teil 2	**Legend (Part II)**	May 5, 2009	Nov 1, 2009	T.Wharmby	S.Brennan

With the appearance of Mossad officer Michael Rivkin, Tony finds himself being forced to question Ziva's loyalty to NCIS. Meanwhile, in Los Angeles, Special Agent Callen goes undercover to try to catch a terrorist cell while OSP psychologist Nate Getz discovers the startling truth about Gibbs and Special Agent Lara Macy's relationship. The NCIS team members soon find themselves racing against the clock to stop Rivkin as they attempt to capture a member of the terrorist cell but it's not easy as Rivkin is making things hard for them by putting all the members of the terrorist cell to sleep one by one before they can get a chance to arrest one. The episode ends with Callen being critically injured in a drive-by shooting and also Ziva being in bed with Rivkin, implying that they might have slept together. *Source:* [1]

Tony: Are we fighting?
Ziva: If we were you would be on the floor bleeding.
Tony: Okay, I accept that as a likely outcome.

Source: [3]

No.	German Title	US Title	Air Date USA	Air Date GER	Directed by	Written by
6.137	Geheimpoker	**Semper Fidelis**	May 12, 2009	Nov 8, 2009	T.Wharmby	J.Stern

After a security breach at the SECNAV's residence leads to the death of an ICE agent, Gibbs and the team are forced to work with ICE and the FBI to find his killer. Meanwhile, Tony finally comes face-to-face with Michael Rivkin and attempts to arrest him for operating on U.S soil which foreign agencies are forbidden to do and for also killing the cell handler and the ICE agent but the two get into a tough brawl which ends when Tony is forced to shoot Rivkin in self-defense when Rivkin tries to stab him with a piece of glass. *Source:* [1]

Abby: The bug stomp. Classic movie move. Sounds like a Tony.
McGee: Nah. It was a Jules.
Abby: A Jules? What is a Jules? I'm going to have a word with this Jules if we ever have the good fortune of meeting.
McGee: I'd like to be here for that.

Source: [3]

No.	German Title	US Title	Air Date USA	Air Date GER	Directed by	Written by
6.138	Heimkehr	**Aliyah**	May 19, 2009	Nov 15, 2009	D.J.North	D.Smith

With Rivkin later dying in hospital from his injuries despite Ziva's efforts to help him and Ziva's own apartment being destroyed in an explosion, Gibbs, Vance, DiNozzo and Ziva travel to Israel, having been summoned there at the request of Eli David, the enigmatic and powerful head of Mossad and also Ziva's father who is demanding answers in regards to Rivkin's death. As tensions rise, and based on information he gets from McGee and Abby who back in Washington are busy working on the laptop found in the wreckage of Ziva's home, Gibbs decides to leave Ziva in Tel Aviv where it is later shown that she has once again been recruited into Mossad and is embarking on a mission to stop a terrorist cell, taking Rivkin's place on the team. However the episode ends in a cliffhanger when it's shown that Ziva has been captured by the terrorists in Somalia that Rivkin had been investigating and the leader, Saleem Ulman is torturing her for information on NCIS. *Source:* [1]

Tony: "Ok. Stop right there. If this is about my Twitter page, I just want to clarify - I'd had a couple of cocktails and what can I say? Sometimes I get a little chatty."

Source: [3]

Season 7 (Episodes 7.139- 7.162)

The seventh season of NCIS started on September 22, 2009 with NCIS: Los Angeles premiering afterwards. At the end of season 6 Ziva had left the NCIS team in Israel, returning to work as a Mossad officer. In the closing seconds of the sixth season, Ziva was shown to have been captured and tortured for information about NCIS.

In the first episode of season 7, Ziva was rescued by Gibbs, Tony and McGee and upon her return to Washington, she eventually became an NCIS Agent after resigning from Mossad for good. Much of the season's story arc then focused on the Mexican Drug War and Colonel Merton Bell, a suspected murderer who hired the lawyer M. Allison Hart to represent him. Hart quickly became a thorn in Gibbs's side by regularly showing up and protecting possible suspects while they were being investigated, claiming that they were her clients.

The season drew to a close as Gibbs was later kidnapped by someone working for Paloma Reynosa, the daughter of the late Pedro Hernandez, a drug dealer Gibbs himself shot dead twenty years previously as Hernadez had been responsible for killing Gibbs's first wife Shannon and daughter Kelly. While being held prisoner, Paloma informed Gibbs that he would work for her or she would have everyone he ever knew and cared about die if he didn't go through with her demands.

It also ended on a cliffhanger with Paloma herself travelling to Stillwater and confronting Jackson Gibbs in his shop, leaving his fate unknown.

Source: [1]

Original Air Date USA   September 22, 2009 – May 25, 2010 on CBS

Original Air Date German Language   February 28, 2010 – October 31, 2010 on Sat 1

Episodes Season 7

No.	German Title	US Title	Air Date USA	Air Date GER	Directed by	Written by
7.139	Der Joker	**Truth or Consequences**	Sep 22, 2009	Feb 28, 2010	D.Smith	J.Stern

Several months have passed since Gibbs left Ziva in Israel, and no-one at NCIS has heard anything from her since. Concerned that something might have gone wrong, Tony, McGee and Abby track down her last known whereabouts, and discover that she was on a mission to take out terrorist Saleem Ulman in Northern Africa. Tony and McGee track him down to get answers about Ziva's disappearance, but are quickly taken prisoner by Saleem. Unfamiliar with NCIS and Tony's mission, Saleem administers a truth serum and questions Tony extensively about the inner workings of the agency, how he was able to find his base of operations and why he traveled so far in his quest. Unable to keep quiet due to the serum's effects, Tony recaps the three months at NCIS since Ziva disappeared, and reveals that NCIS is under the impression that Ziva is dead. He tells Saleem that he traveled to Northern Africa to seek vengeance on the parties responsible. Saleem then demands that Tony reveal the identities of all NCIS agents in the region, and threatens to kill a hostage if he doesn't speak. To Tony's surprise, the hostage is Ziva. However, just as Saleem is about to execute Ziva, Tony tells Saleem one last thing: Gibbs is in Northern Africa too, and Saleem is about to die. Gibbs had been lying in wait the entire time, and just then takes a sniper shot, not only killing Saleem but also the other guards watching over Ziva, Tony and McGee, allowing them to escape. After they all return to the office, everyone stands up and welcomes the team back. *Source:* [1]

```
McGee: I am not your home theater guy.
Tony: Don't be redonculous. Of course you're my home theater guy.
Tony: It's computers. It's your thing. If I had a thing I'd show it off all the time.
Gibbs: There's rules against that DiNozzo.
```

Source: [3]

No.	German Title	US Title	Air Date USA	Air Date GER	Directed by	Written by
7.140	Wie ein Vater	**Reunion**	Sep 29, 2009	Mar 7, 2010	T.Wharmby	S.Binder

The team investigates a bachelor party where all three guests are murdered and left in very mysterious circumstances. One of the victims is found hanging, another is found drowned in the toilet, the third suffered from alcohol poisoning and all three are found with their heads shaved, post mortem. After a thorough investigation the team zeros in on a suspect, a police officer that had been bullied by the three victims during high school. The way that all three victims were found corresponds with the way they had tormented the cop, right down to shaving his head. They also discover that the three victims had used their Navy connections to set up the illegal sale of a decommissioned aircraft, and that the bachelor party was actually a front for the deal to go down during. The team figures the police officer had finally taken his revenge and not only killed his tormentors, but also stole their profits from the aircraft heist. However, after the officer turns up dead, the team learns that the real culprit also attended the same high school as the original three victims, and had framed the cop so they could steal the money from the aircraft job. Meanwhile, Ziva deals with her feelings towards Tony and apologizes for ever doubting him. *Source:* [1]

```
Tony: Hey, you missed a shot there, sidekick.
McGee: I am not your sidekick, Tony.
Tony: And yet, you are.
McGee: No, I am not, because you're not the boss.
Tony: When Gibbs isn't here, I'm the boss.
Gibbs: Gibbs is here.
Tony: Hey, Boss.

Ziva: I was not sure what to say.
Tony: Well did it have to be said in the men's bathroom?
Ziva: I'm sure it had to be said.
```

Source: [3]

Episodes Season 7

No.	German Title	US Title	Air Date USA	Air Date GER	Directed by	Written by
7.141	Der Insider	**The Inside Man**	Oct 6, 2009	Mar 14, 2010	T.Wharmby	F.Cardea & G.Schenck

When political blogger Matt Burns is found dead after being pushed off a bridge while following up on a tip, NCIS takes a special interest in his murder investigation. On his blog, Burns had accused NCIS of covering up the murder of a young Naval officer, Rod Arnett, who Burns suspected of insider trading. NCIS concluded that Arnett's car accident was just that, an unfortunate car accident. However, unable to oversee jurisdiction over the Burns' murder, NCIS reopens Arnett's case. Things become even more complicated when they exhume Arnett's body only to find that his body had been stolen. The team suspects that Burns stole Arnett's body so that he could fuel the conspiracy that NCIS was covering up a murder. It's discovered that Arnett gave insider information to an unassuming sandwich shop owner that he befriended while taking the train everyday. Hoping no one would ever suspect the two of them as conspiring together they agreed to split the $2 million earning. As it turns out, the sandwich shop owner, afraid his scheme with Arnett was about to be exposed, placed the tip to Burns and met him at the bridge to kill him. In the meantime, Ziva resigns from Mossad as she wishes to become a full NCIS Special Agent, but, in order for this to happen, Gibbs needs to sign a consent form. The episode ends without revealing whether Gibbs signs the form. *Source:* [1]

```
McGee: Is that pastrami?
Tony: Mmmmhmmm.
McGee: Can I have some?
Tony: Nuhuh.
McGee: Come on! You know I didn't have lunch!
Tony: Want my pickle?
McGee: I hate pickles.
Tony: I know...
McGee: (After Tony stuffs remainder of sandwich in his mouth.) I hope you choke on that.
```

Source: [3]

No.	German Title	US Title	Air Date USA	Air Date GER	Directed by	Written by
7.142	Damokles	**Good Cop, Bad Cop**	Oct 13, 2009	Mar 21, 2010	L.Libman	D.North & J.Stern

When the remains of AWOL marine Daniel Cryer are found off the coast of Tanzania by a fishing boat, Ziva's account of Mossad's operation to take down Saleem Ulman is called in to question. It turns out that Cryer had deserted the Marines to become a soldier of fortune, and had been part of the team that Mossad had sent after Saleem. Ziva's story that the ship they had been traveling on had gone down in a storm is proven false by the location of Cryers body, and the fact that he was shot to death confirms that something other than a storm had been responsible for the sinking of the ship. Using the location of Cryer's body as a guide, the Navy is able to salvage the ship in question and discovers that the entire crew had been shot to death. Vance presses Ziva for more details, but her team leader, Malachi Ben-Gidon, shows up at NCIS and demands that Ziva return to Mossad's control. Vance agrees on the condition that Malachi debriefs them on the rest of the mission. Malachi agrees and tells them that their cover had been blown and they were forced to kill everyone on the ship, and that Ziva had killed Cryer because he had been responsible for their discovery. However, when Ziva sets the record straight and tells them it was Malachi who had shot Cryer before asking questions, Vance sends him back to Israel. Through all of this Ziva was trying to get a permanent position on the NCIS team, and after proving her loyalty is finally accepted as an NCIS agent. *Source:* [1]

```
Abby: No plan, Just go, find along the way, if you look for something specific....
McGee: ...then there's only 1 right answer.
```

Source: [3]

Episodes Season 7

No.	German Title	US Title	Air Date USA	Air Date GER	Directed by	Written by
7.143	Böse Streiche	**Code of Conduct**	Oct 20, 2009	Mar 28, 2010	T.O'Hara	R.Steiner & C.Waild

On Halloween night the team investigates what looks to be the unfortunate suicide of Lance Corporal James Korby who is found dead in his car. However, they soon discover that Korby was murdered as his organs were frozen with liquid nitrogen and that when he attempted to breathe, the nitrogen entered his lungs, suffocating him. However it's also discovered that Korby has scar-tissue from a previous poisoning and Gibbs suspect that the entire squad, fed up of Korby's jokes attempted to kill him. Someone got Korby to drink the nitrogen and staged his death to look it like a suicide. Tony can't shake the hunch that Sara, Korby's wife and a three-time marine widower, is involved, suspecting her of being a Black Widow. It's soon revealed that Private Singer, who belonged to Korby's unit, was having an affair with Korby's wife Sara. Sara also confesses to coming home to confront Korby right around the time of the crime but getting cold feet at the last second. Just as Tony is about to cuff Sara for Korby's murder, Gibbs realizes that Sara had nothing to do with Korby's death because there was someone else with a real motive: Rachel, Korby and Sara's teenage stepdaughter. Having been about to cash in on a pretty hefty trust fund and inheritance, Rachel knew the only way she could do it was by murdering Korby and then framing Sara for his death. -In the meantime, Ziva attempts to come to terms with her new role as an NCIS Special Agent and the Probie of the team as Tony begins referring to her as Probie, something she begs him not to do for her sanity but Tony continues to do it anyway. Later, in true Halloween style, Ziva gets her own back on Tony by pretending to bow down to him and as a gift gives him a cup of coffee but when Tony drinks it and smiles at her, it's shown that his teeth have turned blue. *Source:* [1]

Tony: Probies, talk louder, I can hear you in there.
Ziva: McGee has been at NCIS for six years. I have been here four. We ARE agents, so can you PLEASE stop calling us ...
Gibbs: Problem, Probie?

Source: [3]

No.	German Title	US Title	Air Date USA	Air Date GER	Directed by	Written by
7.144	Das Boot	**Outlaws and In-Laws**	Nov 3, 2009	Apr 4, 2010	T.Wharmby	J.Stern

When Gibbs' boat mysteriously shows up in the San Diego harbor with two dead men in it, Vance, Gibbs and Ducky travel to San Diego knowing this investigation needs to be handled with extreme sensitivity. It turns out Gibbs dropped his boat off to Franks in Mexico but Franks is nowhere to be found. Franks shows up at Gibbs' house with his daughter in law, Leyla (Franks' deceased son's wife), and granddaughter in tow. It is revealed that the two dead men worked for a private military company that was hired by Leyla's mother, Shada, a powerful tribal leader in Iraq, to kidnap and bring back her daughter and granddaughter to Iraq. It was her way of trying to re-establish a relationship with her estranged daughter. Franks takes full responsibility for the shooting but further investigation reveals that it was Leyla who shot and killed the men when she saw them approaching Franks. In the end, the private military company, headed by Col. Merton Bell, is also held responsible for bounty hunting in Mexico, and Leyla and her mother come to terms. *Source:* [1]

Tony: That's --
Abby: Uh-huh!
McGee: It's no longer in --
Abby: Nuh-uh!
Ziva: This is Gibbs' boat.
Abby: This is the crime scene! It was flown here on a C130 cargo plane along with two bodies and all the evidence, and now it is mine. It is all mine! So I can figure out the mystery!
McGee: What mystery? Who the dead guys were?
Ziva: Or who killed them.
Tony: Or how they ended up on the boat. Abby: Sure, you guys should work on that! While I figure out how he got it out of the basement!

Source: [3]

Episodes Season 7

No.	German Title	US Title	Air Date USA	Air Date GER	Directed by	Written by
7.145	Der letzte Schuss	**Endgame**	Nov 10, 2009	Apr 11, 2010	J.Whitmore, Jr.	G.Glasberg

When a doctor is found murdered, Director Vance shows up at the crime scene, claiming he's seen the type of murder before. The director confirms that the killer was a North Korean assassin, named Lee Wuan Kai (first seen in the NCIS: Los Angeles episode "Killshot"). The team finds that Kai has left her DNA on the victim's body for them. The director is completely surprised and shocked when Kai calls him at home and is sitting in his driveway. As the investigation continues, the team discovers that Kai is in town to kill a North Korean official. Meanwhile, McGee's new love interest, Amanda turns out to be working for the North Korean government and is shot by Kai before dying in McGee's arms. They discover that Kai is in D.C. to kill all the men who made her into an assassin as a child. Vance returns to his home to find Kai pointing a gun at his wife. Kai reveals that she is there because she wants Vance to kill her in order to finally end her pain. The director lowers his gun to help her, but his wife finishes the job instead. . *Source:* [1]

No.	German Title	US Title	Air Date USA	Air Date GER	Directed by	Written by
7.146	Unplugged	**Power Down**	Nov 17, 2009	Apr 18, 2010	T.J.Wright	S.Binder & D.North

Shortly after an attack on an internet service provider, the power to all of Washington DC is down. When the body of a Navy Armed Forces Entertainment worker is found at the site of the attack, NCIS is called in. However, without power, the team cannot use their modern electronics and must solve the case the old fashioned way. They finally discover that the dead USO worker was in fact an undercover National Security Agency agent, one of the two people who had universal access to every retinal scanner in the United States. They then arrest one of the security guards at the service provider, as he is the true mastermind. He kidnapped the agent to gain access to the server room and cut power to the entire city so that he could secretly steal top secret personal and military data and sell it off the black market. The team then reflects on how much richer life is without electronics, until power is restored and they dive right back into their computers except for Gibbs who is more than happy to take a break from electronics for a change. *Source:* [1]

McGee: Do you see this? Nine hours, 21 minutes! *[shoves his watch in Ziva's face]*
Ziva: Has it been that long? *[takes the watch away and breaks it]*
McGee: Why did you do that??
Ziva: Because it was either you or the watch!
McGee: It's just, what's taking so long, you know?
Ziva: Look, I'm sure we're not the only ones that need to be rescued. Plus, things could be a lot worse.
McGee: Yeah, how's that?
Ziva: We could be stuck here with Tony.
Tony: *[from outside the elevator]* I heard that! I find it very interesting that the two of you left together late last night!
Ziva: Just ignore him. He's like an annoying bug. Eventually he'll just go away.
McGee: Ziva, it's been five years. Trust me, he's not going anywhere.

McGee: It's just like a tardis.
Tony: A tard what?
McGee: A tardis, the machine that Dr. Who uses to time travel with...

Tony: Sorry, the whole city's been de-duracelled.

Source: [3]

Episodes Season 7

No.	German Title	US Title	Air Date USA	Air Date GER	Directed by	Written by
7.147	Kinderspiel	**Child's Play**	Nov 24, 2009	Apr 25, 2010	W.Webb	R.Steiner

After the body of a Marine is discovered in a corn field, the team investigates at a military intelligence base that uses genius children to crack military codes. The team discovers that one of the children is making collages that contain codes with important military secrets in them, secrets that are being sold. A second dead body points to the woman running the organization, but when the young girl escapes from the safe house (Ducky's house) and runs home to her mother, the team must race to save her from her would-be murderer. Meanwhile, Ducky attempts to convince Gibbs and the team to spend Thanksgiving at his house, in spite of previously made plans. *Source:* [1]

Ducky: *(in the corn field)* Ah fresh corn! That gives me an idea. Why don't we have corn chowder as the first course?
Tony: Poker.
McGee: Sister.
Ziva: Neighbors.
Gibbs: Later.

Source: [3]

No.	German Title	US Title	Air Date USA	Air Date GER	Directed by	Written by
7.148	Die Ehre der Familie	**Faith**	Dec 15, 2009	May 2, 2010	A.Brown	G.Glasberg

The team works to solve the murder of a Reverend's son and they soon figure out he may be involved in a hate crime. Gibbs' father returns for Christmas and Gibbs tries to figure out why he has a sudden change in behavior right before the holidays. An old friend of Abby asks McGee for a favour - her nephew (who is living with her) wants to see his mother for Christmas, who is currently on a Marine ship in the Indian Ocean, but only McGee can make it happen. Gibbs figures out that it was the victim's brother who was the culprit, since he couldn't accept his brother's conversion to Islam. Gibbs also discovers that his father killed a man attempting to rob his store and he came to ask for advice on how to deal with killing another man. *Source:* [1,]

McGee: It's freezing this morning.
Tony: Man up, chilly willy. Feel that warm blood coursing through your veins. Get in touch with your inner McGrizzly Adams.
McGee: Well I've got hand warmers.
Tony: Give me one.
McGee: No.
Ziva: I'm not cold at all.
Tony: The coldblooded David, like a lady Komodo dragon; ice queen, frigid and deadly.
Ziva: And I remembered to wear my thermal underwear.
Tony: I'll give you fifty bucks for it right now.
Ziva: It wouldn't fit. You're too big.
Tony: *[desperately]* It'll stretch. Turn 'em over.

Tony: How many languages do you speak?
Ziva: Including the language of love, ten.

Abby: Like you said, whoever did this had speed, strength, and agility.
Tony: I have many of those qualities myself.
Ziva: Ha!
Tony: Where is your spirit, probette?
Ziva: Bah humbog!
Tony: Bah-what?

Source: [3]

Episodes Season 7

No.	German Title	US Title	Air Date USA	Air Date GER	Directed by	Written by
7.149	Rocket Man	**Ignition**	Jan 5, 2010	May 9, 2010	D.Smith	J.Stern

The episode starts with two forest rangers finding a body at the site of a forest fire. The team investigates and finds out that the pilot was flying a jet-pack and crashed. An attorney who dislikes Gibbs tries to keep him from talking to her clients. Ducky discovers that the victim had been poisoned and was already dead long before he put the jetpack on, leading to the team to suspect a third party. They figure out that it was the commanding officer, who stole technology from private companies and the Navy to build his own jet-pack and killed the victim to keep him quiet. Later, Gibbs discovers that the sly attorney was sent by an old enemy. ... *Source:* [1]

```
Ziva: Slow drivers.
Tony: Bad drivers.
Ziva: What is so hard? You go as fast as possible, when something gets in your way, you turn.
Tony: You're quoting Better Off Dead. I told you to watch that.

McGee: It has a range of at least a kilometer.
Tony: I don't speak Canadian. How far is that?
```
Source: [3]

No.	German Title	US Title	Air Date USA	Air Date GER	Directed by	Written by
7.150	Der doppelte Tony	**Flesh and Blood**	Jan 12, 2010	May 16, 2010	Arvin Brown	F.Cardea & G.Schenck

The episode starts when a Saudi prince manages to escape an assassination attempt while attending flight school in the United States. The team is tasked with the investigation as well as protecting the prince. Meanwhile, Tony's father appears, much to Tony's discomfort. His father is a business associate of the prince's father, and is trying to sort out a business deal. Later, the team discovers that the assassins weren't terrorists, but was in fact the prince's brother, who disliked his carefree lifestyle. However, the brother manages to escape the country due to his diplomatic immunity. Tony finds out that his father is actually nearly broke. However, he's unwilling to confront his father. Before he leaves, Tony's father tells Tony that despite their rocky relationship, he has always loved him. *Source:* [1]

```
Gibbs Rule #6: Never say you're sorry. It's a sign of weakness.

Tony: I have to break one of your rules, boss. Number six: never say you're sorry. I let things
get out of control in the hotel room.
Gibbs: Ah, it's covered. Rule eighteen.
Tony: Oh, yeah. It's better to seek forgiveness than ask permission. Am I forgiven?
Gibbs: No. You've been distracted by your father.
Tony: It's that obvious?
```
Source: [3]

No.	German Title	US Title	Air Date USA	Air Date GER	Directed by	Written by
7.151	Wie im Flug	**Jet Lag**	Jan 26, 2010	May 23, 2010	T.Wharmby	C.Waild

While transporting a government witness back from Paris, Tony and Ziva's assignment quickly encounters turbulence when they learn a hit man may be on their flight home. With the help of the rest of the team on the ground, as well as a botched attempt on the witness's life, Tony and Ziva deduce that the assassin is one of the flight attendants. After successfully apprehending her, they discover that the man who hired her was in fact the witness's fiance, who would be implicated in her testimony but in the process of arresting him, Gibbs's right arm is broken, forcing him to do everything with his left hand for the time being. *Source:* [1]

Episodes Season 7

No.	German Title	US Title	Air Date USA	Air Date GER	Directed by	Written by
7.152	Kobalt 60	**Masquerade**	Feb 2, 2010	May 30, 2010	J.Whitmore, Jr.	S.Binder

The team finds themselves in a race against time when a terrorist group threatens to detonate "dirty bombs" in the D.C. area. As the team tries to track down the bombs, their investigation is hampered when Hart returns to represent one of their suspects. Despite this, they manage to discover that the entire bomb plot was an elaborate hoax set up by a private intelligence agency to scare Congress into approving a bill that would award private defense contractors billions of dollars in funding. *Source:* [1]

Tony: First the plague, now radiation poisoning. I'm starting to think someone really has it in for me.
McGee: I was there, too, near the car, you know.
Ziva: We all were.
McGee: But don't let that stop you from thinking about yourself.
Tony: This isn't about me! It's about my little DiNozzo makers! They've been nuked!
McGee: I know!
Tony: Do you?! I mean, sure, Tim, you're kids are going to be smart, [Ziva rolls her eyes and walks away] but mine have a shot at being really beautiful.

Source: [3]

No.	German Title	US Title	Air Date USA	Air Date GER	Directed by	Written by
7.153	Vollgas	**Jack-Knife**	Feb 9, 2010	Jun 6, 2010	D.Smith	J.Stern

When a Marine is found dead, Gibbs, Fornell and the team hit the open road to bust an illegal trucking operation. With Werth's help, they manage to infiltrate the operation and stop the ringleaders from stealing a pair of very valuable cars. However, further investigation reveals that the owner of one of the cars was involved in a fatal hit and run accident, and that the owner was responsible for the Marine's murder in order to keep him quiet. *Source:* [1]

Gibbs Rule #27:   There are two ways to follow someone.
                          1st way - they never notice you;
                          2nd way - they only notice you.

Gibbs: Get Ziva and DiNozzo out of bed.
McGee: What?!
Gibbs: Wake 'em up.
McGee: Oh. Oh, right. Get them out of bed because it's the middle of the night and they're asleep.
Gibbs: *[looks at McGee like he's gone mad]* Yes.
McGee: Individual beds. Get them out of individual beds. I was confused. I thought we were talking -- ...
Gibbs: Need some sleep yourself, do you, McGee?

McGee: *(after waking up, with Tony and Ziva staring at him)* I'm awake.
Ziva: We didn't say anything.
McGee: But you did something, didn't you? What did you do? Did you try to put my hand in this water?
Tony: That's a little juvenile.
McGee: You drew something on my face, didn't you? You drew on my face.
Tony: No. I suggested stripping you naked, putting a tag in your too and dragging you down to Autopsy, so when you woke up you'd think you were dead, but Ziva thought it was in poor taste.
McGee: Well, thank you, Ziva.

Source: [3]

Episodes Season 7

No.	German Title	US Title	Air Date USA	Air Date GER	Directed by	Written by
7.154	Schwiegermuttertag	**Mother's Day**	Mar 2, 2010	Sep 5, 2010	T.Wharmby	G.Glasberg & R.Steiner

Secrets arise when Gibbs's former mother-in-law surfaces as a witness in a murder investigation. At first, the crime appears to be a simple robbery gone awry, but deeper investigation reveals that there's more to the story. The victim, a Navy captain, was involved with the same drug cartel that killed Gibbs' first wife and child. His mother-in-law eventually admits that she killed the captain in revenge for her daughter and granddaughter's death, and Gibbs' tells her he murdered their real killer as well. Despite the confession, Gibbs cannot bring himself to arrest his own mother-in-law. He convinces Allison Hart to defend her, and then on purpose makes crucial legal mistakes on arresting her (not reading her her rights, questioning her without legal counsel), so Hart in her typical hardball style convinces him swiftly to let her go. *Source:* [1]

Tony: All right, McNosy, what do you got?
McGee: From what I can gather, Gibbs and JoAnn Fielding are very estranged.
Ziva: The woman lost her daughter and granddaughter. Now her fiancé died in her arms and her former son-in-law is investigating! Show some sympathy!
Tony: Maybe she's cursed! Like a Kennedy!
McGee: Minus the grassy knoll.
Ziva: I heard about that! The shooter was really in the book suppository!
Tony: Depository.

Ziva: That's what I said.

Source: [3]

No.	German Title	US Title	Air Date USA	Air Date GER	Directed by	Written by
7.155	Zwei Leben	**Double Identity**	Mar 9, 2010	Sep 12, 2010	M.Horowitz	F.Cardea & G.Schenck

Gibbs and the team investigate the shooting of a Marine and uncovers more to his life than anyone would have ever imagined. The Marine had been declared MIA after a reconnaissance mission in Afghanistan, somehow obtained millions of dollars, and married another woman under a false identity. The victim's commanding officer reveals that in Afghanistan, they stumbled across a money cache. The victim took the money for himself and disappeared. The team then deduces that a private investigator the commanding officer hired to find the victim was the shooter, as he intended to blackmail the victim. It is also shown that Ducky's mother has passed on, sometime in 2010. *Source:* [1]

No.	German Title	US Title	Air Date USA	Air Date GER	Directed by	Written by
7.156	Der Schatz der Calafuego	**Jurisdiction**	Mar 16, 2010	Sep 19, 2010	T.O'Hara	L.D.Zlotoff

The team and Coast Guard Investigative Service join forces when a Navy diver seeking sunken treasure is murdered. Both teams suspect a wealthy doctor who was funding the treasure hunting expedition is the culprit, but the evidence just doesn't add up. Eventually, they figure out that the diver was scamming the doctor, fooling him into withdrawing cash from his accounts to find a nonexistent treasure. The diver killed the doctor and faked his own death using the body. Both the NCIS and CGIS teams apprehend the diver and the doctor's wife, who was his accomplice. *Source:* [1]

Gibbs: I wanted to see how Jensen lived.
Tony: It says a lot about a man. Take your house for instance: clean, no nonsense, stoic.
Gibbs: Stoic? My house is stoic?
Tony: Understated, then?
Gibbs: I planted some roses last weekend. Red ones. Are red roses stoic?

Tony: Well, they're prickly and thorny.

Source: [3]

Episodes Season 7

No.	German Title	US Title	Air Date USA	Air Date GER	Directed by	Written by
7.157	Holly Snow	**Guilty Pleasure**	Apr 6, 2010	Sep 26, 2010	J.Whitmore, Jr.	R.Steiner & C.Waild

Gibbs uses Holly Snow (previously seen in the episode: "Jet Lag") to investigate a murder in the world of call girls, causing tensions within the team. After finding the body of a murdered Navy reporter, the team finds out that he was interviewing a prostitute who used to work for Holly Snow and that there have been a string of similar murders. Holly makes a deal with Gibbs to help his investigation and they track down the prostitute, who reveals that the killer is jealous of her seeing other men. At first the team believes that the killer is one of her clients, but find out it is actually her boyfriend, who is the attorney representing her. The killer kidnaps Holly, blaming her for getting his girlfriend into a life of prostitution and seeing other men. However, he is shot dead by Gibbs before he can harm her. The episode ends with Gibbs and Holly having a simple dinner together as part of their deal. *Source:* [1]

Ziva: You know what, you two? I have actually heard of this. You two are having a seven-year *****.
Tony: Itch. And yes we are.
Ziva: You two are like a married couple.
Gibbs: *(arriving)* Ah, no they're not, they're still speaking. Let's go.

Source: [3]

No.	German Title	US Title	Air Date USA	Air Date GER	Directed by	Written by
7.158	Ein rotes Haar	**Moonlighting**	Apr 27, 2010	Oct 3, 2010	T.J.Wright	S.Binder & J.Stern

When the NCIS team finds a dead Navy petty officer and FBI informant, they call in Agent Fornell to assist with the investigation. Fornell reveals that a string of similar security leaks have been occurring, and they trace the source to a private security company. They also discover that their NCIS polygraph specialist, Susan Grady, works part time at the same company. After retrieving her, the security company's office is destroyed in an explosion and Susan reveals that she stole some polygraph data for personal use. Abby manages to deduce that the killers inadvertently killed themselves in the explosion, leading Gibbs and Fornell to the real mastermind: a federal judge they both had interviewed during the investigation. She went on a secret crusade to kill informants who would take reduced sentences in return for their testimony, and wanted to destroy the polygraph data as it might implicate her involvement. *Source:* [1]

Tony: What's this surprising bit of editorializing coming from the once and future king of dorkland?
Palmer: Hey, I now have a girlfriend.
Tony: The king is dead. Long live the king.

Palmer: It wasn't sand sand, like good sand. It was bad sand. Very bad sand. It made me break out in red welts.
Ducky: It wasn't the sand, Mr. Palmer, but the sand mite.
Palmer: The sand might what?
Ducky: The sand mite bit you.
Palmer: Sand bites?
Ducky: Well, sand mites might bite.
Palmer: I'm grammatically lost.
Ducky: But medically found. The tiny crustacean known as the mite. M-i-t-e.

Fornell: Thanks for doing it my way.
Gibbs: Yeah, don't mention it.
Fornell: I was being facetious.
Gibbs: Yeah, me too.

Source: [3]

Episodes Season 7

No.	German Title	US Title	Air Date USA	Air Date GER	Directed by	Written by
7.159	Rule Nummer Zehn	**Obsession**	May 4, 2010	Oct 10, 2010	T.Wharmby	F.Cardea & G.Schenck

DiNozzo finds himself captivated by a woman he's never met while investigating the death of her brother. The woman is the world renowned reporter Dana Hutton, who has disappeared shortly after her brother's death. At first, the team believes that the murder may be connected with the siblings' work on investigating Private Military Contractors, but begin to suspect that the KGB may be involved when they discovered Dana's brother was killed by a Ricin pellet. It soon turns out that the man who brought Dana Hutton and her brother up was a KGB asset codenamed "Yuri" who owned a bank account on which the KGB stashed $10 million for use in their US intelligence operations. DiNozzo manages to contact Dana and gain her trust, and she helps the team recover Yuri's KGB documents and money, but reveals she had been injected with ricin as well. With the documents, the team find the operative who killed the Huttons as being one of the KGB agents who didn't return to Russia after the Cold War ended and who wanted to get her hands on the money that Yuri had stashed away. *Source:* [1]

Gibbs Rule #10: Never get personally involved in a case.
Gibbs Rule #39: There is no such thing as coincidence.

Gibbs: You okay?
Tony: Not really. I broke rule number ten. Again. Never get personally involved in a case.
Gibbs: Yeah. That's the rule I've always had the most trouble with.

Source: [3]

No.	German Title	US Title	Air Date USA	Air Date GER	Directed by	Written by
7.160	Kalte Spuren	**Borderland (1)**	May 11, 2010	Oct 17, 2010	T.O' Hara	S.Binder

After finding a dead Marine with his feet cut off, as well as a truck full of dismembered feet, the team begins to believe that a serial killer is loose. Meanwhile, Abby is invited to provide a forensic science lecture in Mexico by Alejandro Rivera, and McGee goes along as an escort. While there, Abby is tasked to solve a cold case involving the murder of a drug dealer 20 years ago, and Abby eventually finds out the drug dealer was the one murdered by Gibbs. Back in the United States, the team deduces that the Marine was the killer, acting as a hit man to kill rival drug dealers and kept their feet as proof. One of the drug dealers is apprehended and she admits that she killed him in self defense. Finally, Abby confronts Gibbs about the murder, which Gibbs admits to. They both agree that somebody is trying to dig up Gibbs' past, but Abby is conflicted on whether to drop the case or pursue it and asks Gibbs whether he will love her regardless of what she does. *Source:* [1]

Gibbs Rule #40: If it seems like someone's out to get you, they are.

Tony: I bet Abby could last longer than ten seconds playing random chat.
Ziva: You are obsessed.
Tony: You wouldn't understand.
Ziva: Why is that?
Tony: Because, being irritating is second nature to you. Me, I'm charming.

Tony: I've already earned my pay today.
Ziva: Really? What did you find?
Tony: Haha! No way. I tell you. You tell Gibbs, I got nothing.
Ziva: Look I'm not going to steal your discovery. Okay? I've have my own.
Tony: Really? What do you got?
Ziva: No way! If I tell you, you tell Gibbs.
Gibbs: Gibbs is going to find out anyway. Come on, let's see it.

Source: [3]

Episodes Season 7

No.	German Title	US Title	Air Date USA	Air Date GER	Directed by	Written by
7.161	Ein guter Patriot	**Patriot Down (2)**	May 18, 2010	Oct 24,. 2010	D.Smith	G.Glasberg

The team is shocked when they discover that a charred corpse found on the beach that is revealed to be that of Special Agent Lara Macy, a fellow NCIS agent and a close friend of Gibbs. They discover that the last case Macy worked on before her tragic death was a case regarding the rape of a Navy sailor. While they manage to find the rapist, the case is completely unrelated to the murder. Meanwhile, Abby confronts Gibbs about the murder he committed in Mexico, asking him what to do, and Gibbs simply tells her to do her job and file the full report. Gibbs soon becomes convinced that Colonel Bell is responsible and leaves for Mexico. When he finally arrives, he finds Mike Franks' house has been burned to the ground as well as the bodies of several of Bell's men. Gibbs is then captured by one of Bell's henchmen, who reveals that the body that Gibbs thought was Franks is in fact Colonel Bell. Gibbs is then knocked unconscious before he can ask the henchman who he's really working for. *Source:* [1]

No.	German Title	US Title	Air Date USA	Air Date GER	Directed by	Written by
7.162	Rule 51	**Rule Fifty-One (3)**	May 25, 2010	Oct 31, 2010	D.Smith	J.Stern

Gibbs's captor is Paloma Reynosa, the leader of the Reynosa drug Cartel. Her reason for having Gibbs brought to Mexico is clear: she wants revenge against him for robbing her of her father and threatens to kill everyone Gibbs has ever met, starting with Mike Franks and ending with his father if he does not start working on her behalf. When Alejandro arrives, Gibbs figures out that the two are siblings and also the children of the drug dealer, Pedro Hernadez, whom Gibbs gunned down nearly twenty years previously in revenge for Hernandez ordering the deaths of Gibbs's first wife, Shannon and young daughter, Kelly. Alejandro reopened the case of his father's murder in an attempt to keep Gibbs out of his sister's reach whilst still delivering justice, but things are complicated by the loss of Abby's report from "Patriot Down" - which has been intercepted by Allison Hart to prevent it from reaching Mexico. Meanwhile, Ziva has passed her citizenship test and is expecting Tony and Gibbs to attend her citizenship ceremony. Tony is forced to break his promise to her when the situation escalates, and he is tasked with shadowing Rivera, meeting Mike Franks during the assignment. The episode ends with Paloma traveling to Pennsylvania and entering the store owned by Jackson Gibbs, ending the episode in a cliffhanger and leaving his fate unknown.
It is revealed that Gibbs started writing down all his rules after a suggestion by his late wife and in this episode creates a new rule, the eponymous rule 51: "Sometimes—you're wrong". Tony also mentions that all rules "in the 40s" are for emergencies only. *Source:* [1]

```
Gibbs Rule #13: Never, ever involve lawyers.

Gibbs Rule #44: First things first, hide the women and children.

Gibbs Rule #45: Clean up your messes.

Gibbs Rule #51: Sometimes - you're wrong.
```

Source: 3

Season 8 (Episodes 8.163- 8.186)

The eighth season of NCIS premiered on September 21, 2010 in the same time slot as the previous season and the second season of NCIS: Los Angeles premiered afterwards. The season story arc involved Ziva's largely unseen boyfriend, Ray, and the CIA continuing to meddle in NCIS's day-to-day workings. Notable events included the terrorism and internal affairs threat during the Enemies two-parter, and the arrival of another Major Case Response Team from Rota, Spain, the team that Tony was offered to be lead of in the beginning of season 4. The season ended on a five part story arc involving the Port-to-Port killer that menaced both teams. *Source:* [1]

Original Air Date USA   September 21, 2010 – May 17, 2011 on CBS

Original Air Date German Language   February 13, 2011 – November 8, 2011 on Sat 1

Episodes Season 8

No.	German Title	US Title	Air Date USA	Air Date GER	Directed by	Written by
8.163	Die tapferste Stunde	**Spider and the Fly (4)**	Sep 21, 2010	Feb 13, 2011	G.Glasberg	D.Smith

Following Jackson Gibbs' (guest star Ralph Waite) confrontation with Paloma Reynosa (guest star Jacqueline Obradors), he is put in NCIS protective custody at his son's house. A few months later, the death of a helicopter pilot leads the team back to the Reynosa Cartel's vendetta with Gibbs, leading team members to become targets. Paloma Reynosa, head of the cartel, plays a game of cat and mouse with NCIS as she makes a wide trail through the US, expanding her cartel's influence. Tensions erupt when Alejandro Rivera (guest star Marco Sanchez), calls Abby on her bluff over the sending of the report on the Pedro Hernandez murder and threatens her in front of Gibbs. Knowing of his involvement in the Reynosa Cartel, NCIS leads Rivera into a trap at a safehouse by tricking him into thinking his sister is dead and those responsible are in protective custody. Rivera takes the bait and intends to exact revenge, but ends up fatally shooting his own sister. Meanwhile, Leon Vance, whilst putting the report implicating Gibbs in a place no one will find it, receives a mysterious text message from Eli David, Director of Mossad claiming "I found him".. *Source:* [1]

Ziva: "Hello, Tony. I am back."
Tony: "Well, hello little Miss Sunshine State. Don't you look balmy.
Ziva: "I do not know what balmy is and I doubt it can be good."
Tony: "Any tan lines."
Ziva: "I assure you I don't have any. I was working. A local informant said a Mexican drug shipment came in by boat. A deal closed by the Reynosa family. Rivera even paid a political visit to the mayor."

Ziva: "I thought that was the Irish."
McGee: "Doesn't go well with eggs or bacon. Why you so tan?"
Ziva: "Why you so white?"
McGee: "I've always been like this."
Ziva: "Becomes you."
McGee: "You're lying."

Ziva: "Through my teeth."   *Source:* [3]

Episodes Season 8

No.	German Title	US Title	Air Date USA	Air Date GER	Directed by	Written by
8.164	Der alte Fuchs	**Worst Nightmare**	Sep 28, 2010	Feb 15, 2011	T.Wharmby	S.Binder

A teenage girl is kidnapped from her middle school on the Quantico marine base, prompting NCIS to investigate. Nicholas Mason, the missing girl's grandfather, complicates matters when he arranges a ransom drop without informing NCIS. The team find a trail of dead bodies leading back to Mason, who admits he was a part of a black operations team that worked within the law, but outside the chain of command. Someone is using Mason's granddaughter to lure him out of retirement and lead them to the other team members. The kidnapper is the girl's high school English teacher, who was formerly a member of Mason's team and is seeking redemption for his past actions by killing off his team-mates. Meanwhile, three interns are assigned to NCIS; Abby is suspicious after her last assistant's attempt to kill her, Palmer feels ineffective after Ducky bonds with his intern, and McGee must contend with an intern who shows no interest in field work at all. Using an elaborate ploy, the team manages to trick the kidnapper into revealing where he was hiding the girl and arrest him. Meanwhile, the disobedient intern begins showing an interest in law enforcement and McGee later hands him an NCIS application form. *Source:* [1]

Tony: "What's goin' on here. We being replaced by younger models?"
Ziva: "I am a younger model."
Tony: "If that was intended to hurt me you've succeeded."
Ziva: "And we are not being replaced. They are from Waverly University."
Tony: "Oh yeah. That's right. Director Vance's internship program. It's not a good idea. Feeds McGee's need to have groupies."

Source: [3]

No.	German Title	US Title	Air Date USA	Air Date GER	Directed by	Written by
8.165	Rache ist bitter	**Short Fuse**	Oct 5, 2010	Feb 22, 2011	L.Libman	F.Cardea & G.Schenck

NCIS responds to an emergency phone call after Heather Dempsey, a Marine bomb technician, shoots and kills an intruder in her home. Dempsey initially evades the investigation, but the team quickly find evidence she was not alone at the time. Her lover is revealed to be a senior FBI agent; the intruder a hit man. They learn that Dempsey's brother was shot and paralyzed by a man named Abbott in a gang war, and that the FBI lover recommended protective custody for him after he testified to escape jail time. Dempsey started a relationship with the agent to learn Abbott's new identity and location. When he learned that Dempsey was searching for him, Abbott hired the hitman to kill her before she could kill him. Because hiring the hitman was not part of his immunity deal, Abbott is arrested. Meanwhile, Tony is excited to be chosen as the face of NCIS' new recruitment campaign, but Director Vance decides Gibbs promotes the qualities NCIS is looking for more than Tony does. *Source:* [1]

No.	German Title	US Title	Air Date USA	Air Date GER	Directed by	Written by
8.166	Schmutzige Millionen	**Royals and Loyals**	Oct 12,2010	Mar 1, 2011	A.Brown	R.Steiner

The team is involved in an international incident as they investigate the murder of an American petty officer whose case is connected with a Royal Navy ship. Complications ensue when someone tries to get the ship to depart before NCIS can properly investigate. They discover that the murder was over a large amount of stolen CIA money, used to pay off warlords and dictators in Afghanistan. At first, the team suspects that the Royal Navy liaison officer is responsible, but quickly find out that he is actually an MI6 agent who was framed for the theft. With his help, they track down the real culprit, the corrupt CIA handler who was in charge of the money. *Source:* [1]

Episodes Season 8

No.	German Title	US Title	Air Date USA	Air Date GER	Directed by	Written by
8.167	Feld der Alpträume	**Dead Air**	Oct 19, 2010	Mar 7, 2011	T.O'Hara	C.Waild

The team investigates the death of a radio DJ and a Naval Officer who were both killed live on air, and their job becomes more difficult by the discovery of various suspects. While searching for the murderer, they inadvertently uncover a large domestic terrorist group composed mostly of wealthy homeowners living in a gated community. The terrorist group feel that America should be spending more money defending itself rather than on foreign wars, and attempted to recruit the DJ to their cause. When the DJ refused, they had him killed to silence him. The NCIS team raids the community and arrests all of the members, only to find that the group have planted a bomb at a local softball game attended by numerous high profile politicians. The NCIS team are able to evacuate the crowd from the game before the bomb explodes. *Source: 1*

Ziva: *(noticing that the barbecue is a bomb)* Tony!!!!
Tony: No!!!!!
Tony: This is nice, I missed the old Ziva.
Ziva: I can tell.
Tony: Don't flatter yourself, that's just my knee.
Ziva: *(picks up the baseball gloves and baseball)* Hey Gibbs, have a catch?
McGee: Whoa, look at this. You do know a little something about baseball, huh?
Ziva: Yeah, my father taught me.

Source: 3

No.	German Title	US Title	Air Date USA	Air Date GER	Directed by	Written by
8.168	Genie und Wahnsinn	**Cracked**	Oct 26, 2010	Mar 15, 2011	T.Wharmby	N.Mirante-Matthews

The NCIS team investigate the death of a Navy researcher who was hit by a bus in the middle of a busy street. They are surprised to find that her entire body is covered in elaborate mathematical formulae, but begin to suspect her death was nothing more than an accident after finding evidence that she was becoming increasingly paranoid. Recognizing the researcher as a kindred spirit because they share similar thought processes, Abby becomes fixated on solving her equations and vows to finish to the work that the victim originally started. Unfortunately her new-found obsession soon begins driving a wedge between her and the rest of the team but thanks to Gibbs and the victim's mother, Abby eventually regains her priorites and resumes working on the case. As the team discover that the researcher was being poisoned, Abby deduces that the formula is a method of converting bacteria into fuel. The trail leads back to a jealous co-worker, who poisoned the researcher in order to take her job.
Meanwhile, Tony's latest fling causes trouble when she suggests role playing, but refuses to tell Tony what she has in mind. Her fantasy is later revealed to be Tony Manero from Saturday Night Fever, evidenced by a very uncomfortable Tony attempting to sneak out of the Navy yard in a white disco suit. *Source: 1*

Abby: "McGee. You're here. I've had some breakthroughs. Or, maybe it's more like some little bursts of inspiration because if I had a breakthrough I would have all the answers but I don't. Not yet, but I'm close. I know I am cuz I can feel it, I have a tingling feeling going up and down my spine…"
McGee: "How many Caf Pows you had today?"
Abby: "Um, eleven... teen"
McGee: "Did you even go home last night?"
Abby: "I've been inputting the raw data from the writings trying to crack the code to the formula and then BAM it hit me
McGee: "Then you think we should find him."
Abby: "Lt Thorson, she had a whole life out there somewhere. She was on a journey and it's my duty to follow it. That's how we're gonna find out who killed her. I can't do it alone, McGee. I need you to come with me."

Source: 3

Episodes Season 8

No.	German Title	US Title	Air Date USA	Air Date GER	Directed by	Written by
8.169	Mark 15	**Broken Arrow**	Nov 9, 2010	Mar 22, 2011	A.Brown	F.Cardea & G.Schenck

When investigating a murder of a former Navy Commander and friend of Vice Admiral Chase, the team stumbles across a piece of an old nuclear bomb that had been lost during the Cold War. Because the victim had connections to Tony's father, they track him down and question him. Eventually, much to Tony's annoyance, Gibbs recruits DiNozzo Sr. to use his contacts to infiltrate a private party attended by arms dealers. They discover that the CEO of a salvage company stumbled across the nuclear bomb and plans to sell it on the black market. The CEO is arrested, and both DiNozzos finally reconcile their differences with one another. *Source:* [1]

McGee: "Mmm… Mmmm… Nutter Butter."
Tony: "This is surreal. I feel like I'm in a James Bond movie directed by Fulani. I'm on a stakeout watching my father and Ziva go undercover while you munch on a Nutter Butter."
Ziva: "We are approaching the house."
McGee: "Alright, Ziva. We read you loud and clear."
DiNozzo, Sr.: "You look ravishing, Sophia." (Dinozzo Sr. puts his hand on her back.)
McGee: "Oh… oh… there it is."
Ziva: "Uh, uh."
Tony: "This is the beginning of the end of my career."
McGee: (in the house,) "Getting a solid image off the spy cam broach."
DiNozzo, Sr.: "There's Dan Mayfield. Come on, I'll introduce you to him."

Gibbs: "Come on DiNozzo, give me something."
Tony: "Uh. No luck on the money trail, Boss."
Gibbs: "McGee."
McGee: "Found several IMs in Thorson's email cash. One's a video. It's a man telling her she's an ungrateful ***** and if she leaves him, he will make her life hell."
Tony: "Wow. Mel Gibson much?"
Ziva: "Huh. There was no evidence Lt Thorson had a boyfriend."
Gibbs: "McGee."
McGee: "Yep. Running the IP address. Ok, ah, this is not her boyfriend. It's her boss."

Source: [3]

No.	German Title	US Title	Air Date USA	Air Date GER	Directed by	Written by
8.170	Fremde Feinde	**Enemies Foreign**	Nov 16, 2010	Mar 29, 2011	D.Smith	J.Stern

The team is designated to protect Eli David (Mossad Director & Ziva's father) during a NCIS conference. They must deal with three Palestinian terrorists trying to kill him. The episode ends on a cliffhanger when, after an attack by the terrorists at the conference apparently fails, Vance and David go to a safe house. Gibbs cannot reach them on the radio and Officer Hadar is shown to be lying dead at the safe house. *Source:* [1]

Episodes Season 8

No.	German Title	US Title	Air Date USA	Air Date GER	Directed by	Written by
8.171	Vertraute Feinde	**Enemies Domestic**	Nov 23, 2010	Apr 5, 2011	M.Horowitz	J.Stern

Gibbs arrives at the scene to find Hadar dead, Vance critically injured, and Eli missing. Eventually, the team tracks down Eli, who had gone into hiding to elude his assassins. They then deduce that the man who planted the bomb is an insider at NCIS. During the episode, Gibbs revisits Operation Trident, Vance's first job with NIS and when he met Eli David. Gibbs originally comes to the conclusion that Eli tried to have Vance killed during the op by tipping off his primary target: a Soviet operative called the Russian. When Eli is found, it is revealed that Vance and Eli had actually worked together during the op to stop the Russian and his hit team which was the career builder for Vance. The insider in NCIS was the same person who mounted the operation in Amsterdam and whose plan was foiled by Vance and Eli. It is revealed that the insider is Riley McAllister, former head of the San Diego field office, and that he mounted the operation so that his area of expertise, Russia, would come back into a post-Cold War play which would have allowed him to become Director. He had hired the Russian, the same man that he later sent Gibbs to assassinate in Paris along with Jenny Shepard, to kill Vance and he had set up the bomb at the safe house to have revenge on Vance and Eli. He then tries to kill Vance in his hospital room... *Source: 1*

Tony: "McGyver. It's so obvious. I mean, why didn't I come up with that?"
McGee: "You got any in reserve waiting for the perfect opportunity?"
Tony: "That's not how my mind works. I mean, it's like scat in there.
Ya know?"
McGee: "Ah yes, animal dung. I always figured."
Tony: "Not animal dung. It's like jive, ya know. Bebop. It's unpredictable. I take lead guitar you
take vocals like McGlee McFlee McGflat McJagger."

Source: 3

No.	German Title	US Title	Air Date USA	Air Date GER	Directed by	Written by
8.172	Der Zeuge	**False Witness**	Dec 14, 2010	Apr 17, 2011	J.Whitmore, Jr.	S.Binder

The NCIS team investigates the disappearance of a Navy Petty Officer who is the sole witness in an upcoming murder trial. Meanwhile, Ziva and McGee attempt to discover the reason for Tony's strange behavior. Annie Wersching guest stars as Deputy District Attorney Gail Walsh. *Source: 1*

Ziva: "Ok. So..."
McGee: "So, Gibbs was there, you were there too. But Gibbs was speaking with an Israeli accent.
You sounded like Jimmy Palmer."
Ziva: "I'm not completely comfortable with the fact you had a dream about me."
McGee: "Well, it's not like I can control it."
Ziva: "You're not making me feel any better."

Ziva: "Another dream about work, McGee? Please tell me I was not in it."
McGee: "You weren't but your knives were. What do you think that means?"
Ziva: "Well. I do not want to speculate."

Source: 3

Episodes Season 8

No.	German Title	US Title	Air Date USA	Air Date GER	Directed by	Written by
8.173	Schiffe in der Nacht	**Ships in the Night**	Jan 11, 2011	Apr 26, 2011	T.Wright	R.Steiner & C.Waild

Gibbs and the NCIS team partner with Coast Guard Investigative Service (CGIS) Agent Abigail Borin to investigate the murder of a Marine First Lieutenant on a dinner cruise. The team learns of the victim's wealth, opening up new lines of investigation. The victim was the heir of a multimillion dollar corporation, and was intending to use his ownership to turn the corporation into a charity organization. Piecing together the clues, the team discovers that the victim's death was the result of a conspiracy between his sister, the family lawyer, and the corporation's CFO. Later, one of the victim's squadmates, who is also a lawyer, arrives at NCIS to deliver his last will and testament, which was intended to carry out the victim's wishes to reform his company. *Source:* [1]

Tony: "Two a.m. on a Friday night. In a parallel universe, the Tony DiNozzo that didn't become a cop is walking out of a bar with a beautiful lady he doesn't know the name of...yet."

Ziva: "How romantic."
Tony: "As romantic as your Cuban Casanova."
Ziva: "He's not Cuban."
Tony: "Oh, must be tough to make time for each other. You're stuck here finishing case reports while he's frolicking in the Miami sun."

Ziva: "He travels... a lot... which is why I'm using comp time to take three days off next week to go see him."

Tony: "You can't do that."
Ziva: "Why not? We're adults."
Tony: "No. Not that. You can't use comp days for time off."
Ziva: "According to the OPN Guide lines I can."
McGee: "Tony how long have you been a senior field agent?"
Tony: "I just never thought there was anything very useful in those things."
Ziva: "Even though NCIS employees are salaried, any scheduled overtime hours must be compensated monetarily or with time off."

McGee: "Yeah. I was actually told that they prefer us to take the time off."
Tony: "Well no one told me. They just send me the money."
McGee: "What are you complaining about?"
Tony: "I don't need more money. I need more time. Just think of all the women I could've dated."

Ziva: "I would rather not."
Tony: "Respectfully dated. But it's never too late."
Ziva: "What are you doing?"
Tony: "Tallying up my overtime."
Gibbs: "Well, ya' got more comin' Skippy. Grab your gear."
Tony: "Got another all nighter?"
Gibbs: "You can sleep when you're dead."

Source: [3]

Episodes Season 8

No.	German Title	US Title	Air Date USA	Air Date GER	Directed by	Written by
8.174	Nichts fragen, nichts sagen	**Recruited**	Jan 18, 2011	May 3, 2011	A.Brown	G.Glasberg

A petty officer's recruitment session at a college fair comes to a fatal end, prompting the NCIS team to solve his murder. The team learns of the petty officer's homosexuality, leading Gibbs to classify the murder as a possible hate crime. Ducky's predecessor at NCIS, Dr. Magnus (Bob Newhart), pays a visit. The team tracks down several suspects, but Gibbs eventually figures out that the killer was the father of one of the students the petty officer was advising. The father did not realize the petty officer was trying to help his son deal with his homosexuality, and feared he was attempting to start a relationship with him. Meanwhile, Magnus reveals the true reason for his visit; he is suffering from Alzheimer's disease and he was hoping that coming back to NCIS would help him regain his memories. To help Magnus, Ducky gives him a collection of pictures of all of the people Magnus had helped... *Source:* [1]

No.	German Title	US Title	Air Date USA	Air Date GER	Directed by	Written by
8.175	Die Kunst des Überlebens	**Freedom**	Feb 1, 2011	Jun 21, 2011	C.Ross, Jr.	N.Mirante-Matthews

The team investigates the murder of a marine. They find out his Marine wife (Christina Cox) was abused and that the husband had an affair. They find numerous suspects, but eventually narrow it down to a bar owner that the wife was also having an affair with. He admits to the murder because he felt the marine didn't deserve to have a wife like her. Meanwhile, McGee becomes the victim of identity theft, as somebody starts using his credit card to buy various expensive items. Tony tracks down the identity thief, who turns out to be the son of McGee's landlady. The boy remarks that he stole McGee's identity because he felt he was too boring and didn't take time to enjoy life. Also, since the purchases were clearly the result of fraud, McGee is only liable for $50. Together, Tony and the boy manage to convince McGee to come with them to buy video games. *Source:* [1]

No.	German Title	US Title	Air Date USA	Air Date GER	Directed by	Written by
8.176	Der Schlussstrich	**A Man Walks Into a Bar ...**	Feb 8, 2011	Jun 28, 2011	J.Whitmore, Jr.	G.Glasberg

A naval commander is found dead in his rack aboard ship, apparently murdered. The NCIS team investigates while having to deal with mandatory psychological evaluations conducted by Dr. Rachel Cranston, who is eventually revealed to be the older sister of their former colleague and friend, Agent Caitlin Todd. It is discovered that the commander had actually committed suicide due to facing mandatory retirement and having no other life other than the Navy, and his colleagues had disguised the suicide out of respect for him. *Source:* [1, 2]

No.	German Title	US Title	Air Date USA	Air Date GER	Directed by	Written by
8.177	Die schöne Tochter	**Defiance**	Feb 15, 2011	Jul 5, 2011	D.Smith	F.Cardea & G.Schenck

A botched assassination attempt in Belgravia forces NCIS to protect the Defense Minister's daughter Adriana, who is studying in the U.S. While the team is busy guarding Adriana, Gibbs attempts to investigate the death of the Marine who was killed protecting the minister. Meanwhile, Adriana begins developing a crush on McGee, but she is suddenly kidnapped by two armed attackers. Furious at their failure, Vance orders the team to solve the case in 48 hours or he will take McGee and Dinozzo's badges. The team discovers that Adriana, who disagreed with her father's policies, arranged her own kidnapping to pressure him. However, one of the conspirators becomes greedy and decides to hold her for ransom. Fortunately, the team is able to rescue her, but are unable to arrest her for her role in the plot due to diplomatic immunity. McGee is left to wonder if Adriana really did have feelings for him or if it was all just an act. *Source:* [1]

Episodes Season 8

No.	German Title	US Title	Air Date USA	Air Date GER	Directed by	Written by
8.178	Max Destructo	**Kill Screen**	Feb 22, 2011	Jul 12, 2011	T.Wharmby	S.Kriozere & S.D.Binder

The discovery of some extracted teeth and dismembered digits in a purse results in an NCIS investigation when they are identified as belonging to a Marine. As the team tries to track down the killer, an investigator from an electronic security firm arrives, having traced the source of a number of computer hackings to NCIS. This makes McGee nervous as he had regularly illegally hacked into government computers under Gibbs' orders. The team manages to track down Maxine, who is the dead Marine's girlfriend and is an avid gamer and computer expert. She begins to take a liking to McGee. However, McGee tries to maintain his distance due to the events in "Defiance". She reveals that she had accidentally uncovered some sort of encrypted code in an MMORPG which turns out to be a program capable of hacking the Pentagon. The team tracks down the programmer responsible and shuts down his program, but he is found dead. Gibbs and McGee deduce that the investigator that arrived earlier was behind the killings, since news of such a threat to American security could ruin his career. Later, Dinozzo manipulates events to get McGee to start dating Maxine. *Source:* [1]

No.	German Title	US Title	Air Date USA	Air Date GER	Directed by	Written by
8.179	Das Geld anderer Leute	**One Last Score**	Mar 1, 2011	Jul 26, 2011	M.Weatherly	J.Stern

NCIS discovers that one of its former investigative assistants found brutally stabbed to death was selling details for how to rob a warehouse full of valuable possessions. They discover that the warehouse contains items seized from a former Navy officer (JoBeth Williams) who used a Ponzi scheme to cheat many people out of their money. While investigating the warehouse, the team finds that something hidden in one of her desks was stolen. In order to find the killer, Gibbs makes a deal with the officer to downgrade her sentence to house arrest in return for divulging his identity. However, it is a ploy by Gibbs to lure out the real killer, a robber who lost his money trying to launder it through the officer's accounts. The officer grabs her notebook containing the accounts where she hid her money and flees, technically breaking her house arrest agreement. Gibbs and Ziva swoop in, arresting both the killer and the officer while at the same time getting the evidence they needed to put her away for life. Meanwhile, budget cuts cause personnel to be reorganized in NCIS, including the transfer of the Spain team to Washington DC. Tony immediately becomes infatuated with the new team leader, who apparently returns his feelings. *Source:* [1]

No.	German Title	US Title	Air Date USA	Air Date GER	Directed by	Written by
8.180	Das Geständnis	**Out of the Frying Pan**	Mar 22, 2011	Aug 2, 2011	T.O'Hara	Carroll, Steiner & Waild

Director Vance has Gibbs and his team assigned to the case of a drug-addicted teenager accused of patricide. Gibbs begins to question Vance's motives when the NCIS team begin to find inconsistencies in the investigation that lead him to believe his suspect is innocent. Tensions between Gibbs and Vance - fuelled by budget cuts and re-assignments in previous episodes - come to a head when Vance admits the victim was a close friend. After a lengthy investigation, NCIS discover that the boy's runaway mother had recently tried to re-enter his life, and killed his father in a rage when he refused to let the two meet. . *Source:* [1]

Episodes Season 8

No.	German Title	US Title	Air Date USA	Air Date GER	Directed by	Written by
8.181	Ein offenes Buch	**Tell-All**	Mar 29, 2011	Aug 29, 2011	K.R.Sullivan	A.Bartels

A dying message from a naval officer attached to the Defense Intelligence Agency leads Gibbs' team in search of a manuscript containing military information. As the team investigates further, they find the body of a murdered FBI agent, and discover that both victims were involved in the writing of a book exposing secret anti-terrorist operations. However, the team is forced to track down the anonymous author of the book when Navy intelligence officers destroy all copies of the book. With the author's help (who is also a former Marine Lieutenant who was discharged for a failed anti-terrorist operation), the manage to arrest an arms dealer who had stolen a shipment of military weapons, but find out that she wasn't the killer. With this new information, as well as new evidence from Abby, Gibbs deduces that the FBI agent's husband is the killer, since he mistakenly believed that his wife was having an affair. *Source:* [1]

No.	German Title	US Title	Air Date USA	Air Date GER	Directed by	Written by
8.182	Der Hafenmörder	**Two-Faced**	Apr 5, 2011	Sep 5, 2011	T.Wright	Mirante-Matthews&Steiner

The body of a seaman is found wrapped in plastic and doused with a hospital-grade cleanser, hallmarks of a serial killer known as the "Port-to-Port" killer who kills service personnel when they make landfall. Vance creates a task force to catch the killer, appointing Barrett as lead investigator as she had been tracking the killer since he struck in Rota, Spain. Tensions arise within the MCRT when Gibbs suspects Barret and DiNozzo are sleeping together, compromising the loyalties of the team. Ziva discovers her boyfriend Ray is a secret CIA liaison to NCIS and questions the entire nature of their relationship when she catches him in a lie. After several dead ends and the discovery of another victim (bringing the known total to five), the episode ends with Ziva and DiNozzo in a bar, discovering a human eyeball floating in a glass of gin and tonic sent by an unidentified patron. *Source:* [1]

No.	German Title	US Title	Air Date USA	Air Date GER	Directed by	Written by
8.183	Spiel der Masken	**Dead Reflection**	Apr 12, 2011	Oct 17, 2011	W.Webb	G.Schenck & F.Cardea

The Major Case Response Team investigates a murder in the Pentagon that was caught on camera. Complications arise when the killer himself is found dead in an apparent car accident, but Ducky claims it was impossible for him to have committed the murder that was caught on tape as he died two days earlier; eventually the team discovers the real killer was using an advanced silicone mask to impersonate the deceased so he could tamper with evidence implicating him in a botched special forces mission. Meanwhile, after trying to figure out the mystery of the eye from "Two-Faced", E.J. and Palmer discover that the eye from the previous episode can open MTAC when scanned. *Source:* [1]

Episodes Season 8

No.	German Title	US Title	Air Date USA	Air Date GER	Directed by	Written by
8.184	Besser spät als nie	**Baltimore**	May 3, 2011	Oct 24, 2011	T.O'Hara	S.Binder

After sending the NCIS team a message in the form of the eye in "Two-Faced" - revealed to belong to a person whose identity is classified - the Port to Port Killer seems to have struck with another victim: Danny Price, formerly DiNozzo's partner in the Baltimore P.D. homicide squad. Believing that the Port to Port Killer may have a connection to DiNozzo, the team begins to concentrate on his time in Baltimore. Inconsistencies in the autopsy reports lead them to suspect there is a copycat killer on the loose, and it is eventually revealed that a mistake caused by Palmer in a report sent out to law enforcement agencies gave the copycat killer the necessary knowledge to replicate the Port to Port Killer with near-perfect accuracy. Because of Palmer's mistake, NCIS is able to catch a would-be copycat before he can kill, as well as find Price's murderer - DiNozzo's former captain in Baltimore. The episode is intercut with flashbacks showing DiNozzo's first meeting with Gibbs in which DiNozzo arrested Gibbs while he was working undercover on a money laundering case. DiNozzo joins NCIS after finding himself unable to work with Price in the Baltimore PD, but unwilling to expose his former partner. *Source:* [1]

No.	German Title	US Title	Air Date USA	Air Date GER	Directed by	Written by
8.185	Schwanengesang	**Swan Song**	May 10, 2011	Oct 31, 2011	T.Wharmby	J.Stern

While chasing the Port to Port Killer, NCIS is placed on high alert when evidence comes to light that he has infiltrated the Navy Yard. They learn that his latest victim survived because somebody intervened and lost an eye in the process: the team's on-again, off-again enemy, Trent Kort. Kort names the Port to Port Killer as Lt. Jonas Cobb (Kerr Smith), the first member of a CIA assassination team who cracked under inhumane training. Kort was sent to locate Cobb and eliminate him. As the NCIS team close in on Cobb, they suffer a personal tragedy when Mike Franks is killed after attempting to apprehend him. With Cobb injured, armed and unaccounted for, Gibbs confronts Leon Vance over his decisions in recent weeks. Vance admits that the decision to put E.J. Barrett in charge of the case came from higher up. Gibbs realizes that Cobb identifies with him, and is likely targeting E.J. The episode ends with E.J. ignoring Vance's orders and attempting to apprehend Cobb. However, Cobb ambushes E.J. and they both get into a struggle, which E.J. begins to slowly lose. *Source:* [1]

No.	German Title	US Title	Air Date USA	Air Date GER	Directed by	Written by
8.186	Operation Frankenstein	**Pyramid**	May 17, 2011	Nov 8, 2011	D.Smith	G.Glasberg

Having learned the identity of the Port-to-Port killer after the death of Mike Franks, Gibbs and his team prepare for the worst when he makes his final strike close to the heart of NCIS, leading Ziva into a trap. When Ziva is found by McGee, DiNozzo, Gibbs and Ray Cruz, she reveals that it was misdirection while the killer, Lt. Jonas Cobb, infiltrates NCIS to target the people he holds responsible for turning him into a killer as a part of "Operation Frankenstein": Leon Vance, Trent Kort and the Secretary of the Navy. Everything he has done since killing his first victim in Spain has been with the sole intention of finding them - but knowing that the Secretary of the Navy is under twenty-four hour protection, Cobb changes tactics and instead targets E.J. Barrett who is not only the person who has been investigating him from the beginning of his killing spree, but is also the Secretary of the Navy's niece. The NCIS team are able to track Cobb back to the facility where he was put through his training and is seen "training" Trent Kort, Jimmy Palmer and Barrett. He claims he only ever did what he thought was right, but refuses to surrender and is shot and killed by Gibbs and Vance. The Secretary of the Navy resigns over the affair, Trent Kort goes into hiding in Israel and Mike Franks is given a state funeral in a coffin built by Gibbs. The episode ends with DiNozzo being given a classified assignment to "handle" an unknown person and that an NCIS agent is suspected of selling classified information. *Source:* [1]

Season 9 (Episodes 9.187- 9.210)

The ninth season of NCIS premiered on September 20, 2011, in the same time slot as the previous season and the third season of NCIS: Los Angeles premiered afterwards.

Season nine introduced several new recurring guest stars, most notably Dr. Samantha Ryan, a love interest for Gibbs. By the end of the season, NCIS and the Navy had found themselves under threat from a new and dangerous enemy: insurance CEO-turned terrorist, Harper Dearing, who lost his son in a fire aboard a Navy ship and is out for revenge against the Navy for not solving the problem that led to the fire and then not updating ships with the same problem. He also has a grudge against NCIS, as his son wouldn't have been on the ship if they had not transferred him. Managing to get a hold of powerful explosives, Dearing started firebombing Navy ships. However, towards the end of the season, Dearing stepped up his game: he had Director Vance abducted. Whilst NCIS found him quickly, it transpired that Dearing was only after Vance for his car, managing to rig up explosives in the car seat so that Vance would unknowingly deliver a car bomb to the Navy Yard. By the time Gibbs realized, it was nearly too late; the bomb detonated, resulting in major damage to the NCIS building, as well as many deaths and injuries and leaving the fates of Gibbs, Tony, McGee, Abby, Ziva and Vance unknown. Upon learning of the destruction, Ducky suffered a heart attack on the beaches of Miami. The finale aired on May 15, 2012.

The 200th episode of NCIS was aired on February 7, 2012.   *Source: 1*

Original Air Date USA   September 20, 2011 – May 15, 2012 on CBS

Original Air Date German Language   January 29, 2012 – Oct 23, 2012 on Sat 1

Episodes Season 9

No.	German Title	US Title	Air Date USA	Air Date GER	Directed by	Written by
9.187	Phantom 8	**Nature of the Beast**	Sep 20, 2011	Jan 29, 2012	T.Wharmby	G.Glasberg

Set over the course of several months, the episode follows a series of events surrounding the investigation given to Special agent Tony DiNozzo by SECNAV in "Pyramid", culminating in the death of an NCIS agent. Secretary Jarvis assigned Tony to the investigation after a dead Navy Captain was found with an incision in his arm. After Dr. Donald "Ducky" Mallard discovers security footage of Special agent Erica Jane "EJ" Barrett removing a microchip from the body of Special agent Gayne Levin, suspicion falls on her.

The Major Case Response Team begin to suspect EJ is the target of Tony's investigation, but EJ confides to Tony that Levin asked her to remove the microchip. The team learns that the microchips provide access to a classified Navy fleet, known as the 'Watchers'... *Source: 1*

Ziva: "Tonight we should all go out and celebrate."
McGee: "You mean a wedding down."
Ziva: "No. There is no wedding. I mean Palmer's not getting married until next Spring."
Gibbs: "It's called a 'wetting down'...means you're paying."

Source: 3

Episodes Season 9

No.	German Title	US Title	Air Date USA	Air Date GER	Directed by	Written by
9.188	Für immer jung	**Restless**	Sep 27, 2011	Jan 29, 2012	J.Whitmore, Jr.	S.D.Binder

A Marine named Thomas Hill collapses at his homecoming party, having been drugged and stabbed before arriving. As the NCIS team start digging through his past, they discover Hill's adopted younger sister is a twenty-seven year-old serial con artist who runs away from her foster families shortly before her "eighteenth" birthday. The evidence leads them to her uncle, the one pulling the strings in the scam, who killed Hill when he discovered the deception.

Meanwhile, Tony begins to feel remorse for schoolyard bullying during his time at boarding school, and enlists McGee's help in making amends. However, by the end of the episode, it is revealed that Tony was the victim of bullying and not the perpetrator. *Source:* [1]

Tony: "I have not been moping…feeling a little dejected, apathetic, perhaps"
McGee: "That's actually the definition of the word moping."
Ziva: "Then I guess you won't need this."
McGee: "Or this."
Tony: "What are this's?"
Ziva: "Gifts to cheer you up."
Tony: "Well. I have been feeling a little mopey. Thank you. Very sweet of you… Oh… two tickets to female mud wrestling? Thanks. I'll have to put a pin in that. An original recipe Probie...very sweet… very nice. Two more tickets to female mud wrestling. How old do you guys think I am?"

Ziva: "Physically or mentally?"
Gibbs: "DiNozzo. I got a gift for ya."
Tony: "Dead body?"
Gibbs: "Yep."
Tony: "Thank you, Boss. A gift I can use. Only thing I need to do right now is to keep working. See? This is what I need...work…keep me busy."

McGee: "Good. Think we can still get refunds."
Tony: "Never said I didn't want them."

Ziva: "No McGee. You do not have bags under your eyes. They're just trying to get your sheep."
McGee: "Goat. You sure because I've noticed in the past week…"

Ziva: "Why on Earth would you try to find the man that you strung up by his underwear? To do it again?"

Gibbs: "So Duck…she crazy or not?"
Ducky: "Crazy is not a technical diagnosis."
Gibbs: "Well I'm not a technical guy, Duck."

Source: [3]

Episodes Season 9

No.	German Title	US Title	Air Date USA	Air Date GER	Directed by	Written by
9.189	Das ANAX-Prinzip	**The Penelope Papers**	Oct 4, 2011	Jan 31, 2012	A.Brown	N.Mirante-Matthews

NCIS is assigned the case of Paul Booth, a Navy lieutenant who is found with McGee's business card from his days in Norfolk. Booth was a friend of McGee's grandmother, Penelope Langston, who developed a research project for the military known as the ANAX Principle before the outbreak of the Vietnam War. The ANAX Principle was then shut down for four decades before being restarted. It uses specially-bred caterpillars to create a genetically-engineered plague. Booth's killer is revealed as Max Ellsword, one of the original researchers of the ANAX Principle, who killed the lieutenant when Booth planned to reveal the program to the press. At the end of the episode McGee and his grandmother speak of how Gibbs reminds them of McGee's father. McGee ultimately decides to call his dad who he hasn't spoken to in seven years.
Meanwhile, Jimmy Palmer struggles with plans for his upcoming wedding. *Source: [1]*

McGee: "I'm talking about tough love tactics, Tony…the veneer of impenetrability."
Tony: "The skill of turning one word into a rallying cry."

McGee: "Well, Boss. I'm trying to penetrate Tellis's top secret files but the code is overly complicated it's almost indecipherable."
Gibbs: "Decipher it."
McGee: "Well that's just it. I…I can't. I mean I will. I will. I am."

Source: [3]

No.	German Title	US Title	Air Date USA	Air Date GER	Directed by	Written by
9.190	Der unsichtbare Dritte	**Enemy on the Hill**	Oct 11, 2011	Feb 7, 2012	D.Smith	G.Schenck & F.Cardea

An assassin who has evaded arrest over a lengthy period of time, "The Cooler", flees a news camera crew, but is placed in a fatal coma when hit inadvertently by a passing van during escape. Gibbs and his team subsequently discover the Cooler was contracted to assassinate Geoffrey Brett, a Navy Lieutenant Commander. Brett initially refuses a protective "detail" and then flirts with Ziva, who he later leaves stranded. Sifting through Brett's finances, the NCIS team find millions of dollars that have been stolen from the Navy in an account established under the name, "George Kaplan"; Kaplan's name was allegedly responsible for the payment to kill Brett. It is eventually revealed that Kaplan's female money manager, Drew, is paying off her gambling debts by embezzling from Kaplan and was also responsible for funding the "hit" on Brett. When Brett hears Kaplan's name, known only to Drew, he eludes Ziva in order to find Kaplan's money manager, who is later found hanged from an alleged suicide. Ducky suspects the apparent suicide is murder as Tony, an aficionado of older movies, remembers that "George Kaplan" is a phony identity in the 1950 film, North by Northwest. In a final interrogation scene, Brett confesses to accumulating money for his daughter's medical care and future (Ziva had previously admired a photo of Brett's daughter in a wheelchair), and then asks for a lawyer. In an episodic subplot, Abby volunteers to become a kidney donor and is accepted by a the clinic where her brother had also successfully volunteered. It later emerges that Abby's brother did not apply to be a donor and the siblings are puzzled, with dead parents and a senile aunty unable to assist. Gibbs helps Abby to track down the identity of the mysterious stranger, whose name is Kyle. The episode also reveals that Abby was adopted by her parents and in a previous scene, in which Abby contemplates a locket and an old-fashioned photo of a woman, is explained. Abby visits Gibbs at the conclusion of the episode to share her discovery. *Source: [1]*

Tony: "Who do you know that needs a kidney?"

Abby: "Oh I don't know 'em. I just volunteered."

Source: [3]

Episodes Season 9

No.	German Title	US Title	Air Date USA	Air Date GER	Directed by	Written by
9.191	Im sicheren Hafen	**Safe Harbor**	Oct 18, 2011	Feb 14, 2012	T.O'Hara	R.Steiner & C.J.Waild

Abigail Borin returns to NCIS when a U. S. Coast Guard Petty Officer, Cooper, is shot while inspecting an incoming vessel. The NCIS team discover that a Lebanese family seeking asylum has stowed away on the boat. As Ziva begins to bond with the family, evidence emerges that Cooper was shot with ammunition sold to the Lebanese government, and Gibbs begins to suspect a political connection. NCIS discover that Cooper was killed in order to force the vessel to dock at Norfolk, where a bomb on board would be detonated, destroying half the Norfolk naval base. The plot was masterminded by Hakim, one of the asylum seekers, as revenge for the death of his sister during an air strike during the Lebanese Civil War. However, his mother successfully manages to talk him down. Meanwhile, the team tries to find the perfect girlfriend for Gibbs, but once they decide on a candidate, Gibbs revealed that he had already dated her, but broke up because "perfect is boring". *Source:* [1]

Tony: "Wait. I think I have a solution."
Ziva: "What? A pet for Gibbs? A…a new hobby?"
Tony: "A new woman."
Ziva: "What're you talkin' about?"
Tony: "A new playmate for Gibbs."

Gibbs: "Ziva. Sometimes people do the wrong things for the right reasons."
Ziva: "People always think their own reasons are right, especially parents."

Source: [3]

No.	German Title	US Title	Air Date USA	Air Date GER	Directed by	Written by
9.192	Mehr über Mary	**Thirst**	Oct 25, 2011	Feb 21, 2012	T.Wright	S.Williams

An NCIS case changes from accidental death to murder when evidence reveals that a Navy lieutenant died of forced over-hydration. The team discovered that the victim, Jason Simms, had been drugged with ecstasy, causing severe dehydration; this led him to over-hydrate, causing water toxification. When a second victim, Alcott, is found bound to a tree and also dead by way of water toxification, NCIS realize that both Simms and Alcott had failed marriages, and had been members of outreach programs and targeted by a serial killer.
Meanwhile, Gibbs meets Ducky's new love interest, Mary, a woman he met online. McGee realizes that Mary is connected to the same program as Jason and Alcott, and is responsible for their deaths. Ducky is disturbed by his misplaced judgement of Mary, feeling guilty that he did not see her deception sooner. *Source:* [1]

Ziva: "Oh, Ducky you are my hero."
Ducky: "That's me… The Sir Galahad of caffeinated beverages."

Ducky: "As I thought. Water intoxication."
Gibbs: "Drunk on water?"
Ducky: "Seeming intoxicated was the least of his problems Jethro. Pryor to his near miss with the truck our Lieutenant here was well on the way to drowning in his own skin."

Gibbs: "Duck. I wish I had that Yogi Berra book of quotes for any occasion."
Ducky: "Jethro, psychotic behavior is so bizarre, yet I just can't understand how I coulda' missed it. I'll never trust my judgment again."

Source: [3]

Episodes Season 9

No.	German Title	US Title	Air Date USA	Air Date GER	Directed by	Written by
9.193	Das magische Dreieck	**Devil's Triangle**	Nov 1, 2011	Feb 28, 2012	L.Libman	S.D.Binder & R.Steiner

Gibbs and Fornell are approached by their mutual ex-wife, Diane, when her current husband disappears under suspicious circumstances. Both NCIS and the FBI are brought into the investigation. They soon realized that he was kidnapped to create a lone virus for distribution at a charity football game involving in five branches of the armed forces. Based on the level of pathogens in the equipment used to manufacture the virus, Abby is able to determine that the target is actually the VIP box, where some of the most powerful people in the armed forces are present. The kidnappers are led by a Department of Homeland Security agent, who was paid off by someone inside the military-industrial complex. With the threat over, Fornell and the FBI take control of the case.
Meanwhile, Tony is concerned that he is going prematurely bald, and Ziva and McGee express interest in Gibbs' relationship with Diane. *Source:* [1]

Gibbs Rule #69: Never trust a woman who doesn't trust her man.

Tony: "What I find interesting is how the same woman landed both Gibbs and Fornell."

Ziva: "Why? They're very much alike."
Tony: "I don't think so. Gibbs is wild savannah untamed. This Diane lady must have serious game to have landed a wild beast like that. Wonder what her game is."

Source: [3]

No.	German Title	US Title	Air Date USA	Air Date GER	Directed by	Written by
9.194	Der leere Sarg	**Engaged (Part I)**	Nov 8, 2011	Mar 6, 2012	J.Whitmore, Jr.	G.L.Monreal

A C-130 carrying the bodies of Marines killed in Afghanistan crashes. NCIS is given twenty-four hours to identify the bodies before they are released to their families, but complications arise when one of the bodies cannot be identified, and Gabriella Flores, a Marine who was killed in an attack on a local school-building project, remains unaccounted for. Accessing satellite footage of the bombing, the team realize that Flores is still alive, having tried to save two young girls — but moments later, she is captured by insurgents. The episode ends with NCIS preparing a rescue mission to save Flores. *Source:* [1]

Ziva: "Something's on your mind. I can see your wheels churning."
Tony: "Butter churns David. Wheels turn."

McGee: "Oh come on Tony. A bucket list?"
Tony: "Hey!! No snooping McSteve Austin. My life is none of your business, you bionic eyeballs."

Ziva: "You're writing about buckets?"
Tony: "It's a bucket list, Ziva. It's a list of things I'd like to accomplish before the end of the fourth quarter.
Life is short. I've gotta start making it count."

McGee: "Ride a ferris wheel naked?"
Tony: "Actually I've already done that. I should cross that off. Do you have a pen?"

Source: [3]

Episodes Season 9

No.	German Title	US Title	Air Date USA	Air Date GER	Directed by	Written by
9.195	Der Vorhof der Hölle	**Engaged (Part II)**	Nov 15, 2011	Mar 13, 2012	T.Wharmby	G.Glasberg

Gibbs and Ziva travel to Afghanistan in search of Gabriella Flores where they discover that a group of teachers in Flores' school-building project have become sympathetic to the Taliban cause, believing that the education program causes children - particularly young girls - to question their heritage and their place in society. Gabriella Flores is successfully rescued, but her commanding officer dies in the process. In order to make a political statement, the cell is planning a terrorist attack in Washington, plotting to blow up school buses carrying three hundred students from a private girls' school while on a field trip. Gibbs and his team track down the sole remaining terrorist (by tricking the terrorist's younger brother into revealing his knowledge of the attack, telling him that his older brother was killed in an ambush by the FBI, and that his sister committed suicide), and McGee jams the terrorist's cell phone from making calls, preventing the terrorist from detonating the bombs. *Source:* [1]

Tony: "Ah, McGee. I love the smell of coeds in the morning."
Tony: "I used to thrive on all night stake outs and sub zero surveillance. Maybe this is a sign something is missing from my life."

Tony: "I hate libraries."
McGee: "Another one of your fears?"
Tony: "Don't mock me."
McGee: "Yeah. What's a library smell like?"
Tony: "Lonely smart people."

Source: [3]

No.	German Title	US Title	Air Date USA	Air Date GER	Directed by	Written by
9.196	Die Sünden meines Vaters	**Sins of the Father**	Nov 22, 2011	Mar 20, 2012	A.Brown	G.Schenck & F.Cardea

Tony's father is accused of murder and Tony is sidelined during the investigation. After searching for clues, the team discovers that DiNozzo Sr was actually framed for the alleged death as a lawyer had committed the crime with his assistant who had drugged DiNozzo Sr, resulting in temporary memory loss. The episode ends with both DiNozzos spending Thanksgiving at Gibbs' house. *Source:* [1]

Gibbs: Didn't see this one coming.
Ducky: How could you? This is going to be a sticky one.
Gibbs: Blunt force trauma?
Ducky: Why do you need me? I'll know more when I get him out of the trunk.

McGee: "Don't give up hope, Tony."
Tony: "I gave up hope when he started dating girls younger than me, and that was in the late '80s."

Tony: "How'd it go with my father last night?...Where is he? "
Gibbs: "Autopsy."
Tony: "You shot him? Can't say I blame you."

Source: [3]

Episodes Season 9

No.	German Title	US Title	Air Date USA	Air Date GER	Directed by	Written by
9.197	Schüsse im Schnee	**Newborn King**	Dec 13, 2011	Mar 27, 2012	D.Smith	C.J.Waild

When a Navy captain is killed in a hotel room, NCIS must track down and protect his very pregnant companion from unknown assailants. They discover that his companion was a Marine who had had a romantic relationship with an Afghani native with strategically important land holdings in Afghanistan. With the father's death, the unborn child is due to inherit his land. Gibbs and Ziva manage to eliminate the Russian mercenaries sent to kidnap the child. They were hired by Afghani elders to prevent the child from falling into the hands of the United States, who they feared would use the child as a bargaining chip to gain control of their land. Meanwhile, Jimmy has problems of his own when he brings his future father-in-law to work. He is initially rude and unappreciative towards the team, wondering why Jimmy hasn't gotten a better job in the private sector. Angered, Jimmy chastises his father-in-law and tells him about all the good he can achieve in NCIS, convincing him to bless their marriage. *Source:* [1]

```
Ziva:  "You did not tell us that Wendy sent you a Christmas card."
Tony:  "Wendy who?"
McGee: "Your Wendy...Baltimore Wendy".
Ziva:  "Your former fiancee."
Tony:  "Oh yeah, that. What are you doing reading my Christmas cards? "
Ziva:  "It was pinned on the wall behind your desk".
Tony:  "People usually do that so that others can enjoy them".

McGee: "You know you never mentioned why you broke off the engagement with Wendy."

Tony:" Who said that I broke it off? "
McGee: "What? She left you at the altar?"
Tony:  "Didn't say that either."
```

Source: [3]

No.	German Title	US Title	Air Date USA	Air Date GER	Directed by	Written by
9.198	Geisterjagd	**Housekeeping**	Jan 3, 2012	Apr 9, 2012	T.O'Hara	S.Williams

The investigation of a Navy Commander's murder leads the team to E.J. Barrett to reopen their investigation into Agent Stratton. In addition to contending with the bitter feelings about E.J. leaving him in the earlier ambush, DiNozzo is forced to confront his status with Ziva. The team learns that Stratton is still after Agent Barrett. They reveal to the ONI Director that they know he is in league with Stratton, who is actually a rogue black ops agent named Cole. They trick the Director into filtering false information to Cole, who then kills the Director to tie up loose ends. Using E.J. as bait, the team manages to arrest Cole. With the threat to her life now over, E.J. decides to return to her family, finally ending her relationship with DiNozzo. Afterwards, DiNozzo and Ziva finally agree to try and pursue a relationship, but at that moment Ray finally calls Ziva. *Source:* [1]

```
McGee: "Morning."
Ziva:  "Hey."
Tony:  "Meh."
McGee: "I never thought I'd end up being known as the cheerful one at the office."

Tony:  "Wait, what?"
Ziva:  "Are you saying we're not cheerful?"
McGee: "Last couple weeks, I'd say more, I don't know, surly?"
Ziva:  "Surly?"
Tony:  "Surly you're McStaken."
```

Source: [3]

Episodes Season 9

No.	German Title	US Title	Air Date USA	Air Date GER	Directed by	Written by
9.199	Ein verzweifelter Mann	**A Desperate Man**	Jan 10, 2012	Apr 16, 2012	L.Libman	N.Mirante-Matthews

NCIS investigates the death of Navy lieutenant Maya Burris, whose body was found at a construction site. Ziva thinks about her future and has a life-changing decision to make when Ray asks her to marry him. However, Ziva later finds out that the murdered lieutenant was killed by Ray, who went rogue from the CIA in order to complete an assassination he had botched overseas. Ray is arrested and Ziva breaks up with him since she no longer feels she can trust him. *Source: [1]*

Ziva: "I did not say no. I just have to make sure that I am ready. That we are *both* ready."

Tony: "Nobody's ready for marriage - trust me. If they were, the divorce rate wouldn't be 50% - not to mention the murder rate."

Source: [3]

No.	German Title	US Title	Air Date USA	Air Date GER	Directed by	Written by
9.200	Was wäre wenn …	**Life Before His Eyes**	Feb 7. 2012	Apr 23, 2012	T.Wharmby	G.Glasberg

During a routine stop in a diner for his morning coffee, Gibbs finds himself shot. He then suddenly finds himself inside a spectral version of the diner where he sees various characters from the past and present, both living and dead. He meets Mike Franks, who tells him that this is an opportunity for him to reflect on his past actions. He shows him an alternate future where Kate hadn't died, where Kate and DiNozzo are married with a newborn baby, but as a result Ziva stays with Mossad and is eventually arrested by NCIS. Gibbs then meets his mother, and he reaffirms that he had always loved her. Disgraced NCIS Agent Riley McCallister then appears and questions Gibbs' decision to murder Pedro Hernandez. Gibbs has Mike show him the future where he had never killed Hernandez, and it is revealed that he would have left NCIS and become a broken, reclusive alcoholic who pushes away any attempts to reach out to him. Finally, he meets Shannon and Kelly, who show him a future where they had never died. Gibbs would have stayed a Marine, but would have been killed in action overseas. Through this experience, Gibbs learns that he should not regret the choices he has or had not made.

This experience is related to a case one day before the shooting, where a Petty Officer and civilian contractor are found shot aboard a drydocked warship. They were attempting to steal the ship's military hard drives and sell them to the Chinese. However, the third accomplice, Michael Rose, eventually balks and is forced to kill his co-conspirators in self defense. Michael's son, Steven, pleads to Gibbs that his father was trying to do the right thing, and he was just misguided. Gibbs decides not to help Michael. On the day that Gibbs is shot, he draws his pistol but refuses to fire when he realizes that the shooter is Steven. Steven fires, but only hits Gibbs in the shoulder. Steven is subdued by several bystanders and he apologizes for shooting Gibbs. The next day, McGee tells the rest of the team that he turned down Director Vance's offer for a promotion to Okinawa since he feels there is still a lot of good he can do where is right now. Despite being injured, Gibbs returns to work, freshly inspired by his near death experience. *Source: [1]*

Tony: "Riva. Viza. No no no, Tiva."
Ziva: "Ziva. My name is Ziva David."
Tony: "Ah, Ziva, the Icy Israeli. I followed you to a hotel pool once."
Ziva: "Clearly I made an impression. Cannot say the same about you."

Source: [3]

Episodes Season 9

No.	German Title	US Title	Air Date USA	Air Date GER	Directed by	Written by
9.201	Superhelden	**Secrets**	Feb 14, 2012	Aug 20, 2012	L.Libman	S.D.Binder

When a Navy Captain is found dead with an unusual costume under his uniform, Tony must work with Wendy Miller, a journalist who is also his ex-fiancée, to find the killer. It is revealed that Wendy had called off the marriage at the last minute and neither she nor DiNozzo talked to each other for over nine years. The team discovers that the murdered Captain was a Real Life Superhero, a member of a group of costumed community activists and vigilantes. In addition, a failed assassination attempt on Wendy's life leads the team to believe that the case involves one of her stories. Eventually, Gibbs and the team realize that a number of other Superheroes were killed in surrounding districts, and figure out that they were carried out by a corrupt real estate investor who feared that the crime fighting activities of the Superheroes would raise the land values of the property he wanted to purchase. Afterwards, DiNozzo asks Wendy why she left him, and she admits that she wasn't ready for commitment at the time. However, she does leave open the option of restarting their relationship. *Source:* [1]

Tony: "Um, Ziva got a speeding ticket! And I sometimes get coffee for free. But I tip big! All right, let's have it."

Gibbs: "Let's go. Dead Navy captain."
Ziva: "Do you ever get the feeling that he enjoys being smacked in the head?"
McGee: "I'd rather not think about it."

Tony: "Sorry, I'm just--"
McGee: "Really pensive."
Tony: "Confused."
McGee: "Why, because you made out with your ex-fiance today?"
Tony: "What are you talking about?"
McGee: "Lipstick. It's not your color."

Tony: "Eagle eye, McGee"

Source: [3]

No.	German Title	US Title	Air Date USA	Air Date GER	Directed by	Written by
9.202	Geheimniskrämer	**Psych Out**	Feb 21, 2012	Aug 27, 2012	D.Smith	G.Glasberg & R.Steiner

Dr. Robert Banks, a prominent Navy psychologist, is found dead from an apparent suicide, and happens to be one of Dr. Cranston's patients. Cranston believes that Banks was murdered, and the team finds evidence that her suspicions are correct. They then begin investigating Banks' work as a psychological warfare agent. However, the Psy Ops Director, Dr. Samantha Ryan, is reluctant to give Gibbs any useful information. Believing that Ryan is hiding something, Gibbs reveals that he knows where her son goes to school, which is supposed to be classified information. Ryan then gives Gibbs the necessary clues to solve the case in return for him keeping her son's whereabouts a secret. The team finds out that the murder was perpetrated by his daughter, who wanted the money from his life insurance policy, and one of Banks' co-workers who she seduced into helping her.
Afterwards, Ryan calls Gibbs in the middle of the night, telling him that he has a special gift for making people feel safe, and asks him out for breakfast, to which he replies that he knows a diner that is open 24 hours. *Source:* [1]

Gibbs Rule #42: Don't ever accept an apology from someone that just sucker-punched you.

Tony: "Boss local LEO'S outside say there's a woman outside who claims to be the victims doctor."

Gibbs: "Let her in."
Tony: "Doctor.. Kate's sister."

Source: [3]

Episodes Season 9

No.	German Title	US Title	Air Date USA	Air Date GER	Directed by	Written by
9.203	Der schmale Grat	**Need To Know**	Feb 28. 2012	Sep 3, 2012	M.MacLaren	G.Schenck & F.Cardea

When Chief Petty Officer Wiley is murdered before he can divulge information about infamous arms dealer Agah Bayar, Special agent Leroy Jethro Gibbs is immediately on the case. As he and his team investigate, they discover that Wiley sold top secret information about America's stealth communication network to Bayar. However, Gibbs is then approached by the DIA and ordered to halt the investigation. Gibbs then decides to pursue Bayar's mistress. Meanwhile, the young and bumbling Probationary agent Ned Dorneget tries to butter up Gibbs in hopes of joining the team. Gibbs decides to send him and Special agent Timothy McGee to pick up the mistress, but it is revealed that she is an SVR agent, and quickly escapes custody. McGee accuses Dorneget of getting seduced by her, but Dorneget counters by admitting that he is gay. Gibbs and Director Leon Vance then deduce that the entire case was a DIA plot to leak faulty information to the Russians in order to sabotage their stealth communication research, using Wiley as the patsy. The plan begun to go awry when Wiley was busted for drug possession and tried to talk to Gibbs forcing the Russians to kill him to save their operation. Bayar, who was aware of the plan, acted as the middleman while the SVR agent was the courier. Source: [1]

Tony: "Boss local LEO'S outside say there's a woman outside who claims to be the victims doctor."

Gibbs: "Let her in."
Tony: "Doctor.. Kate's sister. Tony: McGee, what's Ziva doing?"
McGee: "Memorizing her speech."
Tony: "Speech?"
McGee: "Director Vance volunteered her to speak at a high school career day."
Tony: "In what language, Vulcan?"
Ziva: "I can hear you, Tony. I do not need you making this worse. Back up."
McGee: "I think you mean back off."
Tony: "Why are you so uptight, Ziva?"
Ziva: "Public speaking is not my thing. It makes me nervous."
Tony: "Nervous? What are you talking about? I've seen you take down armed terrorists without breaking a sweat."

Ziva: "I'm trained for that."

Source: [3]

No.	German Title	US Title	Air Date USA	Air Date GER	Directed by	Written by
9.204	Verräterische Zeiten	**The Tell**	Mar 20, 2012	Sep 10, 2012	T.Wright	G.L.Monreal

In the episode, Gibbs must work together with both Secretary of the Navy (Matt Craven) and Dr. Samantha Ryan (Jamie Lee Curtis) to find out who leaked top secret information. They believe that Wickes, a close personal friend of the Secretary and CEO of military contractor Wickes Steel, might be involved. In order to to confirm their suspicions, they fake the Secretary's assassination. While Ryan believes that Wickes is guilty, Gibbs believes otherwise. As the team investigates further, they track down the hacker responsible for obtaining the top secret information, and find out that the leaked information was just a ruse to distract them. The hacker's real objective was to hack into a secret AUTEC account that was inactive and had accrued over $300 million in interest. Further investigation reveals that Wickes' half brother was responsible for plot, as he believed the money could have helped save their company from bankruptcy. Meanwhile, Gibbs and Ryan's relationship between each other begins to grow closer. Source: [1]

Episodes Season 9

No.	German Title	US Title	Air Date USA	Air Date GER	Directed by	Written by
9.205	Der gute Sohn	**The Good Son**	Mar 27, 2012	Sep 17, 2012	T.O'Hara	N.Mirante-Matthews & S.Williams

In the episode, NCIS Director Leon Vance is personally involved in a case when Gibbs suspects his brother-in-law, Michael Thomas, to be the killer of a Petty Officer. When trying to find the victim's girlfriend, they discover that she had been sleeping with another sailor from the same ship and apprehend him. Both sailors were friends and had gotten in a fight over the girlfriend. However, Gibbs still suspects Michael is guilty, due to his criminal record, but Vance maintains that even though Michael had a tough childhood, he is still innocent. When more evidence implicating the second sailor surfaces, Vance takes Michael back to his house, though his wife is reluctant to accept Michael due to his past. Further investigation reveals that the sailor was innocent,and that the victim had been involved in a illegal gambling den that was scamming its players. Fingerprints reveal that Michael was involved in the gambling ring. Vance confronts Michael with this information, and Michael admits his involvement, and that he killed the victim in self defense when he accused him of cheating him out of his money. Vance, tired of Michael's repeated failures and lies, finally but reluctantly turns his back on him and has him arrested. *Source:* [1]

Ziva: "I'm worried, McGee. What if he's sick?"
McGee: "He'd be whining. He always whines when he's sick."
Tony: "You two really suck at whispering. Believe it or not, I can hear you. I'm not sick. Every once in a while I just need to power down, be still, reflect on this little trip through the cosmic rip. I need to find my deep calm."

McGee: "Yeah, he's sick."

Source: [3]

No.	German Title	US Title	Air Date USA	Air Date GER	Directed by	Written by
9.206	Missionare	**The Missionary Position**	Apr 10, 2012	Sep 25, 2012	A.Brown	A.Abner

After the corpse of a Marine lieutenant falls out of the sky, Tony helps Ziva and her mentor, Monique, look for missing Navy Chaplain Wade in Colombia. Chaplain Castro, who is one of Wade's colleagues, also decides to travel with them. They theorize that Wade had been kidnapped by a local drug cartel while vaccinating villagers, and narrowly escape an ambush. Chaplain Castro reveals that part of the reason why she is helping them is because she was supposed to have performed Wade's mission. Meanwhile, Gibbs and McGee try to track down the plane that dropped the body. Ryan informs him that the vaccination mission was a covert CIA operation to obtain the DNA of cartel leaders. Tony, Ziva, and Monique manage to rescue Wade from the cartel and escape Colombia. Monique decides to stay behind, admitting that she is involved in something too serious to reveal. Jimmy Palmer chooses his best man but in a surprise twist, he chooses Abby to be his Best Woman much to her delight. *Source:* [1]

Gibbs: "Cause of death."
Ducky: "You've gotta be kidding. Well, stabbed, blunt force trauma, shot..."
Tony: "Not to mention the whole plummeted to Earth thing."

Ducky: "Mr. Palmer, I would no sooner care to plan your bachelor party than actively seek a root canal. That's not to say that I'm not deeply honored. But take my advice: mentors make terrible wingmen."

Tony: "McGee's idea of an incredible party is a bunch of free corn nuts and an Xbox marathon."
McGee: "Sounds pretty good to me."

Source: [3]

Episodes Season 9

No.	German Title	US Title	Air Date USA	Air Date GER	Directed by	Written by
9.207	Aquamarin	**Rekindled**	Apr 17, 2012	Oct 2, 2012	M.Horowitz	C.J.Waild & R.Steiner

The NCIS team deal with an arsonist, which has links to the mysterious Watcher Fleet. While investigating, the team up with arson investigator Jason King, who DiNozzo feels uncomfortable around. They find that the arson was to cover the up the theft of a top secret Navy file codenamed "Aquamarine". When a second fire occurs on board a cargo ship, the team goes to investigate as well. Jason saves DiNozzo's life after accidentally setting off a trap. Closer investigation reveals that the ship contained faulty wiring that could cause the entire ship to explode under the right conditions. DiNozzo finally reveals his past with Jason. He saved Jason's life from an arson fire, but was forced to abandon his sister, and Jason has resented him ever since. When they finally track down the arsonist, he reveals that he was hired to steal the file, but is killed by a carbomb. The team recovers the stolen files, and finds out that Aquamarine was a list of Navy ships that had been installed with the faulty wiring. The Watcher Fleet so far had only been able to retrofit a third of the affected ships. While Gibbs has NCIS warn the Navy about a possible terrorist attack, DiNozzo sets the record straight with Jason, telling him that he had to make a choice, and that rescuing him was his inspiration to become a police officer in the first place. Meanwhile, the U.S.S Brewster falls victim to an arson attack. *Source: 1*

McGee: "Nice look, Tony. What is that? Blue collar meets Ivy League?"
Ziva: "Chic farmhand?"
Tony: "Ring a ding ding. I call it 'practical playboy'."

Tony: "Thanks, I'm going for a new look. Crime-scene chic. Actually earning some style points."
Gibbs: "One more word about your boots and you're gonna find mine up your ass, DiNozzo."

Source: 3

No.	German Title	US Title	Air Date USA	Air Date GER	Directed by	Written by
9.208	Auftrag in Neapel	**Playing With Fire**	May 1, 2012	Oct 9, 2012	D.Smith	G.Schenck & F.Cardea

In the aftermath of the arson attack aboard the U.S.S Brewer, the NCIS team discovers evidence of it being caused by the same arson explosive from earlier. Fortunately, the explosive went off prematurely only causing minor damage to the ship and two casualties, including the bomber. They also discover that a similar explosive was found on the U.S.S Benjamin Franklin stationed in Naples, Italy. Ziva and DiNozzo team up with NCIS Agent Stan Burley to apprehend the bomber who they manage to capture, though Burley is injured in the process. After interrogation, Gibbs discovers that the mastermind of the bombings is an investment fund CEO named Harper Dearing. After finding out that Dearing has been missing for over a year, Gibbs declares him NCIS' most wanted fugitive.
Meanwhile, Ducky admits to Gibbs that he is in a moral dilemma since he inherited a large sum of money from his deceased mother, but does not know what to do with it. Ultimately, he decides to make Gibbs the executor of his will, and intends to donate much of his newfound wealth to a charity meant to provide scholarships to the children of US Marines. *Source: 1*

Tony: "Andiamo, bambina!" *(Let's go baby)*
Ziva: "Dove?" *(where?)*
Tony: "Gear up! We're leaving for Naples."
Ziva: "Naples, Italy?"
Tony: "Si. I'm going home to grab some clothes. You should do the same. We're hopping the military flight from Andrews Air Force Base."
Ziva: "Is this one of your practical jokes?"
Tony: "Nope. Gibbs orders...It's a good thing you canceled your Pilates weekend."
Ziva: "Who told you?"
Tony: "I'm a very special agent. I have my ways."

Source: 3

Episodes Season 9

No.	German Title	US Title	Air Date USA	Air Date GER	Directed by	Written by
9.209	Menschenopfer	**Up in Smoke**	May 8, 2012	Oct 16, 2012	J.Whitmore, Jr.	S.D.Binder

When a bug is found in Probationary Agent Ned Dorneget's tooth, the team goes full force in the effort to arrest Harper Dearing. The team receives multiple suspects, one of which is Dorneget's dentist, which ends up leading to an MTAC call from Dearing himself. He reveals the reason he is doing this is Gibbs' fault. The team discovers that Dearing's son was a Navy sailor who was killed by a manufacturing defect that could have easily been avoided, and that his plans are to take revenge on the Navy by exploiting similar weaknesses. Since Gibbs was in charge of the case, Ryan surmises that Dearing has cast Gibbs as his nemesis. The team pursues a lead from information provided by Ryan that Dearing might be manufacturing defective Navy artillery rounds. However, the plot turns out to be a wild goose chase concocted by Dearing, which leads Gibbs to wonder whether Ryan is really on their side or not. After receiving a text from Dearing, Gibbs calls DiNozzo and finds out that Director Vance is missing. *Source:* [1]

Palmer: "You guys, just give me one hint as to what Abby has planned. It is my bachelor party, okay? I have a right to know."

Tony: "Sorry. She swore us to secrecy, and she scares me more than you."
Palmer: "God. I think I made a big mistake making her my best man."
McGee: "Relax, Jimmy. Everything is fine. Just make sure you're up on your hepatitis vaccinations."

Palmer: "Hepatitis?"
Tony: "And get a good pair of knee pads."
McGee: "And a good helmet."
Palmer: "You guys are messing with me."
Tony: "Are we? Two words."
McGee: "Abby Sciuto."

Tony: "I'm telling you, Ryan was there."
Ziva: "So what if she was? I was happy to gossip when things were just getting started, but now that they are a couple I think we should just back off."

Tony: "How are you not interested in other people's private lives?"

Source: [3]

No.	German Title	US Title	Air Date USA	Air Date GER	Directed by	Written by
9.210	Für Evan	**Till Death Do Us Part**	May 15, 2012	Oct 23, 2012	T.Wharmby	G.Glasberg

After investigating Vance's car, the team locates Vance at a family plot where Vance finds himself next to the body of a sailor killed along with Dearing's son. After picking him up, the team finds another message with a horse jaw that leads them to a retired NCIS agent who handled a case that sent Dearing's son to the destroyer that claimed his life. However, Dearing blows up the agent's house and leaves them a message, soon confronting Dr. Ryan by threatening her son and forcing her to flee when he bails out her jailed ex-husband. Meanwhile, Jimmy is nervous on whether or not to marry with all of this, but Ducky tells him to go through with it, and he will join him, and Jimmy asks Breena to advance the wedding so he could return. Gibbs recruits Cole based on Ryan's profiling of Dearing to lure him into a trap, but Dearing avoids it and leaves a phone call on the Navy Yard. Playing the call makes the team realize there is a bomb in Vance's car, installed when he was abducted, and the whole building is evacuated. Cole attempts to defuse the bomb but is killed in the process when the bomb detonates, damaging part of the NCIS building with Gibbs and his team still inside. Ducky receives a phone call about the attack and is asked to autopsy the bodies, but the shock and stress of the call causes him to have a heart attack and collapse alone on a beach, leaving everyone's fates unknown. *Source:* [1]

Season 10 (Episodes 10.211-10.234)

The tenth season of the police procedural drama NCIS premiered on September 25, 2012, in the same time slot as the previous seasons, Tuesdays at 8pm. The season premiere was seen by 20.48 million viewers, focusing on the aftermath of the bombing of the Navy Yard from the ninth-season finale and culminating with the apprehension of Harper Dearing, who is killed when he attempts to resist arrest.

The season continues with mostly standalone episodes until the "Shabbat Shalom" and "Shiva" story arc, which focuses on the deaths of Eli David and Jackie Vance and sets the rest of the season into motion. Leon Vance and Ziva David soon discover that Mossad Deputy Director Ilan Bodnar was behind the attack, and set out for revenge. They track Bodnar to Berlin, but later learn that he had never left the United States. Going against orders from the Department of Homeland Security, Ziva finds Bodnar on a ship headed for South Africa and kills him. This sparks a massive investigation by the Department of Defense, headed by Richard Parsons. His sneaky and unprofessional methods cause the team to question his true intentions. Everyone soon realizes that he is not interested in Ziva or Vance, but has instead set his sights on Gibbs. Parsons pressures Gibbs to admit that he and his team have broken the law on countless occasions and to come forward and admit everything that he has done. After a long feud, Gibbs is freed of his charges and sent on a top-priority mission, while Ziva, DiNozzo, and McGee resign from the agency.

The season ends with a cut to four months later, showing Gibbs aiming a sniper rifle at FBI agent Tobias Fornell. The season finale aired on May 14, 2013.

Source: [1]

Original Air Date USA	September 25, 2012 – May 14, 2013 on CBS

Original Air Date German Language	January 6, 2013 – Oct 20, 2013 on Sat 1

Episodes Season 10

No.	German Title	US Title	Air Date USA	Air Date GER	Directed by	Written by
10.211	Mit äußerster Härte	**Extreme Prejudice**	Sep 25, 2012	Jan 6, 2013	T.Wharmby	G.Glasberg

The NCIS team regroup in the aftermath of the Navy Yard bombing. Gibbs, Abby, Palmer, and Vance escape the explosion unscathed, while Ducky and McGee are hospitalized. Ziva and Tony remain unaccounted for, trapped in an elevator, though they are able to escape. The FBI is called in to aid in the hunt for Harper Dearing, only for Dearing to set a trap that kills four agents. The President authorises the use of "extreme prejudice" to bring Dearing to justice, but the trail runs cold when Dearing seemingly kills himself to avoid capture. Gibbs is unconvinced, and puts pressure on Dearing's sister-in-law to reveal his location. NCIS raid Dearing's home, only to find that he has once again eluded them. Gibbs convinces Vance that the only way to approach Dearing is to approach him alone; Vance agrees and Gibbs is finally able to confront Dearing, who compares himself with Gibbs and the pain of unjustly losing a child. Gibbs stabs and kills Dearing in self defense before Dearing can shoot him, as the latter man planned to do, and the episode ends two months later with Gibbs passing by a memorial to the victims of the bombing. *Source:* [1]

No.	German Title	US Title	Air Date USA	Air Date GER	Directed by	Written by
10.212	Duftmarken	**Recovery**	Oct 2, 2012	Jan 13, 2013	D.Smith	S.Williams

The NCIS building goes under renovations as the team goes under psych evaluations. Then, they are called into service when the former armory manager is found dead in the river, having disappeared after the bombing. Soon, they discover she was murdered and find that one of the heads of renovation is the murderer, jealous of her boyfriend (an armorer)'s relationship with the manager. Meanwhile, Abby is shown to have nightmares that she is dead in autopsy. Gibbs asks the psychologist to check on Abby. She later tells Gibbs that the nightmares are a result of her fear of being alone, leading Gibbs to advise her to confront her biological brother. She manages to do so and they acknowledge their bloodline. When the psychologist, Miles Wolf (Steve Valentine), confronts Vance, he reveals that he wants the building back to its original standards as he wants to go back in time and prevent the attack, believing he is responsible for the attack. *Source:* [1]

No.	German Title	US Title	Air Date USA	Air Date GER	Directed by	Written by
10.213	Falscher Mond	**Phoenix**	Oct 9, 2012	Jan 20, 2013	T.OHara	S.D.Binder

Realizing that he may have made a mistake in one of his autopsies, Ducky decides to exhume the remains of a deceased Marine to find out the true cause of his death. However, since he is still not cleared for active duty due to his heart attack, Ducky recovers the body without authorization. However, he discovers that the Marine did not die from alcohol poisoning like he had initially thought, but was actually poisoned in a way to make it look like it was alcohol. Meanwhile, the team investigates the death of a Marine sergeant and discovers he is connected to the cold case, as he has a copy of Ducky's exhumation request. Gibbs decides to put Ducky in charge of the case. Under Ducky's leadership, the team discovers that the poisoned Marine had been running a con by selling counterfeit moon rocks to rich buyers. Realizing that some of the buyers had their counterfeit rocks sent to NASA to be examined, the team deduces that one of the NASA scientists was also in on the plot. After closing the case, Ducky feels more confident in his ability to be a lead investigator. Later, Gibbs informs Ducky that he has finally been cleared to resume his duties as chief medical examiner, much to an overworked Palmer's relief. *Source:* [1]

Episodes Season 10

No.	German Title	US Title	Air Date USA	Air Date GER	Directed by	Written by
10.214	Ghostrunners	**Lost at Sea**	Oct 23, 2012	Jan 27, 2013	T.Wharmby	C.J.Waild

NCIS is called in to investigate a helicopter crash when the missing crew washes up on the shore. However, the pilot is still missing. Meanwhile, Ziva dares DiNozzo and McGee to ask out the first woman they see, which happens to be CGIS agent Borin, who is also investigating the crash. After interviewing the two conscious crew members, the team fails to find any information that can point to the exact location of the crash or the pilot. Ducky also notes that besides severe dehydration and exposure, the crew lacks any of the injuries typical with a helicopter crash. Soon after, while looking for any helicopter wreckage on the beach, DiNozzo and McGee find the pilot's corpse and discover that he was shot in the head. When confronted with this revelation, the crew claims that the pilot was mentally unstable and tried to commit suicide after finding out his son was terminally ill. However, Gibbs is skeptical after hearing differing accounts from the pilot's wife and commanding officer. When the fourth crew member regains consciousness, he admits that the pilot didn't try to commit suicide. With this new evidence, the team interrogates the crew again, and they finally crack and admit that they had planned to sell the helicopter. However, the pilot balked and attempted to have them arrested, only to be shot and killed by the buyer. The crew were then forced into a life raft and left to drift far from their supposed crash point. With the crew's testimony, the team tracks down and arrests the buyer and recovers the helicopter. Meanwhile, Ziva reveals to DiNozzo and McGee that she told Borin about the bet, and that it was a ploy to teach them a lesson about not inviting her out to their recreational activities. *Source:* [1]

McGee: Hi, Agent Borin. Uh, I wanted to know...do you like 80's cover bands? Because I have tickets. I mean, Tony got tickets. For us, I mean. Ah, you know, if you want to go, ah...I just figured that since we were both born around...you know, that you would remember the eighties... How old are you?
Borin: Are you asking me out, McGee?
McGee: Well, yeah, I, well, I've got tickets...
Borin: Yeah. Got that part.

Source: [3]

No.	German Title	US Title	Air Date USA	Air Date GER	Directed by	Written by
10.215	Leroy Jethro	**The Namesake**	Oct 30, 2012	Feb 3, 2013	A.Brown	G.Schenck & F.Cardea

The fatal and violent shooting of a Petty Officer in possession of an expensive sports car leads to the team to wonder how he got the car and why he was killed. They manage to trace the gun used in the murder to a local pawn shop, there Gibbs finds a Congressional Medal of Honor on display, despite the fact that selling the medal is illegal. The pawn store owner reveals that she bought the medal from an elderly veteran who needed the money badly. Gibbs discovers that the previous owner of the medal was Leroy Jethro Moore, a close friend of his father and the person he was named after. He remembers that his father and LJ had a falling out many years ago and LJ disappeared afterwards, leading Gibbs to decide to track him down. He finds out from his father that LJ allowed Gibbs' mother to commit suicide by drug overdose in order to end her suffering from terminal cancer, something that Gibbs' father had never forgiven him for. Additional investigation reveals that the deceased Petty Officer worked part time as a valet, and stole the sports car for a joyride. The team also traces ownership of the gun to a local university student. His true target was the car's actual owner, a billionaire entrepreneur who he believed stole his idea for a filesharing network, and the Petty Officer was killed in a case of mistaken identity. The suspect is then quickly apprehended. Meanwhile, Gibbs has his father and LJ meet each other for the first time in years, and convinces them to end their feud, pointing out that all three of them shared common ground in their love for Gibbs' mother. Gibbs' father and LJ finally make amends and renew their friendship, with Gibbs' father buying back LJ's medal and returning it to him. LJ also decides to move back to Stillwater now that the feud has ended. *Source:* [1]

Episodes Season 10

No.	German Title	US Title	Air Date USA	Air Date GER	Directed by	Written by
10.216	Trauma, Teil 1	**Shell Shock (Part I)**	Nov 13, 2012	Feb 10, 2013	L.Libman	N.Mirante-Matthews

The episode begins with two men trying to run from a gang, but they are eventually caught and beaten badly. The gang then drags one of the men into the darkness while the other flees. The next morning, the team is called over to investigate the body of the man who was dragged off, Sergeant Michael Torres. They find out that Torres was with his commanding officer, Captain Joe Westcott, and track down Westcott at Torres' house. Westcott tells the team about the attack, and how he feels guilty about how he didn't try to save Torres. However, Gibbs is not convinced that Westcott is telling the whole truth. More inconsistencies surface when Ducky's autopsy reveals that Torres was not beaten by a gang of men, but only a pair which contradicts Westcott's account. Surveillance footage of the attack does not provide an conclusive evidence either since the tape it was recorded on is corrupted.

Gibbs then has Westcott tell him about the story of how his squad was ambushed by insurgents in Iraq shortly before their tour of duty ended. Several of Westcott's men were killed and Westcott himself witnessed one of his men getting captured. However, rather than try to help him, Westcott fled in fear. Though the captured soldier is rescued by another squadmate, he dies shortly after due to his wounds. Westcott can't forgive himself for succumbing to cowardice, and it is revealed that he suffers from Post Traumatic Stress Disorder, as he is constantly reliving the ambush in his mind.

The team manages to clean up the surveillance footage and see that there were only three men involved in the fight: Westcott, Torres, and another man named Randall J. Kersey, who claims to have never seen Westcott nor has he been outside the country. They surmise that Westcott suffered another PTSD attack and believed Kersey was one of the insurgents and began to assault him. Torres tried to intervene but was knocked down and struck his head on the pavement, dying instantly.

After sending Westcott to therapy to have his PTSD treated, Gibbs has McGee obtain satellite photos of the insurgent base where Westcott had been ambushed. To the team's shock, they discover that Kersey was indeed present at the base as one of the insurgents. They raid Kersey's house, but are too late. Kersey has already fled, but the team discovers evidence that he had already built two bombs and is planning an attack.

Meanwhile, Tony finds an old camera with photos of his mother, who died when he was eight years old. Unfortunately, McGee gets a hold of Tony's embarrassing old high school portrait and Ziva gives him an endless amount of grief. *Source:* [1]

Tony: *(to Ziva)* I guess that she was the first woman to break my heart, and I don't like to talk about things like that. .

Ziva: The Little Prince. 'That which is essential is invisible to the eye.'
Tony: Ziva David, did you just quote a movie?
Ziva: No, I quoted a book. That was made into a movie.

Tony: Looks like our wannabe John Walker Lindh was planning something. Something big.
Gibbs: Not was. Is. Find him!

Source: [3]

Episodes Season 10

No.	German Title	US Title	Air Date USA	Air Date GER	Directed by	Written by
10.217	Trauma, Teil 2	**Shell Shock (Part II)**	Nov 20, 2012	Feb 17, 2013	T.Wright	G.Monreal

With Kersey on the run, Gibbs and the team try to track him down before he can stage his attacks. However, searches of his house and questioning his girlfriend fail to give them any leads. Meanwhile, Ziva begins acting strangely and is frustrated after a failed attempt to get tickets for an opera, which makes DiNozzo curious as he attempts to pry to find out what is troubling her.

With no options left, Gibbs brings back Westcott, hoping he can jog his memory to find out any leads. However, Westcott's PTSD interferes with his memories, and he is reluctant to help. Gibbs then takes him to the convenience store where he and Torres were last seen before Torres' death. Westcott then remembers seeing Kersey enter the store and hand off a piece of paper to a blue haired girl. As Gibbs tries to help Westcott deal with his PTSD, DiNozzo and Ziva stake out the store to see if the blue haired girl comes back. Ziva then finally admits that Thanksgiving is her deceased sister Tali's birthday, and that the holiday has always been difficult for her to deal with. She also reveals that she goes to an opera every year on Tali's birthday, as her sister had wanted to be a singer, but that they were all sold out this year. They then find and intercept the blue haired girl, who turns out to be an unwitting courier for the bomb. She leads the team to Kersey, where he is promptly arrested and his bomb is confiscated.

In interrogation, Gibbs attempts to play Kersey's conscience in order to get him to reveal the location of the second bomb. However, Kersey resists and spits on the pictures of Westcott's slain men. Witnessing this, Westcott flies into a rage and attacks Kersey. He then gets a sudden flashback and remembers seeing a picture of Kersey's girlfriend in the insurgent base, meaning she is his accomplice. Putting together the collected evidence, the team discovers that Kersey's girlfriend is planning to bomb a local senator's Thanksgiving party. Fortunately, they warn the police in time to have the bomb disarmed, and the team intercepts Kersey's girlfriend before she can escape.

With the case closed, Gibbs takes Westcott to see one of his men. They both make amends for what happened in the ambush, and are both determined to work through their PTSD. Westcott apologizes for running from the battle, but the squadmate corrects him, saying that Westcott had never fled from the battle, and in fact was the one to rescue the captured Marine. However, Westcott's guilt made him remember the event incorrectly. Westcott then feels much better about himself now that he knows that he was never a coward.

Back at NCIS headquarters, since Ziva missed the opera she had wanted to go to due to the case, DiNozzo sets up the sound system to play an opera so that she can imagine that she's at the opera with Tali at her side. *Source:* [1]

Ziva: *(to Tony)* Shut up! I'm sick of sitting in this car with you being nice to me!

Ziva: You're such a child. And then you wonder why I cannot talk to you.
Tony: So he's a hilarious veterinarian who likes the opera.
Ziva: Tony, there is no funny veterinarian...There is no one, actually. Only Tali.

Ziva: .... So every year, on her birthday, I go to the opera in honor of her. This year, this year was..."
Tony: Sold out.

Ziva: Abby was so excited Gibbs moved Thanksgiving to tonight.
Tony: Listen, I told the boss that you'd be a little late.

Tony: Did you know that McGee installed a crazy surround sound system in here? I came in one night and he was playing video games...wearing a cape.

Tony: *(music plays)* I know it's not the same, but maybe if you closed your eyes it would be like you're at the opera... and maybe even like Tali's there with you.

Source: [3]

Episodes Season 10

No.	German Title	US Title	Air Date USA	Air Date GER	Directed by	Written by
10.218	Käufer und Verkäufer	**Gone**	Nov 27, 2012	Feb 24, 2013	J.Whitmore, Jr.	R.Steiner & S.Williams

A Naval Officer is murdered while attempting to prevent the kidnapping of his teenage daughter, Lydia, and her friend Rosie. Lydia escapes but witnesses the murder and Rosie is taken.

The team begins a search for the girl, at first suspecting a registered sex offender who had been stalking Rosie online, but he is cleared. Lydia repeatedly tries without success to give a description of the kidnappers. Ziva takes in the young girl as her mother is over-seas and helps her cope with the loss of her father.

After learning that the abduction is related to human trafficking, Gibbs seeks the help of Miranda Pennebaker (Alex Kingston), a woman involved in illegal sales. She denies ever selling human beings but is able to steer him in the right direction.

Later, when one of the kidnappers is found dead after Rosie managed to use his phone to send a text message for help, Gibbs tells Ziva and Abby to stay with Lydia at his house and keep her safe. A man breaks into the house but is quickly taken down and brought in for questioning. Identified as a friend of Lydia and Rosie's families, he confesses to having been approached by human traffickers who had offered him half a million dollars in exchange for helping them find two girls and driving the van used to kidnap them. He had broken into the safehouse after hearing that Lydia might be able to identify him.

With information from the man in custody, the team manages to arrest the kidnappers before Rosie is sold.

Meanwhile, Tony becomes jealous when he learns that Ziva is making plans with Shmeil, a friend from Israel. Shmeil turns out to be an elderly man who has known Ziva since she was three, and they both invite Tony to go with them to dinner. *Source: 1*

Tony: No, I'm talking about the -new- us, here, Ziva. You know, the post-elevator us, the open book, baring our souls, telling each other all kinds of personal stuff.

McGee: Boss, I thought you said you'd wait for me?
Gibbs: Yeah. I tried.

Abby: Well, how about you? I walked in when you were talking about... that... and your family and everything. That was really amazing. I almost fauceted.
Ziva: But you did not. Instead, you walked in with Lydia's cell phone and became an instant hero.
Abby: It's a teenage girl and a smart phone. That is a no-brainer.

Miranda: Still making moonshine down here?
Gibbs: Not for years. Might be fun, though.
Miranda: Smells like...
Gibbs: Wood?
Miranda: Like..varnish.
Gibbs: Quiet reflection.
Gibbs: Zebra can't change its stripes.
Miranda: No. But a woman can.

Tony: Let me get this straight. You've met my father?
Shmeil: Nice kid! And such stories! Oh, many I cannot repeat in mixed company, but he had me laughing.

Ziva: *(about Lydia)* You know, when I was her age, I was about to go into the military.
Abby: A frying pan. It's a little cliche.
Abby: *(to Lydia)* Isn't Bert like the most relaxing thing? He's like the most Zen hippo in the whole universe.
Lydia: I'll bet you were an awesome teenager.
Abby: I was, like, awesomely awkward.

Source: 3

Episodes Season 10

No.	German Title	US Title	Air Date USA	Air Date GER	Directed by	Written by
10.219	Die Wildkatze	**Devil's Trifecta**	Dec 11, 2012	Mar 3, 2013	A.Brown	S.D.Binder

FBI Senior Agent Fornell being shot while leaving a Burgers drive through and he quickly returns fire, killing shooter Navy Seaman Tyler Brown. The team goes to the bar of the matchbook found in Brown's car and the manager informs them that Brown was the bouncer. Gibbs and Fornell are surprised to find their ex-wife Diane Sterling there inquiring about purchasing the bar. They learn that Diane was promoted to IRS Special Agent and is actually undercover on a tax-fraud case investigating the perpetrator behind multiple counts of identity theft for the purpose of filing fake tax returns to get refund checks. She had traced the identity theft to the bar and directs them to the check-cashing storefront where the cashier directs them to an accountant named Oliver Lambert as a possible suspect. They head to a rental house linked to Lambert and find a dead body in a crate full of frozen fish. The man is identified as a bar patron they had spoken to previously and they discover he aided in the identity theft for the operation along with Brown who had checked IDs as the bouncer. Abby uncovers a cell phone in each fish and detects an active one among them which had contact with Lambert's phone. The team goes to the location of the placed call and finds Lambert there bleeding out from stab wounds. He admits he stole the money from the IRS in order to repay a debt he owed. Analyzing the fish shipping manifests leads them to the smuggler and Lamberts client, Avis Gardner. Without enough evidence to tie him to Brown, Diane wires herself and approaches Avis to offer her services as his new accountant. He takes her to the man in charge of the whole operation and he turns out to be the check cashier from earlier. They arrest him and discover he was the one who put the hit on Diane and Fornell when he learned she was posing as Diane Fornell. *Source:⁴*

Ducky: Six shots to the chest! Nice shooting. Jethro, we can safely say the cause of death is...
Fornell: One pissed off FBI agent.

McGee: Look, I'll take the couch. You can have the bed.
Diane: I would rather stand. I'll take the couch.
McGee: Me? Being rude? This coming from the woman who spent the entire car ride over here telling me I had the worst possible haircut for my face?
Diane: Well, it's a simple question. You're an attractive man. I want to know, do you find me attractive?
McGee: Um, you mean physically, or...You're worried something might be wrong with you.
McGee: Look, you're...attractive. At least on the outside.
Diane: *(to McGee)* No! Believe it or not, I think I just need a hug!
McGee: I'm not hugging you.
Diane: You come over here and hug me right now, damn it!
Diane: What kind of a man are you? Here you have a depressed miserable co-worker standing here right in front of you, and you can't even give her a simple hug? Your parents failed.
Fornell: *(about Diane & McGee)* C'mon, people, chop chop! Holy Fourth of July wienie roast! WHAT THE HELL AM I LOOKING AT?
Fornell: Intertwined like horny rabbits! *Source:³*

No.	German Title	US Title	Air Date USA	Air Date GER	Directed by	Written by
10.220	Neues Geld	**You Better Watch Out**	Dec 18, 2012	Mar 10, 2013	T.Wharmby	G.Schenck & F.Cardea

The NCIS team investigates the murder of a man found dead at Patuxent River Station by his wife who had just returned from six months at sea on a deployment. After discovering the man had a $100 bill that has not been put in circulation yet, they team up with the Secret Service to find the rest of the money. They discover that the bill belonged to a batch that was scheduled to be destroyed, and that it was stolen from the landfill. Using that information, the team tracks down the culprit responsible for both the theft and the murder.
Meanwhile, Tony's father, Anthony DiNozzo, Sr., comes to stay with Tony for Christmas, causing some friction between the two, and tries to get him into the spirit of Christmas when he notices that Tony does not have a Christmas tree. Tony then kicks his father out after catching him in bed with a neighbor... *Source:¹*

Episodes Season 10

No.	German Title	US Title	Air Date USA	Air Date GER	Directed by	Written by
10.221	Die Wahrheit hat viele Gesichter	**Shabbat Shalom** (1)	Jan 8, 2013	Mar 17, 2013	D.Smith	C.J.Waild

In the opening scene, a father and son discover a man in a petty officer's uniform dead in a lake while fishing. Back at the NCIS squadroom, Tony, McGee, and Ziva are sifting through a box of old undercover gear that is being thrown out to make more room for supplies. They reminisce about past cases, including one involving Ziva having to wear a prosthetic pregnant belly.

The team is called to the scene at the lake and quickly learns that the victim is not Navy personnel. Rather he is a "government paparazzi" named Tyler Wilkes, a disgraced reporter who had lost credibility after distributing digitally altered photographs in the previous year. It is also found that, at the time of his death, Wilkes had been undercover working a story on alleged drug use in the Navy. The team narrows down four suspects who all confess to the murder, evidently believing that doing so will confuse the investigators and, in turn, clear them. Instead, Gibbs arrests each of them and puts them in separate holding cells.

Ducky, on examining the body, realizes that the death was most likely an accident as the deceased had mono and died from internal bleeding due to a split in his liver. However, the perpetrator still attempted to hide the killing.

At the end of the day, Ziva leaves to find her father Eli is waiting for her at her car in the parking lot. He insists that he is in town to make amends with his daughter and that his intentions are honorable. Despite being suspicious, she cautiously accepts his efforts, though informs Gibbs immediately, who tells Vance. The latter notes that Eli may be nearing retirement but fears that the presence of Iranian ambassador Arash Kazmi, with whom he had a possibly volatile history, will complicate the situation.

Ziva and Eli begin to repair their relationship, spending time together at a coffee shop and looking through photographs. Eli expresses particular interest in a picture of a "pregnant" Ziva, which had accidentally been mixed into the photo stack, asking if it was a boy or a girl. She at first deflects, reminding him that she was only undercover, but quickly admits that she would tell people that the baby was a girl when asked. Eli proceeds to discuss the possibility of retiring in the near future and asks that his visit "be the first step to [his] redemption."

Gibbs and Vance's fears of trouble with Kazmi and Eli are abated when they learn that the two are in fact negotiating a peace agreement. They arrange a meeting to explain that Kazmi had lived in the disputed territories surrounding Israel and that he and Eli had grown up knowing each other through the olive harvest. They request Vance's help with proceeding, who arranges for Eli and Ziva to come to his house for dinner.

Soon after, Ziva discovers that her father had accidentally killed Wilkes when the latter took pictures of him arriving at the airport. Eli had struggled with the reporter over the camera, causing his enlarged liver to burst. She confronts Eli shortly afterwards, who admits that he had covered Wilkes' death to prevent word from getting out that he was in Washington D.C., which would ruin the peace arrangements. Ziva is nonetheless furious and disheartened by this, but agrees to sit across from her father at the dinner table one last time.

Vance's wife Jackie prepares a Shabbat meal, and Eli tries to lighten the tension by saying the blessing and expressing thanks for "life, freedom, and family". However, Ziva is unable to continue and goes outside to call Gibbs. Then, an unknown assailant shoots up Vance's house. Ziva pursues the shooter, wounding him, and is joined by Gibbs, who rushes to the scene after hearing the gunshots. The shooter is cornered but commits suicide before he can talk.

Tony and McGee hurry to the site of the shootout and tend to the victims. However, Ziva returns to the house to find that Eli has been killed and breaks down sobbing, cradling his head and praying in Hebrew.

Jackie is critically wounded and rushed to the hospital. After several hours in surgery, Vance emerges from the operating room and quietly states that his wife is dead. Source: 4

Episodes Season 10

No.	German Title	US Title	Air Date USA	Air Date GER	Directed by	Written by
10.222	Tage der Trauer	**Shiva (2)**	Jan 15, 2013	Mar 24, 2013	A.Brown	C.J.Waild, G.Glasberg & S.Williams

The episode opens depicting a young Ziva praying the Shabbat blessing over candles, with her father standing next to her. Various other family members, now deceased, are shown surrounding her, including her mother, older brother Ari, and younger sister Tali. The memory fades and an adult Ziva appears in a synagogue questioning God, "Why should I not be angry, with all that has been taken?" She further pleads for a sign that she should not lose hope. Tony then enters the room and attempts to offer support, though she declines any expressions of sympathy, saying that she instead needs "revenge."

SecNav Jarvis orders that the deaths of Eli David and Director Vance's wife, Jackie, be kept quiet to avoid an outcry while the identity of the perpetrator is still unknown. Meanwhile, Ducky determines that the shooter was a Swedish mercenary who was hired to perform the killings.

As Ziva and Vance struggle to cope with their losses, both attempt to participate in the investigation despite being prohibited due to their relationships with the deceased. NCIS Deputy Director Jerome Craig is brought in to temporarily replace Vance, and Eli's burial is delayed due to the investigation, causing Ziva further pain as Jewish law mandates that a person be buried within twenty-four hours.

The team firsts suspects Arash Kazmi, the Iranian Eli had met with days earlier to discuss the possibility of peace between their countries, though Kazmi protests his innocence and offers VEVAK files (intel) to support his claims. McGee contacts Gavriela Adel (Georgia Hatzis), a Mossad agent stationed in Jerusalem, who suggests Duane Gustafson, an American millionaire who funded an anti-Mossad group, as a potential suspect. Gustafson, however, insists that his association with anti-Israel organizations is "strictly business".

Because Gibbs is concerned that Ziva will be the next target, Tony takes her to his apartment as a precaution. Still trying to console her, he brings her longtime Israeli friend Shmeil (Jack Axelrod) to stay with them and lets her sleep in his bed. Later, he attempts to soothe her after a nightmare, but Ziva again refuses comfort and insists that she is "fine".

Mossad Deputy Director Ilan Bodnar, described by Ziva as Eli's protegé, arrives at NCIS demanding answers and exasperated that Kazmi has not yet been charged. Ziva, in turn, is infuriated that the team is sharing information with Ilan, a man who considered himself to be like a son to Eli, that was withheld from her, his blood daughter. Tony responds, "Now you are the daughter of a dead man — let yourself act like one."

The NCIS team locates a bank account under the name of "Virtue" that allows them to track the man who hired the hitman while Ziva speaks to Ilan over video chat. Ziva agrees to Ilan's request to meet her at the apartment before Gibbs calls her and asks her about the significance of "Virture". She realizes that the Hebrew word for "virtue" is Ilan's middle name, prompting them to come to the conclusion that he must have been behind the killings. Gibbs and Tony rush to the apartment before Bodnar reaches it, presumably to kill Ziva, but he never shows.

Shortly afterwards, Kazmi's vehicle is bombed and Bodnar disappears.

The Western Wall in Jerusalem, where Ziva was shown praying in the final scenes of the episode.

Eli's body is released for burial that evening, and Tony goes to the airport to see Ziva before she leaves for Israel. He urges her not to seek revenge on her own, and, though she does not renounce her desire to do so, she assures him that for now she is only attending a funeral. They embrace, with Ziva finally accepting comfort for her loss, and Tony reminds her in Hebrew, "At lo levad" ("You are not alone"). The episode ends with Jackie's funeral and Ziva mourning Eli in Israel, visiting the Western Wall, and planting an olive tree. *Source:* [1]

Episodes Season 10

No.	German Title	US Title	Air Date USA	Air Date GER	Directed by	Written by
10.223	Neben der Spur	**Hit and Run**	Jan 29, 2013	Apr 7, 2013	D.Smith	G.Glasberg & G.L.Monreal

The team investigates a car crash where a Marine and a woman are found dead. They initially believe it is a murder-suicide, due to both victims coming from feuding families. However, Abby reveals that both victims were already dead before the car crashed, meaning a third suspect is responsible. Unfortunately, the case reminds Abby of her first "case" as a young girl, where she tracked down another girl, Ricki, to return her teddy bear. However, Ricki cannot take back the bear since it came from her grandfather, with whom her father has cut off all ties. Abby then tracks down the grandfather, but he is unwilling to confront Ricki's father. Remembering her failure to reunite Ricki's family causes Abby to fall into a depression, and she calls in sick for the first time in her career. Meanwhile, the team manages to figure out that the victims were in fact trying to get married, but lost their money to a Ponzi scheme set up by the Marine's cousin. When confronted, the cousin murdered both of them to keep them quiet. Gibbs then meets Abby and encourages her by telling her actions can do good, even if she isn't aware of it. Abby then remembers the final part of her first case, where she gives Ricki her rabbit instead of the bear, with Abby's brother pointing out that Ricki will remember that simple act of kindness forever. In the present, Gibbs gives Abby the fortune she had given him after their first case together, which reads "Today's friend is tomorrow's family" *Source:* [1]

No.	German Title	US Title	Air Date USA	Air Date GER	Directed by	Written by
10.224	Schnee in Kuba	**Canary**	Feb 5, 2013	Apr 14, 2013	T.O'Hara	C.J.Waild

The team captures a master hacker who happens to be second on the most wanted cyberterrorist list and was also responsible for a cyber attack on MTAC which resulted in the death of an undercover agent. The team is interested in interrogating him for the location of the most wanted cyberterrorist, a hacker who is only identified as "MC". Analyzing the hacker's computer, Ziva and DiNozzo investigate a warehouse and find evidence of a bomb containing the ebola virus having been built. In order to get the hacker to talk, Ziva and DiNozzo fly him to Guantanamo Bay in an effort to intimidate him by placing him with terrorists he had previously betrayed. However, once they arrive, the prison's security is compromised, leading to a mass breakout. The prisoners demand Ziva and DiNozzo hand over the hacker in return for their lives. In order to save himself, the hacker reveals how they can find MC. It is then revealed that the entire breakout was a ploy; NCIS only tricked the hacker into thinking they were in Guantanamo Bay when they in fact had never left the United States. Meanwhile, Gibbs and McGee manage to trace the ebola bomb and safely defuse it. Even though the plan was foiled and they have a way of tracking MC, Deputy Director Craig points out NCIS still has to arrest him. *Source:* [1]

Episodes Season 10

No.	German Title	US Title	Air Date USA	Air Date GER	Directed by	Written by
10.225	Zurück zu den Wurzeln	**Herafter**	Feb 19, 2013	Aug 18, 2013	T.Wharmby	N.Mirante-Matthews

The team is called to investigate the death of a Marine private during training, and discover he had suffered a number of wounds from repeated beatings and stabbings. They initially believe the injuries were received due to his participation in an underground fighting ring, but he had not been in a fight in months. The death of another Marine private who shows similar wounds leads the team to the privates' commanding officer. They discover that the CO's brother was tortured and killed in Iraq, and he was trying to "toughen" up his men in preparation for what they might face in battle.

Meanwhile, Vance discovers that Jackie had secretly set up her own bank account and hired a lawyer to draft a Separation of Property letter. Worried, Vance consults Gibbs, who tells him that Jackie was most likely afraid that Vance would die in the line of duty, and prepared accordingly, since Shannon did the same thing when he joined the Marines. Vance is still unsure of what to do with his life without Jackie, though Gibbs reminds him that he still has his two children to take care of, giving him a purpose. *Source:* [1]

No.	German Title	US Title	Air Date USA	Air Date GER	Directed by	Written by
10.226	Allein im Wald	**Detour**	Feb 26, 2013	Aug 25, 2013	Mario Van Peebles	S.D.Binder

Ducky and Palmer are called out to investigate the mysterious suicide of a Navy Lieutenant, but are kidnapped on the way back to NCIS headquarters. They are then forced to perform an autopsy on the lieutenant's corpse in order to find an important item he was carrying. Meanwhile, the rest of the team discovers that the dead lieutenant is in fact a Cuban spy who was stealing classified files, and the people who kidnapped Ducky and Palmer are his handlers. Both Ducky and Palmer manage to escape their captors and are rescued by the rest of the team, who managed to track them. Thanks to a ruse set up by Ducky and Palmer, the team is able to apprehend the lead handler and recover the stolen files. *Source:* [1]

No.	German Title	US Title	Air Date USA	Air Date GER	Directed by	Written by
10.227	Tote Rosen	**Prime Suspect**	Mar 5, 2013	Sep 1, 2013	J.Whitmore, Jr.	G.Schenck & F.Cardea

Gibbs' barber Frankie asks him to find out if his son Cameron, a former Navy enlistee, was the "Dead Rose Slasher" - the nickname given to a serial killer who targets young female drug addicts - due to Cameron's physical resemblance to the photofit issued by the Metro Police. Frankie is worried Cameron might be involved due to his temper. Abby and her friend from the Metro PD's forensics lab pull an all-nighter while Ducky calls in a favor as they try to find out who the murderer is.

At the same time, the team is tasked with tracking down a Marine lance corporal who has absconded to the Caribbean with over $120,000 in cash from the cash sales office he was assigned to. Tony is sent to the Bahamas to stake out for the lance corporal along with probie agent Ned "Dorney" Dorneget and takes the opportunity to "probie" him like he did with McGee during Seasons 1-3, much to Ziva's amusement. *Source:* [1]

Episodes Season 10

No.	German Title	US Title	Air Date USA	Air Date GER	Directed by	Written by
10.228	Marine Dex	**Seek**	Mar 19, 2013	Sep 8, 2013	M.Weatherly	S.D.Binder & C.J.Waild

In Afghanistan, EOD specialist Marine Sergeant Theodore Lemere is shot and killed by a sniper after leading a trapped child out of minefield with the help of his bomb sniffing dog, Dex.

Lemere's widow, Ruby, approaches Gibbs, showing him a video message left behind by Lemere indicating that he might have been deliberately targeted. Abby's analysis of the bullet that killed Lemere appears to confirm this, after tracing the bullet to an American manufacturer. Gibbs suspects that the lead dog handler of a civilian contractor, Beta Co, might be responsible since he and Lemere had gotten in a fight previously, though they lack evidence to prove it. Ruby then receives a gold medallion in the mail, which is revealed to have been looted from Afghanistan. When an thief attempts to break into the Lemere household to steal the medallion, Dex chases the thief away.

Gibbs and McGee decide to take Dex back to Afghanistan to investigate the crime scene while the rest of the team processes the evidence the thief left behind. DiNozzo and Ziva arrest the thief, who was using his contacts in Beta Co to smuggle looted Afghani artifacts into the US. Gibbs confronts the Beta Co contractors, pointing out one of them was a former special forces marksman. The marksman draws his weapon, but is attacked by Dex and shot dead by Gibbs.

At Lemere's funeral, Gibbs approaches Ruby and tells her that due to the wounds he suffered attacking Lemere's killer, Dex has been permanently retired from the Marines, meaning he can stay with Ruby much to her joy. The episode then ends with a phoof of Dex sitting by Ruby's side as the two study the coffin.

Meanwhile, Director Vance is interviewing potential nannies to take care of his children, but keeps rejecting the applicants. He confides in Ziva that he's afraid that if he hires a nanny, he will forget about his wife. Ziva tells Vance that he only he can decide when he can move on from his wife's death. Inspired, Vance finally decides on which nanny to hire. *Source:* [1]

No.	German Title	US Title	Air Date USA	Air Date GER	Directed by	Written by
10.229	Die weiße Bö	**Squall**	Mar 26, 2013	Sep 15, 2013	T.Wright	B.Nuss

In the opening scene, the body of a navy medical officer is found during a storm at sea and quickly determined to have been murdered. The team leaves to investigate at the scene, but McGee is late as a result of being with Adam, a middle school-aged boy he is spending time with through a Big Brothers Big Sisters program. When he arrives at the ship, he encounters his father, John McGee, a 4-star admiral. It immediately becomes apparent that their relationship is somewhat strained.

Meanwhile, Tony and Ziva come across NCIS Agent Stan Burley, who assists in the investigation. Tony shortly afterwards becomes concerned that Burley is attempting to flirt with Ziva, who is "vulnerable" due to her father's recent death, telling McGee, "You see he would use that to his advantage. Swoop right in, like a hawk going after a sweet, innocent, furry little Israeli." However, when Tony speaks with Burley, the latter responds by announcing that he is engaged to be married.

McGee briefly considers quitting the Big Brothers Big Sisters program, but decides against it and encourages Adam to stand up to a bully.

Numerous potential killers are introduced. It is discovered that there was a drug problem on the ship, though all related suspects are cleared. The admiral later becomes a suspect, prompting him to admit that he has cancer, though he is also cleared. Later, it is found that John McGee's aide had killed the medic in order to prevent the news of the cancer from being released.

As the episode closes, McGee decides to attempt to repair his relationship with his father. *Source:* [1]

Episodes Season 10

No.	German Title	US Title	Air Date USA	Air Date GER	Directed by	Written by
10.230	Auf der Jagd	**Chasing Ghosts**	Apr 9, 2013	Sep 22, 2013	A.Brown	N.Mirante-Matthews

After Navy Reserve Lieutenant Callie Daniels comes home to find her house torn apart and her husband Noah missing, the team searches her home and find his severed finger. When they uncover a trust account in Noah´s name with a balance of 2.5 million, they speculate that the perpetrator was after the money. Callie receives a call from Noah´s captor allowing them to trace the line to the perpetrators empty van. The license plate leads them to the vehicle´s owner who explains he had lent the van to his brother Darryl. After seeing that both Darryl and Noah had debit card charges at the same restaurant and at the same time, they question the restaurants owner, Rebecca, who notes that Darryl had hassled Noah about his trust fund money. Abby´s analysis from the crime scene reveals that the struggle was manufactured and that there was another person who helped haul Noah off. Through the FBI´s tip line, the team locates Darryl´s body at a hotel with a suicide note, but when the autopsy debunks the death as a suicide, they listen to the original call with the tip and recognize the voice as Rebecca´s. The team tracks her down and coerces her to confess that she was romantically involved with Noah and was in cahoots with him to stage his own kidnapping and murder so they could abscond with his trust fund, using Darryl as a pawn in their scheme. Meanwhile, Tony discovers Ziva and McGee have been working together to locate Bodnar and Gibbs and Vance give Ziva permission to go to Rome in pursuit of him. *Source:* [4]

No.	German Title	US Title	Air Date USA	Air Date GER	Directed by	Written by
10.231	Berlin	**Berlin**	Apr 23, 2013	Sep 29, 2013	T.O'Hara	S.Williams & G.L.Monreal

As Tony and Ziva head to Berlin to track down Bodnar, the team is visited by newly appointed Mossad Director Orli Elbaz who asks for the team´s help investigating the murder of Mossad Officer Mantel in Virginia by a rogue faction in support of Bodnar. While Gibbs and McGee search the hotel Mantel was staying in, they notice a man in a SUV watching them but he drives away before they can confront him. When Abby discovers that Mantel was using Mossad´s old communication system and that his laptop was rigged with misleading files, they hack into Mossad´s database for answers. Upon seeing that Mantel was red-flagged as a rogue officer, they realize that he was working with Bodnar and that there was never a faction to begin with. After pressing Orli for answers, they put the pieces together to determine that she believed Bodnar was still in the U.S. and gave NCIS a dummy case which would grant permission for Mossad to be on U.S. soil. Orli had Mantel killed and wanted to kill Bodnar before he could be arrested, thereby ensuring that Mossad´s secrets would be kept safe. She also had CIA and Homeland Security searching for Bodnar in Rome in hopes that he would let his guard down, making him easier to track in the states. Meanwhile in Berlin, Ziva and Tony locate the courier scheduled to make a delivery of diamonds to Bodnar, but instead the hand off is made to Bodnar´s brother Yaniv. Just as they are driving back from delivering Yaniv to the Federal marshals, Ziva and Tony are broad-sided by an SUV targeting them *Source:* [4]

Episodes Season 10

No.	German Title	US Title	Air Date USA	Air Date GER	Directed by	Written by
10.232	Rache	**Revenge**	Apr 30, 2013	Oct 6, 2013	J.Whitmore, Jr.	G.Schenk & F.Cardea

As the episode opens, Tony and Ziva are semi-conscious in the aftermath of the crash. Bodnar approaches the vehicle and retrieves the diamonds despite efforts from a dazed Ziva to stop him.

Later, in the ER, she is anxious to resume the search for Bodnar despite having sustained injuries and being instructed to stay out of the field for the time being. She and Tony sneak out of the hospital and return to NCIS headquarters, questioning Abby about the details of the case. Despite Abby's unwillingness to talk, they are able to deduce the location of the rest of the team.

McGee and Gibbs are shown investigating Bodnar's former hideout and processing the body of a man who had apparently assisted Bodnar in exchange for diamonds in payment. They are unable to identify him through facial recognition and eventually learn that this is due to extensive plastic surgery the man underwent. Tony and McGee locate the surgeon and learn that the man was a South African mercenary named Clive Goddard.

Ziva begins to undergo intensive training, evidently in hopes of a confrontation with Bodnar, including forcing herself to practice boxing with an injured shoulder.

Homeland Senior Division Chief Tom Morrow demands that Vance rein in Ziva's efforts and leave the case to Homeland Security. Vance is reluctant to accept this but mildly suggests to Ziva that she back down.

Bodnar contacts Ziva at NCIS and insists that, while he was responsible for the deaths of Eli David and Jackie Vance, he did not kill the Iranian ambassador. McGee is able to pinpoint the area in the background of Bodnar's video as a park in New York and alerts Homeland. However, they quickly realize that the video was a ploy to throw them off and that the background was staged.

Ziva, meanwhile, manages to figure out Bodnar's true location from a note attached to Goddard and confronts him on a ship about to depart. Bodnar insists that he will not be apprehended, and when Ziva refuses to shoot him unarmed, a fight ensues. The team, having become aware of Ziva's absence, rushes to the scene in time to see Bodnar fall to his death.

In the closing scene, Ziva is taken to Vance's office, where she tells him that "it's over". *Source:* [1]

No.	German Title	US Title	Air Date USA	Air Date GER	Directed by	Written by
10.233	Helfende Augen	**Double Blind**	May 7, 2013	Oct 13, 2013	D.Smith	C.J.Waild & S.D.Binder

When Petty Officer Lowry is stopped while chasing a man he insists is following him, Lowry appeals to the team to help him find his pursuer as his recent mugging left him with a concussion and gaps in his memory. Abby finds a crumpled legal disclaimer among Lowry´s possessions, but Lowry is unable to recall what he signed up for. The team stimulates his senses to jog his memory, and his recollection of bratwurst leads them to his pursuer eating the sausage in a warehouse used for a government-funded study on surveillance that Lowry had volunteered for. The warehouse is burned down in a fire before they are able to investigate further, but Gibbs´ realization that Lowry could have motive for getting rid of evidence from the study causes them to search through the surveillance tapes on Lowry. They find that Lowry had inadvertently included his friend in the videos, a marine who was absconding from deploying on a third tour. Lowry confesses he had tried erasing the data in the warehouse in order to protect her and the team arrests him. Meanwhile, when an investigator from the Department of Defense questions the team about Ilan Bodnar´s death, it initially seems as if he is investigating Ziva and then Vance, but it is quickly revealed that Gibbs was his target all along. *Source:* [4]

Episodes Season 10

No.	German Title	US Title	Air Date USA	Air Date GER	Directed by	Written by
10.234	Egal was man tut	**Damned If You Do**	May 14, 2013	Oct 20, 2013	T.Wharmby	G.Glasberg

In the aftermath of Gibbs' arrest, the Department of Defense broadens their investigation into NCIS, placing the future of the entire agency in jeopardy. While the team believe that the investigating agent is looking to capitalise on Gibbs' arrest to make his career, they soon discover that NCIS' pursuit of Ilan Bodnar was used to cover up the CIA's involvement in the assassination of a foreign intelligence head. Instead of letting Gibbs take all the blame for the charges, Tony, Ziva, and McGee take responsibility for what happened and resign. The episode ends with a cut to four months later, showing Gibbs aiming a sniper rifle at FBI agent Fornell. The scene fades to black, where the sound of a gunshot is then heard. *Source:* [1]

Season 11 (Episodes 11.235-11.258)

The eleventh season of the police procedural drama NCIS premiered on September 24, 2013, in the same time slot as the previous seasons, Tuesdays at 8pm. Special Agent Ziva David, portrayed by Cote de Pablo, departed during the season with her final appearance being in "Past, Present and Future". The episode "Crescent City (Part I)", which aired on March 25, 2014, serves as the first of a two-part backdoor pilot of a second spin off to NCIS called NCIS: New Orleans based in New Orleans.

On August 13, 2013, "casting intel" on a new female character named Bishop was published, with filming scheduled to mid-October. Bishop is described as a "twentysomething female[;] bright, educated, athletic, attractive, fresh-faced, focused and somewhat socially awkward. She has a mysterious mixture of analytic brilliance, fierce determination and idealism. She's traveled extensively, but only feels comfortable at home." Emily Wickersham was cast to play the character, named NSA Analyst Ellie Bishop. Wickersham was promoted to the main cast, two weeks prior of her debut appearance. She made her first appearance in "Gut Check".

Source: [1]

Original Air Date USA	September 24, 2013 – May 13, 2014 on CBS
Original Air Date German Language	January 5, 2013 – October 19, 2014 on Sat 1

Episodes Season 11

No.	German Title	US Title	Air Date USA	Air Date GER	Directed by	Written by
11.235	Freund und Feind	**Whiskey Tango Foxtrot**	Sep 24, 2013	Jan 5, 2014	T.Wharmby	G.Glasberg

In the aftermath of the Season 10 finale, Gibbs' team has been left divided as Tony and McGee attempt to adjust to life as civilians while Ziva has returned home to Israel. Parsons' investigation into Gibbs' team continues but things take an intense turn when a hotel bomb explodes, killing SECNAV Clayton Jarvis and seriously injuring Tom Morrow. In the meantime, Vance and Navy Captain Dominick Wayne inform Gibbs that the bombing could involve a terrorist organization a deceased Navy intelligence officer had been investigating.

When Gibbs and Tony were shot at by unknown persons and Ducky and Palmer find a former FBI agent-turned-mercenary hacker-for-hire in their autopsy room trying to access their files, Parsons and the NCIS team soon realize that another mysterious person or group is targeting the entire team one by one. Vance also discovers that Ziva is the next target and Tony must track her down before it is too late. *Source:* [1]

Abby: *[telling McGee about Gibbs being out of town, looks at Delilah]* Can she be trusted?
Delilah: I have a higher security clearance than any of you.
Abby: So did Mata Hari.

Fornell: You know, I'm not gonna kiss you goodnight.
Gibbs: What???
Fornell: Why are you walking me to my car? We breaking up?
Gibbs: If I could I would but unfortunately I trust you.

Source: [22]

No.	German Title	US Title	Air Date USA	Air Date GER	Directed by	Written by
11.236	Zivas Liste	**Past, Present and Future**	Oct 1, 2013	Jan 12, 2014	J.Whitmore,Jr.	G.Glasberg,S.Williams & G.L.Monreal

Gibbs and the team continue the hunt for Parsa and his growing terrorist ring while Tony heads to Israel to track down Ziva. Tony does eventually manage to track down Ziva, but Ziva reveals that after the death of her father, she no longer wants to live the life of an agent and therefore has decided to cut off all ties to her previous life, including NCIS and Tony. Tony is heartbroken at this, as he realizes his romantic feelings for Ziva and tries to convince her to return. However, Ziva's mind is made up. Tony tells Ziva to at least call Gibbs, as he is a "good listener", and returns to the United States.

Meanwhile, Gibbs continue to try and track down Parsa and the men responsible for the bombing that killed SECNAV Clayton Jarvis. They discover that Tomás Mendez, the member of an anti-terrorist business organization, is a potential target, and Fornell is assigned to be his bodyguard. However, Abby and McGee analyze the bomb parts and manages to trace them to corporations owned by Mendez. Gibbs realizes that Mendez is one of the businessmen in league with Parsa. The show then returns to the scene depicted in last few seconds of the season 10 finale, "Damned If You Do" where Gibbs commandeers a sniper rifle, but instead of targeting Fornell, he shoots and kills Mendez before he can set off another bomb.

Afterwards, all charges against Gibbs are dropped, and Tony and McGee are reinstated as NCIS agents. Meanwhile, at home, Gibbs receives a phone call from Ziva. *Source:* [1]

McGee: Hey Abby. Ducky said you pulled some prints off our Jane Doe? Any luck?
Abby: Luck. Is that what you think happens in here?
McGee: No I just meant
Abby: It's Tuesday so no backtracking.

Source: [22]

Episodes Season 11

No.	German Title	US Title	Air Date USA	Air Date GER	Directed by	Written by
11.237	Unter dem Radar	**Under the Radar**	Oct 8, 2013	Jan 19, 2014	D.Smith	G.Schenk & F.Cardea

When an apartment landlord attempts to open a door to deliver mail, he is killed by a bomb wired to the door. Since the apartment belongs to a Navy lieutenant, Gibbs and his team are called in. However, they find that the Navy lieutenant, Terence Keith, is missing after taking leave. Further investigation reveals that Keith had wanted to be a fighter pilot but washed out of flight training. He had also purchased over 200 pounds of C4 explosive and rented a STOL plane. The team deduces that he is planning to use the explosives and the plane to bomb a target. However, because the STOL can fly below radar coverage, it would be next to impossible to find. Fortunately, McGee comes up with the idea to use Twitter to find the plane by asking Twitter users to send a tweet if they see it fly overhead. Using the data they collect, the team figures out that Keith is planning to bomb the U.S.S. Benjamin Franklin, an aircraft carrier that is also carrying several of Keith's classmates who graduated from flight training. Gibbs manages to contact Keith and tells him his plan is doomed to fail, as the carrier has scrambled fighters and its anti-air defenses have locked onto him. Keith turns the plane away, but since he is holding a dead man switch and has nothing left to live for, commits suicide by detonating the bombs.
There are two other sideplots in the episode: Agent Strickland and McGee losing his NCIS ID. Agent Strickland, Mike Franks' last partner, temporarily joins the team while she is waiting to retire in two weeks. However, she is allowed to retire early after she gets injured in the field. Meanwhile, McGee loses his ID and tries to find it, knowing that he would face severe punishment if the loss is found out. He admits this to Gibbs, and later Vance gives him his ID, saying it was found at RFK Stadium where McGee had gone earlier. McGee manages to escape punishment, however, due to his idea to use Twitter to stop the bombing. *Source:* [1]

No.	German Title	US Title	Air Date USA	Air Date GER	Directed by	Written by
11.238	Ehrenmorde	**Anonymous Was a Woman**	Oct 15, 2013	Jan 26, 014	T.O'Hara	S.D.Binder

Marine Sergeant Patricia Moreno is found dead and temporary replacement Agent Grady joins McGee and Tony in the investigation. Still reeling from the loss of Ziva, McGee and Tony plot a way to "chase away" Agent Grady. The body becomes a "Jane Doe" when McGee discovers that Sergeant Moreno died in Afghanistan almost three years ago and the Jane Doe is an Afghan illegal immigrant who had supposedly stolen Moreno's identity. The late Mike Franks' daughter-in-law's name is found on a job application the Jane Doe had filed and the team finds out that Mike Franks had been helping a human rights group smuggle Afghan refugees into the United States. After they find and arrest the killer, the team discovers that their false identities were leaked from a womens' shelter in Afghanistan. Gibbs and McGee travel to the shelter, where they find that one of the girls who had already left the shelter was threatened into leaking the information. Before they leave, however, the shelter is attacked by an Afghan mob. Gibbs manages to hold off the attackers long enough for a UN security team to arrive. Gibbs then arranges for the Afghan women in the shelter to be evacuated to the United States for asylum, as well as obtaining new identities and green cards for the women already smuggled there.
It is revealed through flashbacks that Franks attempted to recruit Gibbs to help him smuggle six Afghan refugees into the United States. However, Gibbs refused to sign an order that would authorize a military transport to evacuate them. Later, he finds out that the same six refugees were killed in a bomb attack due to his inaction, motivating him to rescue the Afghan women in the present.
Meanwhile, McGee and Tony's fears of Agent Grady replacing Ziva prove to be misguided, as Grady is actually applying for a position in San Diego. *Source:* [1]

Episodes Season 11

No.	German Title	US Title	Air Date USA	Air Date GER	Directed by	Written by
11.239	15 Jahre Rache	**Once a Crook**	Oct 22, 2013	Feb 2, 2014	A.Brown	C.Silber

When the body of a cryptoanalyst, Petty Officer First Class Andrew Wells is found dead on the road, Gibbs and the team are called in to investigate. The team at first believes that the murder is related to espionage, but find out that the cryptoanalyst was merely being scouted for a lucrative job in the private sector. Tony stumbles across evidence that implicates Anton Markin, a man he had met when he was still a Baltimore police officer. Tony had recruited Anton as an informant against the Russian mob, but the plan went awry when Anton murdered the Russian gangster he was spying on and went into hiding. As they try and track down Anton, the team finds out that Anton's sister Marie has been abducted as well. After apprehending Anton, Tony asks him why he betrayed his trust and killed the gangster. Anton reveals he killed the gangster in self defense, but was too scared to turn himself in. Tony apologizes for not being there for Anton when he needed him the most, and Anton tells Tony everything he knows. The team deduces that the Russian mob is still looking to get revenge on Anton, and kidnapped Marie to lure him out. The cryptoanalyst was merely killed due to mistaken identity. They confront Anton's boss at the bakery he used to work at and discover the murder weapon, revealing him to be the killer. They manage to find Marie and reunite her with Anton.

Throughout the episode, Tony is suffering from a severe case of insomnia due to Ziva's departure, and hasn't slept in days. However, after the solving the case, he finally calms down enough to be able to sleep that night. *Source:* [1]

No.	German Title	US Title	Air Date USA	Air Date GER	Directed by	Written by
11.240	Öl und Wasser	**Oil & Water**	Oct 29, 2013	Feb 9, 2014	T.Wright	J.Corbett

Abby and McGee arrive to work only to find themselves victims of a prankster. A routine drill on an off-shore oil drill turns into reality when it is bombed and the NCIS team is called to the oil rig when one of the employees, a Marine reservist, is found dead. Gibbs and his team join forces with the Coast Guard Investigative Service and old friend CGIS Agent Abigail Borin. After discovering the blast was caused by a bomb, the team investigates several suspects including a close friend of the reservist, an environmental activist, and a cook with a criminal past, but runs out of leads. However, thanks to a piece of rare sturgeon leather Abby finds, she manages to trace it to briefcase of the oil company's legal counsel, who planned the bombing in order to short sell his company's stock. However, he never intended to hurt anybody.

During the investigation, Borin confides to Gibbs that the case makes her feel uncomfortable, as when she was a Marine serving in Iraq, she was nearly killed by an IED and lost three of her men, which is what caused her to join CGIS. However, she subtly implies that she would be willing to leave CGIS to join Gibbs' team.

Meanwhile, McGee and Ducky confront DiNozzo, who they believe to be the prankster. DiNozzo denies it and when he tries to leave, becomes the victim of a prank himself. It is implied Gibbs was responsible for pranking DiNozzo. *Source:* [1]

Gibbs: You ready to go? I'm driving.
Borin: No. After everything's that happened, I think it's the best for everyone if I just pull out of the case. It's fine. Look, I'm gonna call headquarters, they're gonna send in another agent...
Gibbs: No, Borin. I have it. My case, my call.
Borin: You pulling rank on me, Gunny?
Gibbs: A Marine leaves no man behind.

Source: [22]

Episodes Season 11

No.	German Title	US Title	Air Date USA	Air Date GER	Directed by	Written by
11.241	Alte Flieger	**Better Angels**	Nov 5, 2013	Feb 16, 2014	T.Wharmby	G.Monreal

The team comes to investigate the death of Marine Sergeant Michael Dawson, who was apparently killed trying to stop a robbery attempt. As the team tries to track down the robber, Gibbs receives a call from the police that his father, Jackson Gibbs, had just had his license revoked and needs to be picked up from the station. Gibbs picks up his father, who informs him that they need to go see Walter Beck, an old war acquaintance of his who saved his life during World War II, since he is dying and Gibbs Sr. still has not had a chance to thank him. Gibbs reluctantly leaves the case to McGee and Dinozzo while he assists his father. However, their search leads to an apparent dead end, with Abby not being able to find any record of a Walter Beck in Gibbs Sr.'s squadron. Thinking his father is either lying to him or "confused", Gibbs returns to trying to solve the case.

Eventually, the team discovers that the robbery was a set up, as Dawson was the real target. They track down one of Dawson's old friends, who admits that Dawson was trying to help him overcome his drug addiction and went to confront his dealer, which resulted in Dawson's death. The friend identifies the store owner as the drug dealer, and a quick search of his store gives them all the evidence they need to convict him.

Afterwards, Gibbs confronts his father about making up the story about Walter Beck, pointing out there was nobody in his squadron with that name. Gibbs Sr. corrects him by telling him that Walter Beck was a German pilot, who saved his life despite them being enemies at the time. With this new information, Gibbs is able to track down where Beck is staying, and both Gibbs Sr. and Beck have an emotional reunion, with Gibbs Sr. introducing his son to Beck. *Source:* [1]

Gibbs: Is there any right way to be a son?
Ducky: Just as there is no right way for you to act as his father. The pain of watching a parent age is unlike any other.

Source: [22]

No.	German Title	US Title	Air Date USA	Air Date GER	Directed by	Written by
11.242	Wasserdicht	**Alibi**	Nov 12, 2013	Feb 23, 2014	H.Dale	G.Schenck & F.Cardea

The team goes out to investigate a fatal hit and run near Quantico, and manage to gather enough evidence to lead them to Marine Staff Sergeant Justin Dunne. After being arrested, Dunne requests an attorney, and hires former FBI agent Carrie Clark, who also happens to be an old acquaintance of the team. Dunne tells Carrie that he has an alibi, in that he was involved in a murder outside of the base at the time of the hit and run, and that somebody else must have stolen his truck. Due to attorney-client privilege, Carrie cannot tell Gibbs and the team anything about Dunne's crime other than he has a solid alibi. However, she manages to leave small, subtle clues for the team to follow. The team then discovers Dunne indeed was not driving his truck at the time of the hit and run, and manage to track down and arrest the Marine who stole it.

Gibbs and the team then continue to investigate Dunne's alibi. Eventually, the plot begins to unravel when the team discovers that Dunne is part of a conspiracy with Olivia Chandler, a gold digger, and Wendell Kaiser, a chronic gambler deep in debt. All three individuals met during an Alcoholics Anonymous meeting. Dunne murdered Kaiser's bookie to clear his debt, and Kaiser would murder Chandler's husband so she could inherit his fortune. The plan would be foolproof since the murderers had no connection to their victims while anybody else with a motive would have an airtight alibi. Unfortunately, they have to be careful how to approach the situation without revealing that Carrie had broken her attorney-client privilege. With the help of Homicide Detective Paul Dockry, an old acquaintance of Gibbs, they manage to trick Kaiser in testifying against Dunne and Chandler. Afterwards, Gibbs invites Carrie to dinner, and they both agree that they're not so different in that they are willing to bend the rules and risk their careers in order to do the right thing. *Source:* [1]

Episodes Season 11

No.	German Title	US Title	Air Date USA	Air Date GER	Directed by	Written by
11.243	Teamplayer	**Gut Check**	Nov 19, 2013	Mar 2, 2014	D.Smith	C.J.Waild

During a briefing in the Multiple Threat Assessment Center (MTAC) by the Secretary of the Navy (SECNAV), network security detects an unauthorized electronic signal being broadcast, and the room is placed in lock down. While McGee sweeps the room, DiNozzo scans the four defense contractor representatives the SECNAV was briefing. Nothing is found until DiNozzo comes in close proximity to SECNAV, and his scanner goes off. A pen containing a covert listening device is found on SECNAV, but she cannot remember when or where the pen came from.

As the investigation proceeds, DiNozzo finds a two year old National Security Agency (NSA) threat analysis report that describes the exact scenario of the security breach. Gibbs and DiNozzo visit the National Security Operations Center where they meet analyst Eleanor "Ellie" Bishop, the paper's author. Gibbs brings Bishop back to NCIS to assist in the investigation.

SECNAV is contacted with a demand for $10 million for return of the intel that was recorded by the bug. She approves the payment and tasks the NSA with tracking the electronic funds transfer to catch the extortionist. Bishop's colleague at the NSA follows a lead to a coffee shop where the account was accessed from and is killed.

Abby's forensics work on the bug from the pen leads to a license plate number for the suspected extortionist. Gibbs, DiNozzo and Bishop apprehend him and interrogate him to find he was working with someone else who extorted the government and killed the NSA agent.

Gibbs' team tracks the killer to a private post office and are waiting to arrest him when Bishop arrives. Gibbs calls her to get her to get back in her car. As she tries to explain why she is there, the killer comes out of the post office surprising Bishop. The killer spots her NSA badge, pulls his gun and tries to subdue her. As Gibbs, DiNozzo and McGee rush to help Bishop, they find she has already wrestled the man to the ground and is holding his own gun on him. Investigating the killer further, Bishop determines that the killer was working for one of the defense contractors in the earlier briefing, who was trying to embarrass the SECNAV because she is a civilian who never served in uniform. Later Bishop meets privately with Gibbs and apologizes for not being a team player. Gibbs has pulled Bishop's application to NCIS she made before she started working at the NSA and offers her a joint duty assignment with NCIS. *Source:* [1]

No.	German Title	US Title	Air Date USA	Air Date GER	Directed by	Written by
11.244	Die teuflischen Drei	**Devil's Triad**	Dec 10, 2013	Mar 9, 2014	A.Brown	S.D.Binder

The team investigate the death of a Marine who was reportedly shot by a clown. A number on a cellphone found on the Marine is traced to a hotel room where Gibbs and Tony accidentally chance upon Fornell and his and Gibbs' ex-wife Diane Sterling. The cellphone belongs to an Eddie Macklin but the team keep hitting dead ends with the evidence. However, the case takes an unexpected turn when Gibbs and Fornell discover that "Eddie Macklin" is the alias of Secret Service Special Agent Edward McKenzie and that NCIS had stumbled on a highly classified six month-long undercover operation. *Source:* [1]

Fornell: I'm just sayin' that there's something different this time, maybe because we're ex's. You should try it. I mean, with another one of your ex-wives...not this one 'cause...this one's taken.
Gibbs: Can I go home now?
Fornell: You are the worst advice-giver I've ever met! Don't quit your day job.

Fornell: If you so much as touch a hair on my daughter's head, so help me God, I will find you and I will rip your eyes out of your face and shove them so far down your throat you'll need a proctologist to read the evening paper.

Source: [22]

Episodes Season 11

No.	German Title	US Title	Air Date USA	Air Date GER	Directed by	Written by
11.245	Patient Null	**Homesick**	Dec 17, 2013	Mar 16, 2014	T.O'Hara	S.Williams

The holiday mood is ruined when the team is called up by the Naval Medical Research Center and CDC to investigate a potential bioterrorist threat after eight children from Navy and Marine families are hospitalized in the ICU with similar symptoms. The team finds out the outbreak is not a deliberate attack: a returning serviceman accidentally acted as a carrier for a rare African disease, which can be easily treated. Vance finds himself receiving a visit from his estranged father-in-law, who he bears a grudge against for abandoning Jackie when she was young. However, Vance eventually has a change of heart and allows his father-in-law to make amends. *Source:* [1]

No.	German Title	US Title	Air Date USA	Air Date GER	Directed by	Written by
11.246	Tod aus der Luft	**Kill Chain (1)**	Jan 7, 2014	Mar 23, 2014	J.Whitmore, Jr.	C.Silber

A stolen drone is later revealed to be linked to the elusive terrorist, Benham Parsa, forcing the NCIS team to join forces with the Department of Defense which brings the team back into contact with retired Lt. Colonel Hollis Mann who is also Gibbs' ex-girlfriend. As such, both teams must track down and recover the device before it is used for a large scale attack. As this happens, McGee is struggling with the possibility of asking for time off as he wants to attend a black-tie gala honoring his girlfriend. *Source:* [1]

No.	German Title	US Title	Air Date USA	Air Date GER	Directed by	Written by
11.247	Güterzug nach Miami	**Double Back (2)**	Jan 14, 2014	Mar 30, 2014	T.Wharmby	G.L.Monreal

In an attempt to find the terrorist Parsa, Gibbs and the team track down one of Parsa's minions using evidence from the drone attack in "Kill Chain" while McGee is left struggling to come to terms with what happened at the black-tie gala evening. While the team fails to catch Parsa, they do get a clue on where he might have gone. Meanwhile, McGee confides to Gibbs that Delilah was paralyzed in the attack, but he is determined to stay by Delilah's side. *Source:* [1]

Bishop: So we're looking for a bullet because....?
Tony: Clipped a guy. Could have DNA on it.
Bishop: Parsa's?
Tony: No, driver.
Bishop: Seriously??? How did you get that?
Tony: Well, it's like Gorillas in the Mist. You'll come to understand his grunts.

Source: [22]

No.	German Title	US Title	Air Date USA	Air Date GER	Directed by	Written by
11.248	Parsas Spiel	**Monsters and Men (3)**	Feb 04, 2014	Aug 17, 2014	D.Smith	J.Corbett

The murder of a port authority officer reveals Parsa's possible whereabouts, as the team continues their tireless hunt. Meanwhile, Bishop reveals her past association with the elusive terrorist. *Source:* [1]

Episodes Season 11

No.	German Title	US Title	Air Date USA	Air Date GER	Directed by	Written by
11.249	Kugelsicher	**Bulletproof**	Feb 25, 2014	Aug 24, 2014	L.Libman	C.J.Waild

The team examine a crash and soon discover bulletproof vests associated with the United States Marine Corps but the investigation takes a turn after Abby's tests determine that the supposedly safe vests are actually faulty. *Source:* [1]

Bishop: Can I ask you a question?
Gibbs: Uh-hmm. Just did.
Bishop: You were a sniper. How did you do it?
Gibbs: Pulled the trigger.
Bishop: Right....But, what...what did you think about when you were taking aim?
Gibbs: Smoke checking the target, Bishop.
Bishop: Right, of course.

Source: [22]

No.	German Title	US Title	Air Date USA	Air Date GER	Directed by	Written by
11.250	Schüsse am Sonntag	**Dressed to Kill**	Mar 4, 2014	Aug 31, 2014	T.J.Wright	G.Schenck & F.Cardea

After meeting his father, DiNozzo confronts a man dressed as a Navy commander. The man runs and is followed by DiNozzo who ultimately shoots and kills him. The only witness is DiNozzo's father. *Source:* [1]

Gibbs: What's on your mind?
DiNozzo Sr: Junior and I have hit another rough patch.
Gibbs: Ya think?
DiNozzo Sr: You've been more of a father to him than I have in the last twelve years. He respects you.

Source: [22]

No.	German Title	US Title	Air Date USA	Air Date GER	Directed by	Written by
11.251	Lampenfieber	**Rock and a Hard Place**	Mar 18, 2014	Sep 7, 2014	A.Brown	S.D.Binder

The speakers explode in the dressing room of a military charity event but the team realize someone else was targeted deliberately after finding shrapnel from a World War II-era Mark 24 warhead and that it was accidentally triggered earlier than the intended time of detonation. Meanwhile, Jimmy Palmer prepares to become a father and Tony received an unwanted task from his father. *Source:* [1]

No.	German Title	US Title	Air Date USA	Air Date GER	Directed by	Written by
11.252	New Orleans (1)	**Crescent City (Part I)**	Mar 25, 2014	Sep 14, 2014	J.Whitmore, Jr.	G.Glasberg

A Congressman is found murdered in New Orleans, Gibbs and his team join forces with Fornell's FBI team and the local NCIS field. Gibbs reunites with long-time compatriot and friend NCIS Special Agent Dwayne "King" Pride (Scott Bakula). With that, Gibbs and Bishop head to New Orleans while DiNozzo and McGee stay in D.C. to work the case with Fornell. Things soon become personal as the Congressman was a former NCIS agent and their contemporary and his murder could possibly be linked to one of their old cases. The episode ends with Gibbs, Pride and Agents Meredith Brody (Zoe McLellan) and Christopher LaSalle (Lucas Black) standing in a square while from a hotel room, the unrevealed killer begins taking surveillance photographs of the NCIS team as Gibbs and Pride look on. *Source:* [1]

Episodes Season 11

No.	German Title	US Title	Air Date USA	Air Date GER	Directed by	Written by
11.253	New Orleans (2)	**Crescent City (Part II)**	Apr 1, 2014	Sep 14, 2014	T.Wharmby	G.Glasberg

Another victim is found in the wetlands, dead at least two weeks. His throat had been cut with a steel blade and jet fuel is found in tire tracks near his body. Abby calls Gibbs to say the jet fuel matched the fuel found on the car mats belonging to victim Agent Doyle. A suspect, believed to have been obsessed with Congressman McLane and the Priviliged killer case, is also found dead. Gibbs and Pride track the killer, the son of a McClane contributor, to a military bar and a nearby cemetery, after Gibbs recalls marble dust also being found in Doyle's car. After solving this case, Pride and his team receive another one while Gibbs waits for Bishop in order to return home. *Source:* [1]

No.	German Title	US Title	Air Date USA	Air Date GER	Directed by	Written by
11.254	Trauzeugen gesucht	**Page Not Found**	Apr 8, 2014	Sep 21, 2014	T.O'Hara	C.J.Waild

When Delilah finds an encrypted email relating to the murder of a Navy lieutenant, she is ordered to ignore it but instead she goes to Gibbs and NCIS starts looking into it. The team realizes that the "murder" may not be a simple textbook murder case and that the CIA could be involved. Delilah and Tim discuss their future. *Source:* [1]

McGee: Tony, What are you doing in the closet?
Tony: Finding myself.

McGee: Thanks to Jones, we're able to see local ISP access.
Abby: And somewhere the head of Leroy Jethro Gibbs explodes.

Delilah: I know you and Tim are close.
Tony: We have showered together.

Source: [22]

No.	German Title	US Title	Air Date USA	Air Date GER	Directed by	Written by
11.255	Aussage gegen Aussage	**Alleged**	Apr 15, 2014	Sep 28, 2014	A.Brown	S.Williams

A female Navy officer's rape is brought to light when one of her colleagues is accidentally killed in a bar. It turns out her executive officer was responsible for hers and several other rapes. *Source:* [1]

Bishop: So this is some sort of competition?
Tony: No. Uh-uh. After McGee's recent emancipation from coupledom, we were talking making a fresh start.

Source: [22]

No.	German Title	US Title	Air Date USA	Air Date GER	Directed by	Written by
11.256	Blue	**Shooter**	Apr 29, 2014	Oct 5, 2014	D.Smith	G.Schenck & F.Cardea

A Marine photographer who disappeared prior to his testifying at a court martial is later found dead of an apparent drug overdose. The team is confronted with the situation of homeless veterans in the D,C. area whom the photographer was documenting. Abby decides to help a homeless woman reconnect with her family. *Source:* [1]

Bishop: *[after Tony notices McGee hasn't shaved]* I think beards are sexy. Can an NCIS agent grow one?
Tony: Not you!
McGee: I'm not growing a beard. I went back to the doctor's this morning. She told me I have pseudofolliculitis.
Tony: Is that a Mary Poppins song?

Source: [22]

Episodes Season 11

No.	German Title	US Title	Air Date USA	Air Date GER	Directed by	Written by
11.257	Flucht aus Marseille	**The Admiral's Daughter**	May 6, 2014	Oct 12, 2014	J.Whitmore, Jr.	S.D.Binder & C.Silber

Tony is assigned to escort Amanda, the daughter of the Vice Chairman of the Joint Chiefs of Staff from Marseille due to her extravagant partying ways but when he reaches the local NCIS office he finds all the employees and agents dead but he and Amanda find themselves on the run from a rogue French policewoman. The team back home work on a supposedly separate case involving a corpse found in a septic tank at Norfolk with a link to Amanda's father. Things become complicated when Tony discovers that Amanda's party-girl persona was a mere cover for her work with the Defense Clandestine Service.. *Source:* [1]

McGee: An internet security seminar? You?? Am I being punk'd?
Tony: No. Think about it. Who do you know that surfs more questionable websites than yours truly?
Bishop: Not something to be proud of.
McGee: You've a good point. That's what you get for being a misogynist. What do you get if you kick a dog? A trip to Hawaii?
Tony: Death by Abby.

Abby: Sometimes, I love my job. And sometimes, I have to crawl inside a giant septic tank.
Gibbs: Well, it could be worse.
Abby: How?
Gibbs: I'd have to climb in there with you.

Ducky: Your prognosis?
Palmer: It's not good.
Ducky: I hate to lose a patient.
Palmer: Wait, I think I've found the problem. Looks like the system drive is full. *[camera shot reveals Ducky's smartphone on the autopsy table]* How many apps did you install, Doctor?
Ducky: There's a limit??

Source: [22]

No.	German Title	US Title	Air Date USA	Air Date GER	Directed by	Written by
11.258	Jackson	**Honor Thy Father**	May 13, 2014	Oct 19, 2014	T.Wharmby	G.Glasberg & G.L.Monreal

The team hunts escapees from Navy vessel which served as a classified detention site for indicted terrorists. Special Agent Gibbs learns of his father Jackson's death. This episode pays tribute to the late Ralph Waite, who portrayed Jackson Gibbs. *Source:* [1]

Abby: So what, McGee, you don't check your e-mail anymore?
McGee: What? Did you send me something?
Abby: Yes, a satellite image!
McGee: [checks his e-mail] Abby, this e-mail just came through two minutes ago.
Tony: Two minutes is two years in Abby time. You know that.

Cal: Jackson Gibbs saved my life. I was headed down a bad road when he hired me. He said that, the world was bad enough as it is. You've got no right to...
Gibbs: ...make it any worse.
Cal: You know, no one ever cared enough to say stuff like that to me before.

Source: [22]

Season 12 (Episodes 12.259-12.282)

The twelfth season of the police procedural drama NCIS premiered on September 23, 2014, in the same time slot as in the previous seasons, Tuesdays at 8 pm. This is the first season in which NCIS: Los Angeles did not air after NCIS. This season, NCIS: New Orleans aired after NCIS. The entire season eleven cast renewed their contracts and returned for the new season. The premiere episode aired on September 23, 2014 and was seen by 18.23 million people.

The main antagonist of the season is Sergei Mishnev, played by Alex Veadov. This character first appears in the premiere episode "Twenty Klicks".

In episode four, "Choke Hold", one of Sergei's associates is sent to the United States to kill a Russian scientist that refused to work with him. Anton Pavlenko (previously seen in "Twenty Klicks"), portrayed by Lev Gorn, a Russian counselor, reappears in this episode. Veadov returns as Sergei in "Check" where he "gets personal" with Gibbs by killing Gibbs' ex-wife Diane the same way that Caitlin Todd was killed, stalking Rebecca, another of Gibbs' ex-wives, and staging murders mimicking the deaths of Mike Franks and Jenny Shepard.

Sergei returns again in "Cabin Fever" where he is killed by Tobias Fornell, who was also married to Diane at one point and who was dealing with intense grief and depression following Diane's murder. It is revealed that Sergei and Ari Haswari are half brothers from Ari's mother, whereas Ari and Ziva David were half brother and sister from their father, Eli David.

Source: [1]

Original Air Date USA	September 23, 2014 – May 12, 2015 on CBS
Original Air Date German Language	January 2, 2015 – Autumn 2015 on Sat 1

Episodes Season 12

No.	German Title	US Title	Air Date USA	Air Date GER	Directed by	Written by
12.259	Die Nadel im Heuhaufen	**Twenty Klicks**	Sep 23, 2014	Jan 4, 2015	T.Wharmby	G.Glasberg & S.Williams

Gibbs and McGee escort an NCIS computer engineer with classified information back to the U.S. from Russia. Things go awry when their transport helicopter is shot down over the wilderness of the Kola Peninsula near the Finnish border. The team back at the NCIS field office in Washington, D.C. find themselves having to navigate a diplomatic minefield when the Russian Embassy keeps mum on search and rescue efforts and Abby discovers that the helicopter had been shot down with a Russian missile reportedly stolen by dangerous group of mercenaries with a personal score to settle. *Source:* [1]

No.	German Title	US Title	Air Date USA	Air Date GER	Directed by	Written by
12.260	Anruf aus dem weißen Haus	**Kill the Messenger**	Sep 30, 2014	Jan 11, 2015	D.Smith	G.Schenck & F.Cardea

A lieutenant commander in the United States Navy is murdered before his private meeting with the President of the United States. The team investigates to see if it he was another unfortunate victim of a criminal streak or intentionally targeted for valuable information. Director Vance receives some devastating news. *Source:* [1]

[Tony looks on as Bishop removes the mug shot of Benham Parsa from the "Most Wanted" wall]
Tony: You're gonna keep it as a souvenir?
Bishop: Oh yeah. I've got the perfect place for it. *[tosses it into the recycling bin]*

Source: [23]

No.	German Title	US Title	Air Date USA	Air Date GER	Directed by	Written by
12.261	Die falsche Wahl	**So It Goes**	Oct 7, 2014	Jan 18, 2015	L.Libman	S.D.Binder

Ducky returns to London after a case reveals a connection to his estranged childhood best friend. Agent Bishop accompanies him on the trip, and they interview his friend's family and coworkers. Meanwhile, Ducky recalls the choices he made in the past and the impact they've had on his adult life. *Source:* [1]

Bishop: We also have his yearly salaries, favorite bands and his political positions on everything from the Middle East to Middle-earth.
Tony: Which he's a big fan of, by the way.
Abby: I can handle Middle Earth.

Maggie: Why didn't you ever marry? You had so much love to give.
Ducky: A colleague, a very good friend of mine, lost his soulmate. And then he nearly wrecked his life marrying the wrong woman over and over, trying to find her again. I...chose to skip that part.

Source: [23]

Episodes Season 12

No.	German Title	US Title	Air Date USA	Air Date GER	Directed by	Written by
12.262	Die Schlinge um den Hals	**Choke Hold**	Oct 14, 2014	Jan 25, 2015	T.O'Hara	C.J.Waild

SECNAV places the NCIS team to a counter-terrorism task force after a Navy scientist is dead, and her murderer is being hunted by Russian mercenaries. *Source:* [1]

Bishop: *[catches Tony and McGee reading a men's magazine]* You don't have to change the subject. I'm not the sex police.
Tony: How kind you are.
Bishop: Um, hello? I'm married. I have more sex than the two of you combined.
Tony: From what I hear, that's not how that works.

McGee: I read somewhere that NASA's sending data to the moon at 662 megabits per second. Word is, if by using h color on the light spectrum, that transfer speed could be multiplied. Johns Hopkins. And MIT.
Bishop: Humblebrag.
Dr. Havana: Don't worry, I'm a Caltech man. Sworn enemies don't get extra credit.
Bishop: Aren't both of your mascots beavers?

[The Secretary of the Navy is waiting for Gibbs and Vance in a basement men's restroom]
Secretary: *[looks at the row of urinals]* How do you do it? It's like pigs at a trough.
Gibbs: In some places it really is a trough, ma'am. [he and Vance look at each other] Fenway, Wrigley...
Vance: Mm-hmm, mostly stadiums.

Agent Pendergrast: Call me Leia.
Tony: Like the princess.
Agent Pendergrast: I hate Star Wars.
Tony: Nobody hates Star Wars!
Agent Pendergrast: You do when you're named Leia, Agent DiNozzo.

Agent Pendergrast: If half of what I heard about NCIS is true, you guys must have something the FBI doesn't.

Abby: Who are you what are you doing here and who's the twenty-seventh President of the United States?

Tony: *[flirting with Agent Pendergrast]* You know what "Tony" is spelled backwards? Y not?

Source: [23]

Episodes Season 12

No.	German Title	US Title	Air Date USA	Air Date GER	Directed by	Written by
12.263	San Dominick	**The San Dominick**	Oct 21, 2014	Feb 1, 2015	A.Brown	C.Silber

Special Agent Gibbs and CGIS Agent Borin discover the body of a man who is a missing crew member from a ship that is 60 nautical miles away. Once aboard the ship, Gibbs realizes that it has been commandeered by pirates, but all is not what it seems. *Source:* [1]

McGee: The trainee returns. How did it go?
Bishop: I won't talk about it.
McGee: That good, huh?

Gibbs: What's your name?
Petty Officer Felton: Petty Officer Felton
Gibbs: What's your first name?
PO Felton: Patricia
Gibbs: call you Patty?
[PO Felton groans]
Gibbs: *[grins]* You hate being called Patty.

Bishop: What'd we do...boss?
McGee: Please stop calling me that.

Abigail Borin: It's Hostage Negotiation 101, DiNozzo. Keep them stalled, keep them calm, keep them talking.
Tony: Just like dating.

Ducky: *[talking to the corpse in his autopsy room]* I know in the end we all must die. I'm not a religious person but I find desecration of the human body to be positively indecent.
McGee: *[walks in holding coffee]* Parents aren't known for their decency, Duck.
Ducky: *[stares at McGee, speechless]* Uh....
McGee: Is something wrong?
Ducky: No, Timothy but I request that you dispense with the coffee before joining me.

Abby: Gosh, I just got chills.
McGee: Why is that?
Abby: You're just....changing...right in front of our eyes. Your gruff manner, your clipped replies. You're no longer McGee. You're McGibbs.

Tony: Hey...still here, Borin? Admit it, I'm growing on you.
Borin: Like a barnacle.

Tony: 35 seconds...running out of time, Boss.
Gibbs: Jaime, you've got two choices. You drop the weapon and I diffuse the bomb. Or I shoot you and I diffuse the bomb.
[...]
Tony: The bomb thing, that was kinda fun right. Next time, you might want to give us a heads up tough, because I didn't pack a diaper.

Tony: *[enters squad room and sees McGee working at his desk]* Well, McGee, I just want you to know I'm proud of you. You didn't blow anything up and there were no international incidents.

Source: [23]

Episodes Season 12

No.	German Title	US Title	Air Date USA	Air Date GER	Directed by	Written by
12.264	Meister der Irreführung	**Parental Guidance Suggested**	28. Okt. 2014	8. Feb. 2015	T.J.Wright	J.Corbett

A woman whose Navy SEAL husband's name is on a jihadist hit list has been murdered, and the team must figure out if her death was the result of a terrorist attack or something much more sinister. One of Tony's old friends, ATF Special Agent Zoe Keates, is introduced. *Source: 1*

Bishop: It's not that I don't want to dress up, ok? It's....it's just that Jake and I can't agree on a costume.
Tony: Phew...marriage. Here we go. [Bishop glares at him] Halloween used to be a single guy's paradise. Now it's been twisted and co-opted into some kind of couples thing.

Tony: What can I say? Women find me alluring.

[The team are out under cover with Tony and Bishop posing as yoga practitioners]
Bishop: Didn't know you practiced yoga.
Tony: Oh yeah, balanced mind, balanced life. I've been reading Sting's biography. He's a Renaissance man.
McGee: *[via microphone]* Please, I just ate.
Tony: I reject your negative energy, McGee.

Source: 23

No.	German Title	US Title	Air Date USA	Air Date GER	Directed by	Written by
12.265	Hundemarken	**The Searchers**	Nov 11, 2014	Feb 15, 2015	T.Wharmby	G.L.Monreal

After the murder of a retired Master Sergeant, NCIS uncovers a fraudulent charity that preys on those searching for missing military personnel. Meanwhile, Bishop agonizes over her probationary exam results. *Source: 1*

Ducky: Today is a difficult day.
Bishop: It is?
Palmer: You've been training for nine months now. Nine months! Magical time frame isn't it? To think, in three months, Breena and I are gonna have our own little human [Ducky rolls his eyes] who hopefully enjoys long walks. *[notices Bishop and Ducky]* Sorry, this is about you.

Tony: Money...the root of all evil.

Abby: Gibbs, Gibbs, Gibbs, Gibbs, Gibbs! I have news, I have lots of news, I have big news.

Tony: *[about the cat he adopted]* He's like the feline version of me.

McGee: Abs, I have pulled two all-nighters in a row and I've nothing left to give.
Palmer: *[enters Abby's lab with two Caf-Pows]* I have two things left to give and they're both Caf-Pows. Pow! Pow!
Abby: Jimmy, you are a lifesaver. *[glares at McGee]* You. Drink.

Price: *[while being handcuffed by Tony]* It was self-defense. I wouldn't dare...I was just scaring him, he came at me. I'm telling you, it was self-defense.
Gibbs: You gave him false hope. You murdered a United States Marine. There is no defense for that.

Source: 23

Episodes Season 12

No.	German Title	US Title	Air Date USA	Air Date GER	Directed by	Written by
12.266	Die Heldin	**Semper Fortis**	Nov 18, 2014	Feb 22, 2015	D.Smith	M.R.Jarrett & S.J.Jarrett

Gibbs looks for a way to clear a Navy Hospital Corpsman of charges after she has illegally helped the victims of a hit and run. Abby's relationship with Burt hits the 2-month mark. *Source:* [1]

Gibbs: If I could

Source: [23]

No.	German Title	US Title	Air Date USA	Air Date GER	Directed by	Written by
12.267	Eingeschneit	**Grounded**	Nov 25, 2014	Mar 1, 2015	B.Rooney	S.Williams

While weather worsens outdoors, DiNozzo, Bishop, and her husband, Jake (Jamie Bamber), are stuck at Dulles Airport working on a case involving a terrorist threat. *Source:* [1]

Bishop: *[to a woman looking at the snow outside the window]* Pretty, isn't it?
Woman: Oh, yes dear. It's just lovely. It's lovely how it turned a one-hour drive into three, soaked a brand new pair of my shoes right down to the toes. Simply spectacular.
Bishop: Well, at least you'll be getting away from it for the holiday.
Woman: I'm going to Calgary.

Tony: Flight delays make nice people cranky and cranky people crankier.

[Ducky and Palmer walk into the hotel room (crime scene) covered in snow]
Ducky: It ain't a fit night out for man nor beast.
Palmer: And yet I'm the one who had to get out and push the van, Shakespeare.
Ducky: That was W. C. Fields, Mr. Palmer, in The Fatal Glass of Beer. And I predict you will be pushing it again on the way back.

Jake: Gees, when you're looking for bad guys ...
Tony: ... they all look like bad guys.

Source: [23]

No.	German Title	US Title	Air Date USA	Air Date GER	Directed by	Written by
12.268	Krampus	**House Rules**	Dec 16, 2014	Mar 8, 2015	T.O'Hara	C.J.Waild

When a DDoS attack crashes the Internet in Washington, D.C., NCIS asks for help from three hackers they had previously encountered: Ajay Khan ("Canary"), Kevin Hussein ("Twenty Klicks"), and Heidi Partridge ("Page Not Found"), and the case makes McGee think about Gibbs' rules and his strained relationship with his dying father. *Source:* [1]

Episodes Season 12

No.	German Title	US Title	Air Date USA	Air Date GER	Directed by	Written by
12.269	Schach	**Check**	Jan 6, 2015	Mar 15, 2015	Al.Riley	S.D.Binder

Two of Gibbs' wives return, whilst the team are forced to investigate murders of both Navy Personnel and friends, killed in ways mimicking the deaths of Mike Franks, Jennifer Shepard, and Caitlin Todd. *Source:* [1]

No.	German Title	US Title	Air Date USA	Air Date GER	Directed by	Written by
12.270	Die Heimkehrer	**The Enemy Within**	Jan 13, 2015	Mar 20, 2015	J.Whitmore, Jr.	G.Schenck & F.Cardea

NCIS hunts down a homegrown terrorist after a rescue mission in Syria reveals that an American was involved in the kidnapping of a social worker. McGee and Bishop question Tony's recent habits as ATF Special Agent Zoe Keats returns to work the case and turns out to be his girlfriend. Meanwhile, Tobias Fornell is struggling with the loss of Diane and raising Emily alone. *Source:* [1]

No.	German Title	US Title	Air Date USA	Air Date GER	Directed by	Written by
12.271	Die Ehre eines Helden	**We Build, We Fight**	Feb 3, 2015	Mar 29, 2015	R.Carroll	J.Corbett

The team's investigation into a petty officer's death leads to the discovery that he is gay, and the investigation gets Hollis Mann involved when the victim was being considered for the Medal of Honor. Meanwhile, Breena goes into labor and gives birth to a daughter: Victoria Elizabeth Palmer. *Source:* [1]

No.	German Title	US Title	Air Date USA	Air Date GER	Directed by	Written by
12.272	-	**Cadence**	Feb 10, 2015	-	T.Wharmby	C.Silber

When a Marine private is found dead, the investigation leads Tony and Bishop to the private's former school (and also Tony's), where they discover some dark secrets lurking in the academy. Bishop and Jake ask Gibbs, Tony, and McGee to dinner. *Source:* [1]

Episodes Season 12

No.	German Title	US Title	Air Date USA	Air Date GER	Directed by	Written by
12.273	-	**Cabin Fever**	Feb 17, 2015	-	B.Rooney	S.Williams

When an explosion at a summit for global terror results in the death of a Navy Petty Officer, the NCIS team investigates. Gibbs later opts to sit out for the duration of the case to help Fornell, who is on the verge of self-destruction following the death of his wife. Eventually, the NCIS team discovers that Sergei Mishnev is the half-brother of deceased terrorist, Ari Haswari. Sergei's regime of terror eventually comes to an end when he is shot dead, this time at Fornell's hands. *Source:* [1]

No.	German Title	US Title	Air Date USA	Air Date GER	Directed by	Written by
12.274	-	**Blast from the Past**	Feb 24 2015	-	D.Smith	D.J.North

When a murder victim is discovered to have an ID Gibbs used for undercover operations twenty years earlier, the investigation leads to the discovery that several former undercover IDs have been leaked for use by Serbian intelligence. *Source:* [1]

No.	German Title	US Title	Air Date USA	Air Date GER	Directed by	Written by
12.275	-	**The Artful Dodger**	Mar 10, 2015	-	T.O´Hara	G.L.Monreal

Following the murder of a lieutenant in an Admiral's office, the team's investigation leads them to tracking down a painting that contains a listening device planted by terrorists. Tony's father returns after his fiancee left him and soon joins the case. *Source:* [1]

No.	German Title	US Title	Air Date USA	Air Date GER	Directed by	Written by
12.276	-	**Status Update**	Mar 24, 2015	-	H.Dale	C.J.Waild

After a thief is murdered in a Marine's home, the team's investigation leads them to a joint effort with the DOD and Delilah to hunt down a terrorist. *Source:* [1]

Episodes Season 12

No.	German Title	US Title	Air Date USA	Air Date GER	Directed by	Written by
12.277	-	**Patience**	Mar 31, 2015	-	T.J.Wright	S.D.Binder

When a supposed petty officer and a woman he is transporting are murdered, the team's investigation leads Gibbs and Tony to bring in McGee and Bishop on a cold case they have been working years on - an unsolved bombing from 1979, and the current case may help them not only prove who is responsible, but where the bomber is. *Source:* [1]

No.	German Title	US Title	Air Date USA	Air Date GER	Directed by	Written by
12.278	-	**No Good Deed**	Apr 7, 2015	-	A.Brown	G.Schenck & F.Cardea

When a Marine is discovered to have been shot with a weapon gone missing from an ATF sting, NCIS discovers the victim had been pursuing a woman abducted by a rogue ATF informant. Meanwhile, things get complicated with Tony when his father comes back down to meet Zoe. *Source:* [1]

No.	German Title	US Title	Air Date USA	Air Date GER	Directed by	Written by
12.279	-	**Lost in Translation**	Apr 14, 2015	-	T.Wharmby	J.Corbett

After a Marine captain is found tortured and killed, the team's investigation leads them to an Afghani citizen who worked as a translator for the deceased, and his brother who is a ruthless Taliban operative. Bishop's past comes to light when she and Gibbs travel to Afghanistan. *Source:* [1]

No.	German Title	US Title	Air Date USA	Air Date GER	Directed by	Written by
12.280	-	**Troll**	Apr 28, 2015	-	D.Smith	S.Williams

When a tech working for ONI is found dead, the team reunites with Ned Dorneget to investigate her computer activity and their investigation soon leads them to a rough intersection with NSA and then to something even bigger - a terrorist organization recruiting youths. *Source:* [1]

Episodes Season 12

No.	German Title	US Title	Air Date USA	Air Date GER	Directed by	Written by
12.281	-	**The Lost Boys**	May 5, 2015	-	J.Whitmore, jr.	G.L.Monreal

NCIS search for a terrorist organization known as "The Calling", a group that recruits young children and teenagers through the Internet while the agency itself suffers a tragedy when Agent Ned Dorneget is killed in an explosion at a hotel in Cairo, Egypt. *Source:* [1]

No.	German Title	US Title	Air Date USA	Air Date GER	Directed by	Written by
12.282	-	**Neverland**	May 12, 2015	-	T.Wharmby	G.Glasberg

Following a deadly bombing oversas, the NCIS team works with several law enforcement agencies, including the CIA, to track a global terrorist group that is recruiting teens via the internet. *Source:* [24]

Actors

Thomas Mark Harmon *(NCIS - role: Leroy Jethro Gibbs)*

(born September 2, 1951 in Burbank, California) is an American actor. Since the mid-1970s, he has appeared in a variety of television, film and stage roles following a brief career as a collegiate football player with the UCLA Bruins. Since 2003, Harmon has starred as Leroy Jethro Gibbs in the hit CBS series NCIS.

Harmon was the youngest of three children. His parents were Heisman Trophy winner and broadcaster Tom Harmon and actress and artist, Elyse Knox (née Elsie Lillian Kornbrath). Harmon has two older sisters, actress and painter Kristin Nelson, the former wife of singer Ricky Nelson, and actress-model Kelly Harmon, who was once married to car magnate John DeLorean. His maternal grandparents were Austrian immigrants.

Following high school graduation in 1970, Harmon spent his first two years of college at Pierce College in Los Angeles. After gaining his associate's degree, he transferred to the University of California, Los Angeles, and was the starting quarterback for the UCLA Bruins football team in 1972 and 1973. In his first game for UCLA in 1972, he engineered a stunning upset of the two-time defending national champion, Nebraska Cornhuskers. The Bruins were an 18-point underdog to the top-ranked Huskers, but won 20-17 with a late field goal under the lights in Los Angeles. As a senior, Harmon received the National Football Foundation Award for All-Round Excellence in 1973. In his two years as quarterback in coach Pepper Rodgers' wishbone offense, UCLA compiled a 17–5 record (.773). Harmon graduated from UCLA with a B.A. in Communication cum laude in 1974.

Even though he considered "advertising or law" as careers after college, Harmon became an actor and has spent much of his career portraying law enforcement and medical personnel. Other than athletics/sports appearances, one of his first national TV appearances was with his father Tom Harmon, in a commercial for Kellogg's Product 19 cereal, for which the latter was the longtime TV spokesman. As an actor, his first credit came courtesy of his sister Kristen's in-laws, Ozzie Nelson and Harriet Nelson, in an episode of Ozzie's Girls. This was followed by guest-starring roles on episodes of Adam-12, Police Woman, and Emergency! in mid-1975 ("905-Wild" centered on two L.A. County Animal Control Officers and was a backdoor pilot episode for a series, but did not sell). Producer/creator Jack Webb, who was the packager of both series, later cast Harmon in Sam, a short-lived 1977 series about an LAPD officer and his K-9 partner. Also in 1977, Harmon received an Emmy nomination for Outstanding Supporting Actor in a Miniseries or a Movie for his performance as Robert Dunlap in the TV movie Eleanor and Franklin: The White House Years. In 1978 he appeared in three episodes of the acclaimed mini-series, Centennial, as Captain John MacIntosh,an honorable Union cavalry officer.

During the mid-1970s, Harmon made guest appearances on shows such as Laverne & Shirley and The Hardy Boys/Nancy Drew Mysteries and had supporting roles in the feature films Comes a Horseman (1978) and Beyond the Poseidon Adventure (1979). He then landed a co-starring role on the 1979 action series 240-Robert as Deputy Dwayne Thibideaux. The series centered around the missions of the Los Angeles County Sheriff's Department Emergency Services Detail, but was also short-lived.

In 1980, Harmon gained a regular role in the primetime soap opera Flamingo Road, in which he played Fielding Carlisle, the husband of Morgan Fairchild's character. Despite initially good ratings, the series was canceled after two seasons. Following its cancellation, he landed the role of Dr. Robert Caldwell on the prestigious NBC Emmy-winning series St. Elsewhere in 1983. Harmon appeared in the show for almost three seasons before leaving in early 1986 when his character contracted HIV through unprotected intercourse, one of the first instances where a major recurring television character contracted the virus (the character's subsequent off-screen death from AIDS would be mentioned two years later). In the mid-1980s, Harmon also became the spokesperson for Coors Regular beer, appearing in television commercials for them.

Harmon's career reached several other high points in 1986. In January, he was named People magazine's Sexiest Man Alive. Following his departure from St. Elsewhere in February, he played the lead in the TV movies Prince of Bel Air, co-starring with Kirstie Alley, and The Deliberate Stranger, in which he played serial killer Ted Bundy. With his career blossoming, he gained a role in the 1986 theatrical film Let's Get Harry and the lead role in the 1987 comedy Summer School, again co-starring with Kirstie Alley. Returning briefly to episodic television in 1987, Harmon had a limited engagement on the series Moonlighting, playing Cybill Shepherd's love interest Sam Crawford for four episodes. He then starred in the 1987 TV movie After The Promise. In 1988, he co-starred with Sean Connery and Meg Ryan in the 1988 feature film The Presidio, and also opposite Jodie Foster in the film Stealing Home. Despite several high profile roles, Harmon's film career never gathered momentum and, after a muted reception to his 1989 comedy Worth Winning, he returned to television, appearing in various television movies.

Harmon's next regular television role would be as Chicago police detective Dickie Cobb for two seasons (1991–1993) on the NBC series Reasonable Doubts. In 1993, he appeared in one episode in the role of a rodeo clown on the CBS comedy/western series Harts of the West with future cast mate Sean Murray, who plays McGee on NCIS.

In 1995, Harmon starred in the ABC series Charlie Grace, in which he portrayed a private investigator. The series lasted only one season, after which he returned to ensemble medical shows on the series Chicago Hope, in which he played Dr. Jack McNeil from 1996-2000. He also portrayed astronaut Wally Schirra in one episode of the 1998 mini-series From the Earth to the Moon.

In May 2002, he portrayed Secret Service Special Agent Simon Donovan on The West Wing in a four-episode story arc. The role gained him his second Emmy Award nomination, exactly 25 years after his first nomination. Harmon appeared in a guest starring role in two episodes of JAG in April 2003, which introduced the character of NCIS agent Leroy Jethro Gibbs; since 2003, Harmon has starred as Gibbs in the CBS drama NCIS. During his time on the show, he was reunited with three of his former Chicago Hope co-stars, Rocky Carroll, Lauren Holly, and Jayne Brook. Since 2008, he has also been a producer/executive producer. Also in 2003, Harmon had a supporting role in the remake of the comedy film Freaky Friday.

Harmon also starred in several stage productions in Los Angeles and Toronto. At the Cast Theatre in Los Angeles he performed in Wrestlers and The Wager. In the late eighties he was part of the cast of the Canadian premier of Key Exchange. Several productions of Love Letters provided him the opportunity to play alongside wife Pam Dawber.

Harmon received the 2,482nd star of the Hollywood Walk of Fame on October 1, 2012.

He worked as a carpenter before making a success of his acting career. On NCIS, his carpentry skills are alluded to through his character's hobby of building boats in his basement.

Harmon has been married to actress Pam Dawber since March 21, 1987. The couple have two sons: Sean Thomas Harmon (born April 25, 1988, who played a young Gibbs in NCIS Season 6 Episode 4 and Episode 15, Season 7 Episode 16, Season 9 Episode 8 and 15), and Ty Christian Harmon (born June 25, 1992). Harmon was the brother-in-law of Ricky Nelson and is the uncle of actress Tracy Nelson and singers Matthew and Gunnar Nelson of the pop duo Nelson. Harmon dated singer Karen Carpenter in the 1970s.

In 1987, Harmon filed for custody of his nephew Sam based on grounds that his sister Kris was incapable of good parenting. Sam's psychiatrist testified the thirteen-year-old boy depicted his mother as a dragon, complained about her mood swings and how she prevented him from being with his siblings. Harmon later dropped the custody bid.

In 1996, Harmon saved two teenage boys involved in a car accident outside of his home. Harmon used a sledgehammer from his garage to break the window of their burning car, then pulled them free from the flames.

Source: [5]

Awards und Nominations Mark Harmon

People Magazine
1986: Sexiest Man Alive

Primetime Emmy Award
1977: nominated, Outstanding Supporting Actor in a Miniseries or Movie – Eleanor and Franklin: The White House Years
2002: nominated, Outstanding Guest Actor in a Drama Series – The West Wing

Golden Globe Awards
1986: nominated, Best Actor in a Miniseries or Television Film – The Deliberate Stranger
1987: nominated, Best Actor in a Miniseries or Television Film – After The Promise
1991, 1992: nominated, Best Actor in a Television Series Drama – Reasonable Doubts

Screen Actors Guild Awards
1996, 1997: nominated, Outstanding Performance by an Ensemble in a Drama Series – Chicago Hope

People's Choice Awards
2010: nominated, Favorite TV Drama Actor – 2011: nominated, Favorite TV Crime Fighter – NCIS
2014: nominated, Favorite TV Drama Actor

Prism Awards
2014: won, Male Performance in a Drama Series

Source: [5]

Filmography (Selection) Mark Harmon

1975: Emergency! (One episode)
1978: Comes a Horseman
1978: Centennial
1979–1981: 240-Robert
1979: Beyond the Poseidon Adventure
1980: The Dream Merchants
1981: Flamingo Road
1981: Goliath Awaits
1983–1986: St. Elsewhere
1984: Tuareg – Il Guerriero del Deserto
1986: Prince of Bel Air
1986: The Deliberate Stranger
1986: Let's Get Harry
1987: Summer School
1987: After The Promise
1987: Moonlighting
1988: The Presidio
1988: Stealing Home
1989: Worth Winning
1991: Till There Was You
1991: Dillinger
1991: Fourth Story
1991: Long Road Home
1991: Shadow of a Doubt
1991: Cold Heaven
1994: Natural Born Killers - Wyatt Earp
1995: The Last Supper -
1995: Charlie Grace
1995: Magic in the Water
1996–2000: Chicago Hope
1997: Casualties
1998: Fear and Loathing in Las Vegas
2001: Crossfire Trail
2002: The West Wing
2003: Freaky Friday
since 2003: NCIS
2004: Chasing Liberty
2009: Weather Girl
2010: Justice League: Crisis On Two Earths (Voice of Superman)
2011: John Sandford's Certain Prey
2012: Family Guy
2014: NCIS: New Orleans (one episode)

Source: [5]

Michael Manning Weatherly, Jr. *(NCIS - role: Anthony „Tony" DiNozzo)*

(born July 8, 1968 in New York City) is an American actor and director, best known for his roles as Special Agent Anthony DiNozzo on the television series NCIS, and Logan Cale on the television series Dark Angel.

Michael Weatherly raised in Fairfield, Connecticut, by parents Patricia O'Hara, a hospital administrator, and Michael Manning Weatherly, Sr. He graduated from Brooks School in North Andover, Massachusetts, in 1986. Subsequently, he spent some time at American University but he left college to pursue acting. He also had a great passion for music, and played in a band while pursuing his acting career. During this time he, like many young actors, appeared in various small works. One of his is a video shot for a Karaoke CD: A Taste Of Honey's version of "Sukiyaki". Despite not continuing with his band, he contributed the song Bitter and Blue to the second soundtrack album of NCIS.

Weatherly began his professional acting career with a minor television role on The Cosby Show as Theo Huxtable's roommate. He then obtained the role of Cooper Alden on Loving and later, The City, which he would portray from 1992 until 1996.

With various guest spots on television he moved to Los Angeles. After moving, he landed a role as a series regular on the FOX television series Significant Others, with Jennifer Garner. The show only lasted six episodes. He then met director Whit Stillman, who cast him in the 1998 film The Last Days of Disco as Hap, opposite Chloë Sevigny. Michael also had a guest appearance as a Warlock in the series Charmed during its first season in 1998.

He began his movie acting career in 1997 with Meet Wally Sparks, as Dean Sparks. In 2000, he had a role in Cabin by the Lake. This was followed by a role in the independent film Trigger Happy (2001) opposite Rosario Dawson.

He starred in Dark Angel for the two seasons it was on the air. This role earned him three award nominations, two Saturn awards for Best supporting actor on Television in 2001 and 2002, and one Teen Choice award for choice actor in 2001. During filming, Weatherly began a relationship with co-star Jessica Alba, leading to their engagement in 2002, later broken off.

In 2003, he appeared in JAG as Special Agent Anthony DiNozzo. He has continued that role on the CBS TV show NCIS.

In 2004 he starred in the television film The Mystery of Natalie Wood, portraying Robert Wagner. Since 2010 Robert Wagner has made 3 guest appearances on NCIS as Anthony DiNozzo, Sr., the father of Michael's character, Tony DiNozzo.

He was a guest presenter at the Australian Logie Awards of 2007 on 6 May 2007 and was a guest on Rove Live. Weatherly made his directing debut with the Season 8 episode of NCIS titled "One Last Score," which aired March 1, 2011.

Weatherly married his Loving/The City co-star Amelia Heinle, who currently plays Victoria Newman on The Young and the Restless, in 1995.[1] On January 10, 1996, Heinle gave birth to the couple's son, August Manning Weatherly, in New York City. The couple divorced in 1997.

In 2001, Weatherly became engaged to his Dark Angel co-star Jessica Alba, but the couple ended their engagement in 2003. His niece is actress Alexandra Breckenridge.

Weatherly married internist Bojana Janković in September 2009. The couple live in Los Angeles with two German Shepherd dogs, Oriana and Quantum. On January 12, 2012, Weatherly revealed via Twitter that he and Janković were expecting their first child together, a daughter, in April 2012.
On April 10, 2012, Janković gave birth to their daughter, Olivia, in Los Angeles.
On October 29, 2013, a son, Liam, was born.

Source: 6

Filmography (Selection) Michael Weatherly

1991: The Cosby Show (One episode)
1992–1995: Loving
1995–1996: The City
1996: Pier 66
1997: Meet Wally Sparks
1997: Asteroid
1997: Spy Game (One episode))
1998: The Advanced Guard
1998: The Last Days of Disco
1998: Significant Others
1998: Jesse
1998: Grown-Ups
1999: Winding Roads
1999: Charmed (One episode)
1999: The Crow: Stairway to Heaven (One episode)
2000: Cabin by the Lake, Fernsehfilm
2000: Gun Shy
2000: Ally McBeal (One episode)
2000: Grapevine (One episode)
2000: The Specials
2000–2002: Dark Angel
2001: Venus and Mars and Trigger Happy
2003: JAG
since 2003: NCIS
2004: The Mystery of Natalie Wood
2005: Her Minor Thing
2010: Charlie Valentine
2012: Major Crimes (One episode)
2014: Whose Line is it Anyway?
2014: NCIS: New Orleans (One episode)

Source: 6

Pauley Perette *(NCIS - role: Abigail „Abby" Sciuto)*

(born March 27, 1969 in New Orleans) is an American actress, best known for playing Abby Sciuto on the U.S. TV series NCIS. She is also a published writer, a singer and civil rights advocate.[7] Perrette also co-owns the "Donna Bell's Bake Shop" in Manhattan.

Perrette raised all over the southern United States. She told Craig Ferguson, on The Late Late Show with Craig Ferguson, that she lived in Georgia, Alabama, Tennessee, North Carolina, South Carolina, New York, New Jersey, and California.[citation needed] In a 2011 interview with the Associated Press, Perrette confessed her early ambitions were to work with animals, be in a rock and roll band or be an FBI agent. She attended Valdosta State University in Valdosta, Georgia, where she studied criminal justice, and later moved to New York City to study at the John Jay College of Criminal Justice. While in New York she held a variety of jobs: "Not only was I bartending in club-kids scene, with a bra and combat boots and a white Mohawk, but I also wore a sandwich board on roller skates passing out fliers for Taco Bell in the Diamond District." Perrette also worked as a cook on a Manhattan dinner cruise boat.

Perrette has worked for years in television and film, mostly doing commercials, voice-overs, music videos and short films, and worked as a bartender in New York City. It was while working odd jobs in New York a friend introduced her to an advertising agency director. From then on, according to Perrette, "I started booking commercials like crazy!." This prompted her move to Los Angeles, where she had a variety of bit parts and made several guest appearances. In 2001, as a recurring character introduced in season two of Special Unit 2, she played Alice Cramer, the Unit's public relations person. She then landed her current role, playing Abby Sciuto, an eccentric forensic scientist, on NCIS, a TV series based on the Naval Criminal Investigative Service. Perrette's initial appearances as the character were on two episodes of JAG aired in spring of 2003 that served as a backdoor pilot and introduced the characters. She has since appeared as Abby in two 2009 episodes of NCIS: Los Angeles. As of August 2011, she had the highest Q Score (a measurement of the familiarity and appeal) of any actor on a U.S. prime time show.

She also appeared as a waitress at Cafe Nervosa in Frasier during season four (in the episode "Three Dates and a Break Up"), and later guest starred in season one of 24. She has made appearances in several films, including The Ring and Almost Famous.

In addition to acting, Perrette is a published poet, writer (her short story "Cheers..." appears in the anthology Pills, Thrills, Chills, and Heartache: Adventures in the First Person), photographer, and spoken-word artist, a lover of music of all kinds, and a passionate advocate for civil rights. In 2007, she produced a documentary about U.S. civil rights attorney and author Mark Lane.

In an 2005 interview with Craig Ferguson, the host of The Late, Late Show, Perrette said she has a lifelong crime obsession. She was an undergrad student in sociology, psychology, and criminal science. She started her master's degree in criminal science before ending up in the entertainment industry. She now plays a forensic scientist, her former career goal.

In the January/February 2010 Performer Q Score, Perrette tied in the top 3 alongside Tom Hanks and Morgan Freeman. She was also the only female to make the top 10.

Perette started appearing in television commercials for Expedia.com in late 2010. She made a guest appearance as a judge on season four, episode six of RuPaul's Drag Race.

Perrette recorded her song, "Fear" (co-written with Tom Polce) under the name "Stop Making Friends". The song was recorded for NCIS: The Official TV Soundtrack which was released on February 10, 2009. "Fear" was featured in a season-six episode of NCIS titled "Aliyah", according to the soundtrack's website.

Prior to this, Perrette was the lead singer in the Los Angeles-based, all-female band Lo-Ball, using the stage name "Pauley P.". A song by Lo-Ball, "Can't Get Me Down", can be heard during the movie Legally Blonde. Perrette appeared in "The Unnamed Feeling" video for heavy metal band Metallica from their album St. Anger.

Most recently, Perrette was the featured vocalist on a song called "Fire in Your Eyes" by B. Taylor, a Las Vegas based hip hop artist.

Perrette was married for three years to actor and musician Coyote Shivers. She has been granted restraining orders against him since leaving him.

Perrette supports many charitable organizations, including animal rescue, the American Red Cross, civil rights, and homosexual rights. During the fall of 2008, Perrette opposed the California ballot initiative Proposition 8, writing a public letter urging Californians to vote against the measure. She is a member of the Hollywood United Methodist Church.

She was engaged with cameraman Michael Bosman, however the two were not legally married; saying they would wait until everyone can get married in the United States. They instead filed for all the legal protections that are available to same-sex couples. The couple had dated for four years, but Bosman did not propose until the legalization of same-sex marriage in California in June 2008. The couple then campaigned very publicly against California's Prop. 8. Perette and Bosman later split, and in December 2011 she announced her engagement to former British Royal Marine and actor Thomas Arklie. She has again announced that the couple will not marry until Proposition 8 is invalidated.

Perrette toured the real NCIS offices on September 30, 2005, accompanied by an Entertainment Tonight camera crew. During the tour, NCIS Regional Forensic Lab director Dawn Sorenson (Abby's real life counterpart) told Perrette, "You make us all look good, so we're grateful."

The character Abby Sciuto was created by Donald P. Bellisario, who "wanted to create...a character who was seemingly an 'alternafreak,' while portraying her as perhaps the smartest, most capable person on television. Not a junkie, killer, loser, or television stereotype." Perrette added some of her own "contributions" to the character, and also conferred with her friend Clint Catalyst, the "author of Cottonmouth Kisses [who is] often brought in as a guest on TV shows when they are doing pieces on goth or alternative culture." Perrette explained that "Clint and I and our 3,000 closest friends all play together...We've never sat around and labeled each other. Sure, there are nights when a certain event leans more towards one style than the other, but it's not like some turf war with gang colors." Like her character, Perrette has often been asked if she's goth or punk, to which her response is "Who cares?" Consequently, she told her employers that her character isn't the type to seek out a label; Abby "wouldn't call herself anything but Abby...What she represents is a smart, capable chick that cannot be reduced to a stereotype."

Perrette worked with America's Most Wanted in February 2004 to present the city of Prattville, Alabama with a check for $10,000, which will be used to supplement the reward offer for information leading to the arrest of the person who killed Shannon Paulk. Paulk was from Prattville, Alabama, near where Perrette had once lived as a child. Perrette also donated $10,000 to Detroit law enforcement officials to be used as a reward for information regarding the disappearance/murder of Raven Jeffries, a 7-year-old Detroit girl. (Perrette's husband was from Detroit.) The story originally aired on America's Most Wanted on September 8, 2007 on Fox. She also asked them for help in finding the person(s) who killed her friend, Lisa Williamson, who was murdered in 2007 after her Detroit home was set on fire.

Perrette was hospitalized in 2014 after "a severe allergic reaction to her [character's] trademark ink-black [hair] color." She told CBS News in Los Angeles that her face had swollen to twice its size and warned that "anyone out there [who] dyes their hair, particularly black, you need to be aware of the symptoms."

Source: [7]

Filmography (Selection) Pauley Perrette

1994: Magical Make Over
1994: Party of five
1996: Frasier
1996–1997: Murder One
1997: Early Edition
1997: The Price Of Kissing
1998: That's Life
1998: The Drew Carey Show
1999–2000: Time of your Life
2000: Almost Famous
2000: Smash
2001: Special Unit 2
2002: The Ring
2002: Dawson's Creek
2002: Haunted
2003: CSI: Crime Scene Investigation
2003: 24 and Ash tuesday
since 2003: NCIS
2004: A Moment of Grace
2005: Potheads: The Movie
2008: The Singularity is near
2009: Satan hates you
2009: NCIS: Los Angeles (2 episodes)
2012: Superman vs. The Elite (Voice of Lois Lane)
2013: Citizen Lane
2014: NCIS: New Orleans (one episode)

Source: [7]

Coté de Pablo *(NCIS - role: Ziva David)*

(born as María José de Pablo Fernández on November 12, 1979 in Santiago de Chile), is a Chilean stage and TV actress and recording artist. She is best known for her role as Ziva David in the CBS television series NCIS, for which she has won an ALMA Award. She also has embarked on a career as a songwriter and vocalist.

De Pablo has a younger sister, Andrea, and a brother who works as a DJ. When de Pablo was 10 years old, her mother, María Olga Fernández, received a job in Miami, Florida, at a Spanish-speaking television network. There, de Pablo attended Arvida Middle School and New World School of the Arts where she studied musical theater. In the 5th grade she found many people could not properly pronounce her first name of "María José," so she asked them to call her "Cote," a common Chilean nickname for "María José." De Pablo then attended Carnegie Mellon University in Pittsburgh, Pennsylvania, where she studied music and theater and appeared in several plays, including And the World Goes 'Round, The House of Bernarda Alba, Indiscretions, The Fantasticks, and A Little Night Music. She graduated in 2000.

After graduation she moved to New York City to find work as an actress, working as a waitress in an Indian restaurant in Manhattan and an Italian eatery in Brooklyn to support herself. She picked up parts in the New York City Public Theater in the TV show All My Children, and in commercials. In 2005 de Pablo was about to make her Broadway debut in The Mambo Kings [7] as Dolores Fuentes, but the show closed after a short trial run in San Francisco. Two days after The Mambo Kings closed de Pablo was asked to audition for NCIS. She was put alongside series star Michael Weatherly to test for chemistry during her second audition; he went offscript by brushing her hair back and commenting, "You remind me of Salma Hayek." De Pablo's response to Weatherly was to stay in character, and she "dismissed him completely." Afterwards, producer Donald Bellisario met with her when she was waiting for a cab to take her back to the airport, and told her she had gotten the part.

De Pablo hosted some episodes of the show Control from 1994 to 1995 on Univision, alongside former Entertainment Tonight host, Carlos Ponce.
De Pablo played the role of Marguerite Cisneros in The Jury (broadcast on the Fox Network). The show was short-lived, screening only ten one-hour episodes.
De Pablo is best known for her role on the CBS nighttime drama NCIS as Ziva David, a former Israeli Mossad Liaison Officer, now a Special Agent for NCIS. De Pablo describes the character as "someone completely different from anyone else on the show because she's been around men all her life; she's used to men of authority. She's not afraid of men."
In 2006 she won an Imagen Award at the Imagen Foundation Awards for Best Supporting Actress in Television for NCIS. In 2008 and 2009 she was nominated for the same award. Also in 2008 and 2009, she was nominated for an ALMA Award for Outstanding Actress in a Drama Television Series for NCIS. In 2011, Pablo was nominated once again for an Imagen Award, but this time it was for Best Actress in Television, not Supporting Actress. She won the 2011 ALMA Award for Favorite Television Actress-Leading Role in Drama.

De Pablo is in a long-term relationship with actor Diego Serrano.
As a consequence of kickboxing during scenes, de Pablo has been injured several times on the show including injuring her neck and back. She currently lives in Los Angeles, California.

Filmography (Selection) Coté de Pablo

1994-95: Control
2000: The $street
2001: The Education of Max Bickford
2002: TOCA Race Driver
2004: The Jury
2005-13: NCIS
2010: The Last Rites of Ransom Pride
2015: The 33 and The Dovekeepers

Awards und Nominations Coté de Pablo

2006: Won an Imagen Award for Best Supporting Actress in Television for NCIS
2008: Nominated for an Imagen Award for Best Supporting Actress in Television for NCIS
2008: Nominated for an ALMA Award for Outstanding Actress in a Drama Television Series for NCIS
2009: Nominated for an ALMA Award for Outstanding Actress in a Drama Television Series for NCIS
2009: Nominated for an Imagen Award for Best Supporting Actress in Television for NCIS
2011: Nominated for an Imagen Award for Best Actress in Television for NCIS
2011: Won an ALMA Award for Favorite Television Actress – Leading Role in a Drama for NCIS
2012: Nominated for an ALMA Award for Favorite TV Actress

Source: [8]

Emily Wickersham *(NCIS - role: Eleanor „Ellie" Bishop)*

(born on April 26, 1984 in Kansas) is an American actress best known for roles on TV including The Sopranos.
In 2013, Wickersham was cast as an NSA Analyst Eleanor "Ellie" Bishop in an NCIS episode which aired November 19, 2013, on CBS. Her character is a replacement for agent Ziva David, who was played by actress Cote de Pablo. De Pablo left the series after eight seasons. Wickersham has been cast as a series regular on NCIS by CBS.
Wickersham, who has Austrian and Swedish origins, was born in Kansas, but grew up in Mamaroneck, New York. Wickersham is the daughter of Mr. and Mrs. John Atwood Wickersham of New York.
She married musician Blake Hanley on November 23, 2010 on Little Palm Island in the Florida Keys.

Filmography (Selection) Emily Wickersham

2006: Late Show with David Letterman / Parco P.I.
2006-07: The Sopranos
2007: The Bronx is Burning / The Gamekillers
2009: Law & Order / Bored to Death / Trauma
2011: Gossip Girl / I am Number Four
2012: Gone
2013: The Bridge
2013-present: NCIS
2014: Glitch

Source: [21]

Sean Harland Murry *(NCIS - role: Timothy „Tim" McGee)*

(born November 15, 1977 in Bethesda, Maryland) is an Australian-American actor. He is best known for playing Timothy McGee in the CBS television drama NCIS and Danny Walden in the military drama JAG which is the parent series to NCIS.

Murray spent his childhood near Coffs Harbour in New South Wales, Australia, and holds dual citizenship in the U.S. and Australia. His mother is Vivienne Bellisario, fourth wife of American television producer and screenwriter, Donald P. Bellisario, making him Bellisario's stepson.

Murray's television credits include a starring role in the UPN sitcom The Random Years and a supporting role as teenager Zane Grey Hart in CBS's comedy/western series, Harts of the West, with Beau Bridges as his father and Harley Jane Kozak as his mother. Lloyd Bridges also starred in the series. The program was set on a dude ranch in Nevada. Murray also appeared in several episodes of JAG and later took on a major role in the show's spin-off NCIS.
Murray has made several television guest appearances, including ER. In addition, Murray has appeared in several feature films including Hocus Pocus (1993), his motion picture film appearance, in which he played Thackery Binx; This Boy's Life; and in Todd Field's Too Romantic.

Murray married Carrie James on November 26, 2005. They had their first child, a daughter named Caitlyn Melissa Murray, on May 3, 2007. The couple's second child, River James Murray, was born in Los Angeles on April 22, 2010.

Source: [9]

Filmography (Selection) Sean Murray

1991: Civil Wars (One episode)
1991: Backfield in Motion
1992: Too Romantic
1993–1994: Harts of the West
1993: River of Rage: The Taking of Maggie Keene
1993: Hocus Pocus
1993: This Boy's Life
1995: Emergency Room (One episode)
1995: Silk Stalkings (One episode)
1995: Trial by Fire
1996: The Lottery
1996: For My Daughter's Honor
1996: Fall Into Darkness
1997: The Sleepwalker Killing
1998–2001: JAG
1999: Touched by an Angel (One episode)
2000: Boston Public (One episode)
2001: Spring Break Lawyer
2002: The Random Years (One episode)
since 2003: NCIS

Source: [9]

David Keith McCallum, Jr. *(NCIS - role: Dr. Donald „Ducky" Mallard)*

(born 19 September 1933 in Glasgow, Scotland) is a Scottish actor and musician. He is best known for his roles as Illya Kuryakin, a Russian-born secret agent, in the 1960s television series The Man from U.N.C.L.E., as interdimensional operative Steel in Sapphire & Steel, and for his current role as NCIS Medical Examiner, Dr. Donald "Ducky" Mallard in the series NCIS.

McCallum was born in Glasgow, Scotland, the second of two sons of Dorothy Dorman, a cellist, and orchestral leader David McCallum, Sr. When he was 10, his family moved to London for his father's move to lead the London Philharmonic Orchestra. Early in the Second World War he was evacuated to Scotland, where he lived with his mother at Gartocharn by Loch Lomond.

McCallum won a scholarship to University College School, a boys' independent school in Hampstead, London, where, encouraged by his parents to prepare for a career in music, he played the oboe. In 1946 he began doing boy voices for the BBC radio repertory company. Also involved in local amateur drama, at age 17 he appeared as Oberon in an open-air production of A Midsummer Night's Dream with the Play and Pageant Union. He left school at age 18 and, following military service with the Royal West African Frontier Force, attended the Royal Academy of Dramatic Art (also in London), where Joan Collins was a classmate.

McCallum became Assistant Stage Manager of the Glyndebourne Opera Company in 1951.
In 1951 he did his National Service where he was commissioned into the Middlesex Regiment and seconded to the Gold Coast Regiment.

He began his acting career doing boy voices for BBC Radio in 1947 and began taking bit-parts in British films from the late 1950s, and his first acting role was in Whom the Gods Love, Die Young playing a doomed royal. A James Dean-themed photograph of McCallum caught the attention of the Rank Organisation, who signed him in 1956.[5] However, in an interview with Alan Titchmarsh broadcast on 3 November 2010, McCallum stated that he had actually held his Equity card since 1946.

Early roles included a juvenile delinquent in Violent Playground (1957), an outlaw in Robbery Under Arms (1957) and as junior RMS Titanic radio operator Harold Bride in A Night to Remember (1958). His first American film was Freud the Secret Passion (1962), directed by John Huston, which was shortly followed by a role in Peter Ustinov's Billy Budd. McCallum played Lt. Cmdr. Eric Ashley-Pitt "Dispersal" in The Great Escape which was released in 1963. He took the role of Judas Iscariot in 1965's The Greatest Story Ever Told. Notable pre-U.N.C.L.E. television roles included two appearances on The Outer Limits and a guest appearance on Perry Mason in 1964 as defendant Phillipe Bertain in "The Case of the Fifty Millionth Frenchman."

The Man from U.N.C.L.E, intended as a vehicle for Robert Vaughn, made McCallum into a sex symbol, his Beatle-style blond haircut providing a trendy contrast with Vaughn's traditional appearance. McCallum's role as the mysterious Russian agent Illya Kuryakin was originally conceived as a peripheral one. However, McCallum took the opportunity to construct a complex character whose appeal rested largely in what was shadowy and enigmatic about him. Kuryakin's popularity with the audience and Vaughn's and McCallum's on-screen chemistry were quickly recognised by the producers and McCallum was elevated to co-star status.

McCallum never quite repeated the popular success he had gained as Kuryakin until NCIS, though he did become a familiar face on British television in shows such as Colditz (1972–1974), "Kidnapped" (1978) and in ITV's science-fiction series Sapphire & Steel (1979–1982) opposite Joanna Lumley. He also played the title character in a short-lived U.S. version of The Invisible Man in 1975. McCallum appeared on stage in Australia in Run for Your Wife during 1987-1988 and the production toured the country. Other members of the cast were Jack Smethurst, Eric Sykes and Katy Manning. McCallum starred with Diana Rigg in the 1989 suspense-thriller TV mini-series Mother Love. In 1991 and 1992 McCallum played gambler John Grey, one of the principal characters in the television series Trainer.

In the 1990s, McCallum guest starred in two U.S. television series: in the first season of the television series seaQuest DSV, he appeared as the law-enforcement officer Frank Cobb of the fictional Broken Ridge of the Ausland Confederation, an underwater mining camp off the coast of Australia by the Great Barrier Reef; he also had a guest star role in one episode of Babylon 5.

In 1994, McCallum narrated the acclaimed documentaries Titanic: Death of a Dream and Titanic: The Legend Lives On for A&E Television Networks. This was the second project about the Titanic on which he had worked: the first was the 1958 film A Night to Remember, in which he had had a small role.

In the same year, McCallum hosted and narrated the TV special Ancient Prophecies. This special, which was followed soon after by three others, told of people and places historically associated with foretelling the end of the world and the beginnings of new eras for mankind.

Since 2003 McCallum has starred in the CBS television series NCIS as Dr Donald "Ducky" Mallard, the Medical Examiner and one of the key characters. In an inside joke, NCIS agent Leroy Jethro Gibbs is asked, "What did Ducky look like when he was younger?" Gibbs responds, "Illya Kuryakin.

According to the behind-the-scenes feature on the 2006 DVD of NCIS season 1, McCallum became an expert in forensics to play Mallard, including appearing at Medical Examiner conventions. In the feature, Bellisario says that McCallum's knowledge became so vast that at the time of the interview he was considering making him a technical advisor on the show.

McCallum appeared at the 21st Annual James Earl Ash Lecture, held May 19, 2005 at the Armed Forces Institute of Pathology, an evening for honoring America's service members. His lecture, "Reel to Real Forensics," with Cmdr. Craig T. Mallak, U.S. Armed Forces medical examiner, featured a presentation comparing the real-life work of the Armed Forces Medical Examiner staff with that of the fictional naval investigators appearing on NCIS.

In late April, 2012 it was announced that McCallum had reached agreement on a two-year contract extension with CBS-TV. The move means he could remain an NCIS regular past his eightieth birthday.

In the 1960s, McCallum recorded four albums for Capitol Records with music producer David Axelrod: Music...A Part Of Me (Capitol ST 2432, 1966), Music...A Bit More Of Me (Capitol ST 2498, 1966), Music...It's Happening Now! (Capitol ST 2651, 1967), and McCallum (Capitol ST 2748, 1968). The best known of his pieces today is "The Edge," which was sampled by Dr. Dre as the intro and riff to the track "The Next Episode".

McCallum did not sing on these records, as many television stars of the 1960s did when offered recording contracts. As a classically trained musician, he conceived a blend of oboe, English horn, and strings with guitar and drums, and presented instrumental interpretations of hits of the day. The official arranger on the albums was H. B. Barnum. However, McCallum conducted, and contributed several original compositions of his own, over the course of four LPs. The first two, Music...A Part Of Me and Music...A Bit More Of Me, have been issued together on CD on the Zonophone label. On Open Channel D, McCallum did sing on the first four tracks, "Communication", "House On Breckenridge Lane", "In The Garden, Under The Tree" (the theme song from the movie Three Bites Of The Apple), and "My Carousel". The music tracks are the same as the Zonophone CD. This CD was released on the Rev-Ola label. The single release of "Communication" reached No. 32 in the UK Singles Chart in April 1966.

He was married to actress Jill Ireland from 1956 to 1967. They had three sons: Paul, Jason (an adopted son who died from an accidental drug overdose in 1989),[13] and Val (short for Valentine). He introduced Ireland to Charles Bronson when both were filming The Great Escape. She subsequently left McCallum, and went on to marry Bronson in 1968.

He has been married to Katherine Carpenter since 1967. They have a son, Peter, and a daughter, Sophie. David and Katherine are active with charitable organizations that support the United States Marine Corps: Katherine's father was a Marine who served in the Battle of Iwo Jima, and her brother lost his life in the Vietnam War. David McCallum has six grandchildren. They live in New York. *Source: 11*

Filmography (Selection) David McCallum

1957: Hell Drivers
1957: Robbery Under Arms
1960: Jungle Street
1962: Freud
1963: Outer Limits
1963: The Outer Limits
1964-1968: The Man from O.N.C.E.L.
1966: Please don´t eat the Daisies
1975: The Invisible Man
1977: King Solomon's Treasure
1978: Kidnapped
1980: The Watcher in the Woods
1983: As the World Turns
1986: The A-Team
1989: Murder, She Wrote
1993: Seaquest
1994: Babylon 5
1997: Team Knight Rider
1999: Sex and the City
since 2003: NCIS
2009: Batman: The Brave and the Bold
2010-2014: Ben 10
2014: NCIS: New Orleans (one episode)

Source: 11

Brian Dietzen *(NCIS - role: Jimmy Palmer)*

(born November 14, 1977 in Barrington, Illinois) is an American actor who has played the supporting role of Jimmy Palmer on NCIS since 2004. In 2012, he was promoted to season regular at the beginning of the show's tenth season.

Dietzen was born in Barrington, Illinois. Later, he studied theatre at the University of Colorado at Boulder's BFA acting program.

Dietzen has appeared in productions of Equus, and Waiting for Godot and joined The Colorado Shakespeare Festival for two years. He was cast in The WB series My Guide to Becoming a Rockstar. The part was a series regular as the drummer of the group. He later teamed up with John Riggi for a two-man show with Steve Rudnick called The Oldest Man in Show Biz.

He performed in the film From Justin to Kelly and has had a recurring role as Jimmy Palmer, a medical examiner's assistant, on the CBS series NCIS, since the first season episode, "Split Decision". Starting in season 10, 2012-2013, he is a featured cast member.

Source: [10]

Filmography (Selection) Brian Dietzen

2002: Boston Public
2002: My Guide to Becoming a Rock Star
2003: From Justin to Kelly
2003: One on One
2004: Purgatory House
since 2004: Navy CIS
2005: Self-Inflicted
2008: Hit Factor
2009: Nowhere to Hide
2013: Mark Leighton
2013: Perception

Source: [10]

Rocky Carroll *(NCIS - role: Leon Vance)*

(born July 8, 1963 as Roscoe Fulton Carroll in Cincinnati, Ohio) is an American actor. He is known for his roles as Joey Emerson on the FOX comedy-drama Roc, as Dr. Keith Wilkes on the CBS medical drama Chicago Hope, and as NCIS Director Leon Vance on the CBS drama NCIS and its spinoff NCIS: Los Angeles.

His acting career is rooted in the theater. In 1981, Carroll graduated from the famed School for Creative and Performing Arts SCPA in Cincinnati Ohio, in the Cincinnati Public School District. Determined to further his knowledge of acting, he attended The Conservatory of Theatre Arts at Webster University in St. Louis, where he graduated with a B.F.A. degree. After graduating, Carroll decided to test the waters by moving to New York City, the heart of the theater community. There, he introduced many young children of color to the works of William Shakespeare by participating in Joe Papp's "Shakespeare on Broadway" series.

Carroll married Gabrielle Bullock on May 25, 1996. They have one daughter, Elissa.

As part of Joe Papp's acclaimed New York Shakespeare Festival, Carroll helped to open doors for actors of color, by taking on non-traditional roles that were rarely portrayed by Black actors in Shakespeare dramas. In 1987, Carroll was introduced to the works of August Wilson. The up and coming and talented young actor was allowed to recreate his role for the Broadway production of Wilson's critically acclaimed story The Piano Lesson. The play not only earned a Pulitzer Prize for Drama, but Carroll earned a Tony and Drama Desk nomination.

He is known for portraying ne'er-do-well musician Joey Emerson on the FOX comedy-drama Roc. He also had a starring role as Dr. Keith Wilkes in the TV series Chicago Hope. Carroll has guest starred in several other TV programs including The Agency, Boston Legal, Family Law, The West Wing, Law & Order, The Game, ER and Grey's Anatomy. Carroll has had roles in many Hollywood films such as Born on the Fourth of July, The Ladies Man, Crimson Tide, The Great White Hype, A Prelude to a Kiss, The Chase, Best Laid Plans and Yes Man .

In the fifth season of the CBS drama NCIS, Carrol was featured in a recurring role as Assistant Director Leon Vance. In doing so, he has been reunited with his Chicago Hope castmates Mark Harmon and Lauren Holly. After the death of NCIS director Jenny Shepard, his character became the new director of NCIS, and replaced Holly in the main cast. In 2009, he also played the role of NCIS Director Vance in the NCIS spin-off NCIS: Los Angeles, while Vance was helping to set up the Los Angeles office of NCIS.

He shares his birthday with fellow NCIS co-star Michael Weatherly.

In addition to being a series regular on NCIS, Caroll has also directed an episode of NCIS, making his directional debut with the Season 12 episode, "We Build, We Fight".

Source: [12]

Lauren Holly *(NCIS - role: Jennifer „Jenny" Shepard)*

(born October 28, 1963 in Bristol, Pennsylvania) is an American-born Canadian actress. She is known for her roles as Deputy Sheriff Maxine Stewart in the TV series Picket Fences, as Mary Swanson in the 1994 film Dumb & Dumber, and as Jenny Shepard on the TV series NCIS. She was married to comic actor Jim Carrey from 1996 to 1997.

Holly was born in Bristol, Pennsylvania. Her mother, Michael Ann Holly, is an art historian and the Starr Director of Research and Academic Program at The Sterling and Francine Clark Art Institute, and former professor at Hobart and William Smith Colleges. Her father, Grant Holly, is a screenwriter and professor of literature at Hobart and William Smith Colleges. She has two younger brothers: Nick and Alexander Innes Holly (1978-1992). Holly was raised in Geneva, New York, and is a 1981 graduate of Geneva High School, where she was a cheerleader. In 1985, Holly earned an undergraduate degree in English from Sarah Lawrence College in New York.[3] Holly, who now lives primarily in Canada with her husband and their three children, became a Canadian citizen in 2008.

In 1992, Holly, her father Grant, and their families established the 'A' Fund at Hobart and William Smith Colleges in memory of her brother, Alexander Holly, whom Holly said "was a boy filled with dreams, hopes, and plans. Although he was only fourteen when he died, he had traveled extensively in Europe and Central America, lived in New York City and Los Angeles, and these experiences produced in him a fascination for architecture and archaeology."

Her acting career began at the age of 20 when she appeared in Hill Street Blues as Carla Walicki for two episodes.At age 23, Holly joined the cast of the ABC television soap opera All My Children as Julie Rand Chandler (1986–1989). She portrayed the comic book character Betty on television's Archie: To Riverdale and Back Again in 1990.

She appeared as Mary Swanson, Lloyd Christmas's love interest in the 1994 Jim Carrey comedy Dumb & Dumber. She portrayed Linda Lee Cadwell, the wife of martial artist and actor Bruce Lee, in 1993's Dragon: The Bruce Lee Story; a doctor in Sydney Pollack's 1995 remake of Sabrina; and Lieutenant Emily Lake in the 1996 comedy Down Periscope with Kelsey Grammer. She starred in the movie Any Given Sunday (1999) along with Jamie Foxx and Dennis Quaid.

She appeared in the music video for Dixie Chicks' single "Goodbye Earl" (2000), along with Jane Krakowski, Dennis Franz, Adrian Pasdar, Michael DeLuise and Evan Bernard.

Holly starred as small-town Deputy Sheriff Maxine Stewart in David E. Kelley's TV series Picket Fences (1992–1996). She was a member of the cast of NCIS as Director Jenny Shepard from 2005–2008, reuniting with her former Chicago Hope co-stars Mark Harmon and Rocky Carroll.

Currently, Holly portrays the "worldly and stunning" lead medical examiner Dr. Betty Rogers, a regular character on the CTV series Motive. In 2014, she was reunited with ex-Picket Fences co-star, Tom Skerritt, to star in the movie, Field of Lost Shoes. Holly is set to star in Oz Perkins (Son of Anthony Perkins) horror film February, along Emma Roberts, James Remar, Evan Peters and Lucy Boynton.

Source: 13

Filmography (Selection) Lauren Holly

1992–1996: Picket Fences
1993: Dragon: The Bruce Lee Story
1994: Dumb & Dumber
1995: Sabrina
1996: Down Periscope
1996: Beautiful Girls
1997: A Smile Like Yours
1997: Turbulence
1998: Vig
1999: Any Given Sunday
1999–2000: Chicago Hope
2000: What Women Want
2000: The Last Producer
2001: Destiny
2001: The Woman Of Camelot
2002: King of Texas
2002: Changing Hearts
2002: Talking to Heavens
2002: Santa Jr.
2002: Pavement
2004: Just Desserts and In Enemy Hands and Caught in the Act
2005: Bounty Hunters
2005: The Chumscrubber
2005: The Pleasure Drivers
2005: Down and Derby
2005: The Godfather of Green Bay
2005–2008: NCIS
2006: Fatwa
2006: Chasing 3000
2006: Raising Flagg
2006: CSI: Miami
2008: Leverage
2009: Crank 2: High Voltage
2009: The Least Among You
2009: The Final Storm
2009: The Perfect Age of Rock 'n' Roll
2009: Before you say 'I do'
2009: Flashpoint
2010: Covert Affairs / You're So Cupid! / Call me Mrs. Miracle / Chasing 3000
2011: Scream of the Banshee
2012: Masque / Layover
2013: Abducted / Field of Lost Shoes / The Town that Came A-Courtin´
2015: Marshall in the Miracle and February

Source: [13]

Sasha Alexander *(NCIS - role: Caitlin „Kate" Todd)*

(born as Suzana Drobnjaković on May 17, 1973 in Los Angeles, California) is an American actress. She played the role of Gretchen Witter, the sister of Pacey Witter on Dawson's Creek, Lucy in Yes Man (2008); and Catherine in He's Just Not That Into You (2009). Alexander also acted as former Secret Service/NCIS Special Agent Kate Todd for the first two seasons of NCIS.

She currently stars as The Chief Medical Examiner of the Commonwealth of Massachusets Maura Isles on the Turner Network Television series Rizzoli & Isles.

Sasha Alexander was born Suzana S. Drobnjaković in Los Angeles, California, to a Serbian mother and Italian father. She began acting in school productions in the seventh grade. She also was an ice skater, but had to stop due to a knee injury. She continued acting through high school and college, and then moved to New York to act in summer stock and Shakespeare festivals. She graduated from the University of Southern California's School of Cinema-Television, where she was a member of the sorority Kappa Alpha Theta, before going on to have a successful acting career in both TV and film.

Alexander got her start on two short-lived series: the medical drama Presidio Med and ABC's twenty-something drama Wasteland. She achieved widespread media attention and critical praise when she appeared on the fourth season of Dawson's Creek as Gretchen Witter, dating the title character, and in an episode of the short-lived Fox comedy series Greg the Bunny, in which she played the part of a lesbian TV Guide reporter and shared an onscreen kiss with Sarah Silverman. Alexander has also appeared in the films Lucky 13, and All Over the Guy as well as He's Just Not That Into You, the independent movie The Last Lullaby, and Yes Man starring Jim Carrey.

Before being cast as Caitlin Todd on NCIS, she appeared on CSI as District Attorney Robin Childs, in the episode "Alter Boys". Alexander joined NCIS as Secret Service/NCIS Special Agent Caitlin "Kate" Todd in 2003. She replaced Vivian Blackadder played by Robyn Lively, who only appeared in the back-door pilot episodes, "Ice Queen" and "Meltdown" on JAG. The official pilot episode "Yankee White" aired September 23, 2003 on CBS.

Alexander's year and a half tenure on the show ended in May 2005 when her character, Kate, was killed off when a terrorist shot her in the head in the last few seconds of the Season 2 finale, "Twilight".[2] The "official explanation" for the actress's departure was that "she asked to be let out of her contract to pursue other opportunities".

In her final two appearances in the "Kill Ari" two-part, Alexander was credited as a Special Guest Star. Chilean actress Cote de Pablo, who plays Ziva David, later permanently replaced Alexander on the show. However, despite having left the show, Alexander made a few further appearances in NCIS with her last one being on the 200th episode, "Life Before His Eyes". However, she wasn't given any official credit of any kind for those appearances, making her appearances in Seasons 1 and 2 as well as her guest appearances in the first two episodes of Season 3 the only ones where she has been credited.

She also had a small role in 2006's Mission: Impossible III. She joined the cast of The Nine in the role of Nick's ex-wife. She also appeared in one episode of Friends ("The One with Joey's Interview"), playing a Soap Opera Digest reporter who interviewed Joey.

Her current television role is that of Boston medical examiner Maura Isles on the TNT series Rizzoli & Isles with Angie Harmon, which debuted on July 12, 2010.

On August 11, 2007, Alexander married director Edoardo Ponti, son of actress Sophia Loren and the late film producer Carlo Ponti, in Geneva, Switzerland. Alexander and Ponti have two children, Lucia Sofia (born May 12, 2006)[7] and Leonardo Fortunato (born December 20, 2010).

Source: 14

Filmography (Selection) Sasha Alexander

1997: Battle of the Sexes
1997: Visceral Matter
1999: Twin Falls Idaho
1999: Wasteland
2000–2001: Dawson's Creek
2001: CSI: Crime Scene Investigation (One episode)
2001: Ball & Chain
2001: All Over the Guy
2002: Friends (One episode)
2002: Greg the Bunny (One episode)
2002: Presidio Med
2003: Expert Witness
2003–2005: Navy CIS
2005: Lucky 13
2006: Mission: Impossible III
2006: E-Ring (One episode)
2006: The Nine (One episode)
2008: Yes Man
2009: He's Just Not That Into You
2009: Love Happens
2009: Tenure
2009: Play Dead
2009: Dark Blue (One episode)
2009: The Karenskys
2010: Coming and Going
2010: Dr. House (One episode)
since 2010: Rizzoli & Isles
2011: Coming and Going
2013: The Girl from Nagasaki
2015: Shameless

Source: 14

Sources Text:

[1] Wikipedia, DL on Nov 29, 2011, Jul 15, 2012, Jun 25, 2013, Jul 9, 2014 and May 10, 2015
via http://en.wikipedia.org/wiki/NCIS_(TV_series)

[2] NCIS Fan Site NCIS FANWIKI, DL on Nov 29, 2011, Jul 15, 2012 and Jun 25, 2013
via http://www.ncisfanwiki.com/page/NCIS%3A+Gibbs+Rules

[3] NCIS Fan Site NCIS FANWIKI NCIS Quotes, DL on Nov 29, 2011, Nov 21, 2012 and Jun 25, 2013
via http://www.ncisfanwiki.com/page/NCIS+Quotes

[4] CBS, DL on Jun 25, 2013
via http://www.cbs.com/shows/ncis/episodes/200764

[5] Wikipedia, DL on Jun 25, 2013, Jul 9, 2014 and May 10, 2015
via http://en.wikipedia.org/wiki/Mark_Harmon

[6] Wikipedia, DL on Jun 25, 2013, Jul 9, 2014 and May 10, 2015
via http://en.wikipedia.org/wiki/Michael_Weatherly

[7] Wikipedia, DL on Jun 25, 2013, Jul 9, 2014 and May 10, 2015
via http://en.wikipedia.org/wiki/Pauley_Perrette

[8] Wikipedia, DL on Jun 25, 2013, Jul 9, 2014 and May 10, 2015
via http://en.wikipedia.org/wiki/Cote_de_pablo

[9] Wikipedia, DL on Jun 25, 2013, Jul 9, 2014 and May 10, 2015
via http://en.wikipedia.org/wiki/Sean_Murray_(actor)

[10] Wikipedia, DL on Jun 25, 2013, Jul 9, 2014 and May 13, 2015
via http://en.wikipedia.org/wiki/Brian_Dietzen

[11] Wikipedia, DL on Jun 25, 2013, Jul 9, 2014 and May 13, 2015
via http://en.wikipedia.org/wiki/David_mccallum

[12] Wikipedia, DL on Jun 25, 2013, Jul 9, 2014 and May 13, 2015
via http://en.wikipedia.org/wiki/Rocky_Carroll

[13] Wikipedia, DL on Jun 25, 2013, Jul 9, 2014 and May 13, 2015
via http://en.wikipedia.org/wiki/Lauren_Holly

[14] Wikipedia, DL on Jun 26, 2013, Jul 9, 2014 and May 10, 2015
via http://en.wikipedia.org/wiki/Sasha_Alexander

[15] Wikipedia, DL on Jun 26, 2013, Jul 9, 2014 and May 10, 2015
via http://en.wikipedia.org/wiki/NCIS_(TV_series)#Ratings

[16] Wikipedia, DL on Jun 26, 2013, Jul 9, 2014 and May 10, 2015
via http://en.wikipedia.org/wiki/NCIS_(TV_series)#Awards_and_nominations

[17] Wikipedia, DL on Jun 26, 2013, Jul 9, 2014 and May 10, 2015
via http://en.wikipedia.org/wiki/List_of_NCIS_home_video_releases

[18] Wikipedia, DL on J Jun 26, 2013, Jul 9, 2014 and May 10, 2015
via http://en.wikipedia.org/wiki/NCIS_(TV_series)#Soundtrack

[19] Wikipedia, DL on Jun 26, 2013, Jul 9, 2014 and May 10, 2015
via http://en.wikipedia.org/wiki/Naval_Criminal_Investigative_Service

[20] Wikipedia, DL on Jun 26, 2013, Jul 9, 2014 and May 10, 2015
via http://en.wikipedia.org/wiki/NCIS_(TV_series)#Other_releases

[21] Wikipedia, DL on Jul 9, 2014 and May 10, 2015
via http://http://en.wikipedia.org/wiki/Emily_Wickersham

[22] Wikiquote, DL on Jul 9, 2014 and May 10, 2015
via http://en.wikiquote.org/wiki/NCIS_(season_11)

[23] Wikiquote, DL on May 10, 2015
via http://en.wikiquote.org/wiki/NCIS_(season_12)

[24] The Futon Critic, DL on May 10, 2015
via http://www.thefutoncritic.com/listings/20150421cbs02/

Other used Sources:

NCIS FAN private website: www.ncisfan.org/

CBS Broadcasting: www.cbs.com/shows/ncis/

Private website with forum: www.forum.navy-cis.de/

Serienjunkies.de: www.serienjunkies.de/ncis/

TV-Serieninfos: www.tvsi.de/krimiserien/navy_CIS.php

Source Poto:

Cover-/Inside-Photos by Jerry Avenaim (http://en.wikipedia.org/wiki/Jerry_Avenaim), DL on Nov 26, 2011
via http://de.wikipedia.org/w/index.php?title=Datei:Mark_Harmon_1_edit1.jpg&filetimestamp=20080805230925

Hinrichsen, Klaus

NCIS Season 1-12
NCIS TV Show Fan Book

May 2015

Klaus Hinrichsen

***

Herstellung und Verlag: Books on Demand GmbH, Norderstedt
Produced and published by Books on Demand GmbH, Norderstedt, Germany
Printed in Germany

ISBN: 978-3-7347-9506-0

Lightning Source UK Ltd.
Milton Keynes UK
UKOW07f1851190515

251889UK00010B/364/P